World
Army Badges and Insignia
Since 1939

This edition first published in the U.K. 1983 by Blandford
Press, Link House, West Street, Poole, Dorset,
BH15 1LL

Reprinted 1986

An omnibus edition of *Army Badges and Insignia of
World War 2, Book One* and *Army Badges and Insignia
Since 1945*

Copyright © 1972, 1973, 1974, 1976, 1983 and 1985
Blandford Books Ltd.

Distributed in the United States by
Sterling Publishing Co., Inc., 2 Park
Avenue, New York, N.Y. 10016

Distributed in Australia by Capricorn Link (Australia) Pty Ltd,
PO Box 665, Lane Cove 2066, NSW

ISBN 0 7137 1386 0

Printed in Hong Kong by
South China Printing Co.

Army Badges and Insignia of World War 2

Book I

Great Britain, Poland, Belgium, Italy,
U.S.S.R., U.S.A., Germany

Guido Rosignoli

BLANDFORD PRESS

POOLE·NEW YORK·SYDNEY

Contents

Introduction

During the last decade I have noticed an increasing interest in military matters; an interest that is growing all over the world. I have also found that in every country the collector concentrates upon the militaria of his own national armed forces and upon that of one foreign army whose exploits have particularly fascinated the popular imagination. The latter, in most cases, is the Nazi German Army.

As, unfortunately, very little contact exists among collectors of different nationalities, there is limited common knowledge about each other's collections. This lack of knowledge often prevents the collector from extending his interest to the many unfamiliar bargains displayed on the stalls of our local markets.

In this book I hope to widen the scope of the collector, and have illustrated and described the badges worn during World War 2 by the armies of seven countries who were major combatants. The order in which they appear has been established by the availability of information and occasionally by printing necessities.

I have supplemented the illustrations with brief historical backgrounds and descriptions of the uniforms on which the badges were worn, although I do not mention the uniforms of special regiments and traditional garments, as they are beyond the scope of this particular volume.

Additional lists of coloured cap bands and trouser stripes have been provided, together with lists of regimental and divisional titles and any other information that could be of use to the military historian.

I regret that space limitations have compelled me to deal solely with the regular armies and, in the case of the Polish and Belgian Armies, to illustrate only the badges of the 1939–40 period.

Uniforms and badges have always been controlled by the official army dress regulations and as the majority of participants entered World War 2 with uniforms and equipment adopted in the early 1930s, I have found it necessary in some cases to show badges in use long before that war.

Although most modern armies nowadays are apparently similar, they differ in their structural organisation, owing to different historical backgrounds and different traditions. Some armies have branches of service, or even rank titles, that have no counterpart in the armies of other nations. For instance, some books published in Britain and the U.S.A. have translated German N.C.O.s rank titles into British and American N.C.O.s rank titles respectively.   I have chosen to translate the ranks literally for what they are.   American terms have been used in the section dedicated to the U.S. Army, so that the term 'shoulder patch' replaces the British 'formation sign', although the American term 'enlisted men' has been generally replaced with the term 'other ranks'.

Where it has been impossible to translate accurately I have employed the foreign term.

G. Rosignoli,
Farnham, Surrey, 1972

Author's Note

I would like to thank the following for the assistance they gave me while I was compiling this book:

The Belgian Embassy

The Embassy of the U.S.S.R.

The Embassy of the U.S.A.

Mr. Henry Brown, M.B.E., General Secretary of the Commando Association

Captain W. Milewski, the Curator, and Captain R. Dembinski of the Polish Institute and Sikorski Museum

Mr. K. Barbarski for his untiring help

Mr. L. Granata of Trieste

Mr. L. Milner of the Imperial War Museum for his help with the German section

Mr. E. C. M. Williams for his help with translations

I would also like to acknowledge both the assistance I have had, and the pleasure I have personally gained, from the many magnificently equipped regimental museums I have visited both here and in Europe.

Since first printing this book some errors to the plate captions have been pointed out. As it has not been possible to alter the plates the alterations are noted here.

Plate 1, top line, Brigadier in both cases should also read Colonel; Plate 73, top line should read Panama Division; Plate 79, Tank Battle badges should read Miscellaneous badges.

9

The Illustrations

The badges illustrated on the following plates are drawn only in approximate proportion to each other. The reader will appreciate that an exact proportion could not have been worked out satisfactorily because of the great variations in sizes of these badges.

As far as the colours of the branches of service are concerned, it should be taken into consideration when reading the text that I have used the colour description of the country concerned.

For instance, although the 'colours' of the Medical Services of Britain, the U.S.A., Belgium, Italy and Poland are a similar shade of red, each country has adopted its own definition of the colour, and so the Medical Service of the U.S.A. has maroon, Great Britain dull cherry, Belgium and Italy amaranth and Poland cherry red.

CAP BADGES AND GORGET PATCHES

Generals   Field-marshal   Generals   Brigadier   Brigadier

OFFICER'S RANK BADGES

Field-marshal   General   Lieutenant-general   Major-general

Brigadier   Colonel   Lieutenant-colonel   Major

Captain   Lieutenant   2nd lieutenant

PLATE 1

WARRANT OFFICERS' RANK BADGES

1. Regimental sergeant-major of the Foot Guards 2. Staff sergeant-major (1st Class) and conductors 3. Regimental corporal-major and Farriers corporal-major of the Household Cavalry and W.O. (1st Class) 4. Regimental quartermaster-corporal and Farriers quarter-master-corporal of the Household Cavalry and quartermaster-sergeant of the Foot Guards 5. Squadron corporal-major of the Royal Horse Guard and W.O. (2nd Class)

NON-COMMISSIONED OFFICERS' RANK BADGES

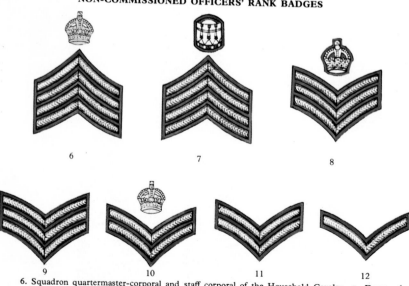

6. Squadron quartermaster-corporal and staff corporal of the Household Cavalry 7. Drum major 8. Corporal-of-horse of the Household Cavalry, quartermaster-sergeant, colour-sergeant and staff-sergeant 9. Sergeant 10. Corporal and lance-corporal of the Household Cavalry 11. Corporal, bombardier (R.A.) 12. Lance-corporal and lance-bombardier (R.A.)

PLATE 2

FORMATION SIGNS

Supreme Headquarters, British and Allied Forces

 G.H.Q. Home Forces

 G.H.Q. India

 Allied Forces H.Q.

 A.L.F.S.E.A.

 S.A.C.S.E.A.

 S.H.A.E.F.

 15th Army Group

 21st Army Group

 C.M.F.

Armies

 1st

 2nd

 8th

 9th

 10th

 12th

 14th

Army Corps

 1st

 2nd

 3rd

 4th

 5th

 8th

 9th(1st)

 10th

 11th

 12th

 13th

 25th

30th

9th(2nd)

PLATE 3

GREAT BRITAIN

FORMATION SIGNS
Armoured Divisions

 Guards

 1st

 2nd

 6th

 7th(1st)

 7th(2nd)

 8th

 9th

 10th

 42nd

 79th

Armoured Brigades

 4th

 6th

 7th

 8th

 9th

 16th

 20th

 22nd

 23rd

 25th

 27th

 31st

 33rd

 34th

 35th

 1st Armd Repl. Group C.M.F.

Army Tank Brigades

 21st(1st)

 21st(2nd)

 23rd

 24th

 25th

36th

PLATE 4

CAP BADGES

Cavalry and Armoured Regiments

L.G.

R.H.G.

K.D.G.

Bays

3 D.G.

4/7 D.G.

5 Innis D.G.

Royals

Greys

3 H.

'4 H.

7 H.

8 H.

9 L.

10 H.

11 H.

PLATE 5

GREAT BRITAIN

CAP BADGES

Cavalry and Armoured Regiments

12 L.

13/18 H.

14/20 H.

15/19 H.

16/5 L.

17/21 L.

22 D.

23 H.

24 L.

25 D.

26 H.

27 L.

R.T.R.

R.A.C.

Recce

PLATE 6

CAP BADGES

Corps, Administrative Departments, etc.

R.A.

R.H.A.

H.A.C.
(Infantry)

H.A.C.

R.E.

R.A.S.C.

R.Sigs

R.A.O.C.

R.A.M.C.

M.P.

M.P.S.C.

R.A.V.C.

A.A.C.

A.D.C.

R.E.M.E.

I.C.

PLATE 7

CAP BADGES
Corps, Administrative Departments, etc.

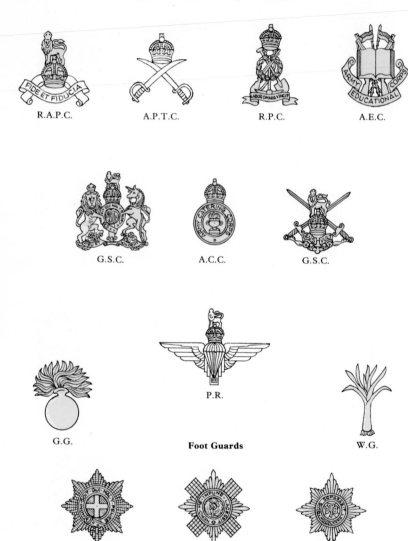

R.A.P.C.

A.P.T.C.

R.P.C.

A.E.C.

G.S.C.

A.C.C.

G.S.C.

G.G.

P.R.

Foot Guards

W.G.

C.G.

S.G.

I.G.

PLATE 8

CAP BADGES

Infantry of the Line

R.S.

Queen's

Buffs.

King's Own

N.F.

Warwick

R.F.

King's

Norfolk

Lincolns

Devon

Suffolk

Som.L.I.

W.Yorks

E.Yorks.

Bedfs. Herts.

PLATE 9

CAP BADGES

Infantry of the Line

Leicesters

Green Howards

L.F.

R.S.F.

Cheshire

R.W.F.

S.W.B.

K.O.S.B.

Cameronians

Innisks.

Glosters.

Worc.R.

E.Lan.R.

Surreys

D.C.L.I.

D.W.R.

PLATE 10

CAP BADGES

Infantry of the Line

Border

R. Sussex

Hamps.

S.Staffords

Dorset

S.Lan.R.

Welch

Black Watch

Oxf.Bucks.

Essex

Foresters

Loyals

Northamptons

R.Berks.

R.W.K.

K.O.Y.L.I.

K.S.L.I.

PLATE 11

CAP BADGES
Infantry of the Line

Mx.

K.R.R.C.

Wilts.

Manch.

N. Staffs.

Y. & L.

D.L.I.

H.L.I.

Seaforth

Gordons

Camerons

R.U.R.

R.Ir.F.

A. & S.H.

R.B.

L.R.

H.R.

PLATE 12

FORMATION SIGNS
Infantry Divisions

 1st
 2nd
 3rd
 4th
 5th
 6th

 9th
 12th
 13th
 15th
 18th
 23rd

 36th
 38th
 40th
 43rd
 44th
 45th

 46th
 47th
 48th
 49th
 50th
 51st

 52nd
 53rd
 54th
 55th
 56th
 59th

 61st
 76th
 77th
 78th
 80th

PLATE 13

GREAT BRITAIN

FORMATION SIGNS

Independent Infantry Brigades and Brigade Groups

1st

24th

29th

31st

32nd

1st

24th

29th

31st

33rd

33rd

36th

37th

38th

56th

61st

70th

36th

37th

38th

56th

61st

70th

71st

72nd

73rd

115th

116th

148th

71st

72nd

73rd

115th

116th

148th

204th

206th

212th

214th

218th

219th

204th

206th

212th

214th

218th

219th

223rd

227th

231st

301st

303rd

304tn

Recce, 4th Division

133rd

H.Q. Pack Transp. Group, C.M.F.

PLATE 14

AIRBORNE FORCES

SPECIAL FORCES CAP BADGES

No 2 Commando   R.S.R.   S.A.S.   L.R.D.G.   'V' Force

Nos 50-52 Commandos

No 6 Commando   P.P.A.

WINGS

1st Glider Pilots   2nd Glider Pilots   S.A.S.

Parachutists

PLATE 15

COMMANDO SHOULDER FLASHES

No 1 Commando

Combined Operations

Commando Signals

Commandos

3 COMMANDO

4 COMMANDO

Nº 6 COMMANDO

5 COMMANDO

V COMMANDO

101 Troop

COMMANDO SBS

Special Boat Service

'V' Force

SPECIAL IV SERVICE

5 Troop

H.Q. Special Service Bde

COMMANDO D

Depot

TWELVE

TWELVE COMMANDO

FIRST COMMANDO BRIGADE

VI COMMANDO

PLATE 16

OFFICERS' RANK BADGES
worn on peaked cap

Generals

Senior officers

Junior officers

collar patches

Generals

Officers

worn on the shoulder straps

Marshal

General of Army

General of Division

General of Brigade

PLATE 17

POLAND

OFFICERS' RANK BADGES
worn on the shoulder straps

Marshal

General

Colonel

Lieutenant-colonel

Major

Captain

Lieutenant

2nd Lieutenant

MONOGRAMS FOR CAVALRY SHOULDER STRAPS

1 L.H.   3 L.H.   2 L.   7 L.   8 L.   11 L.   16 L.   17 L.   19 L.

20 L.   26 L.   27 L.   3 M.R.   6 M.R.   9 M.R.

PLATE 18

WARRANT OFFICERS AND N.C.Os' RANK BADGES

on coloured cap bands

W.O. Staff-sergeant Sergeant Lance-sergeant Corporal Lance-corporal

collar patches

Sergeants Other ranks

shoulder straps

Cadet
(Reg.Army)

W.O. Staff-sergeant Sergeant

Cadet
(Reserve)

Lance-sergeant Corporal Lance-corporal

PLATE 19

POLAND

COLLAR PATCHES

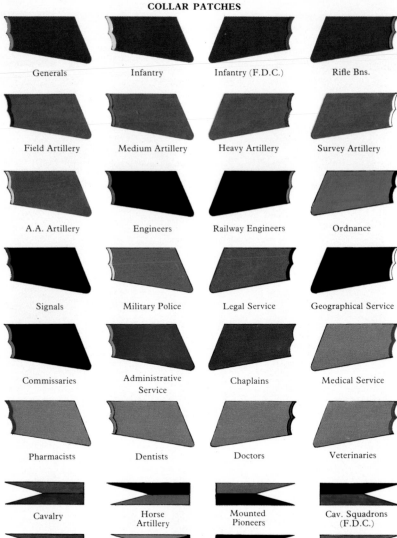

Generals

Infantry

Infantry (F.D.C.)

Rifle Bns.

Field Artillery

Medium Artillery

Heavy Artillery

Survey Artillery

A.A. Artillery

Engineers

Railway Engineers

Ordnance

Signals

Military Police

Legal Service

Geographical Service

Commissaries

Administrative Service

Chaplains

Medical Service

Pharmacists

Dentists

Doctors

Veterinaries

Cavalry

Horse Artillery

Mounted Pioneers

Cav. Squadrons (F.D.C.)

Recce (Mot.Bde)

Anti-Tank (Mot.Bde)

Signal Sq.

Train

Armoured units

PLATE 20

COLLAR PATCHES
Light Horse

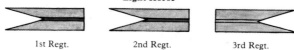

1st Regt.   2nd Regt.   3rd Regt.

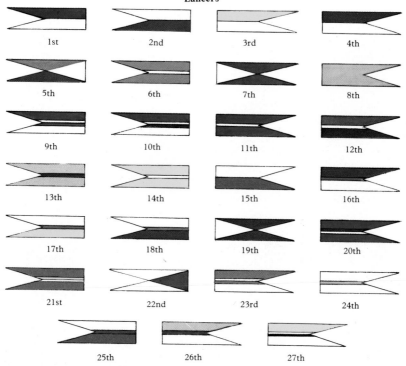

Lancers

1st   2nd   3rd   4th

5th   6th   7th   8th

9th   10th   11th   12th

13th   14th   15th   16th

17th   18th   19th   20th

21st   22nd   23rd   24th

25th   26th   27th

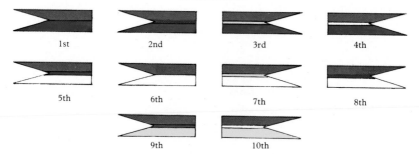

Mounted Rifles

1st   2nd   3rd   4th

5th   6th   7th   8th

9th   10th

PLATE 21

POLAND

COLLAR BADGES

General Staff

Geographical Service

Commissaries

Naval Service

11th Mtn. Division

21st/22nd Mtn. Division

Chaplains

Craftsmen

N.C.O. Schools

Bandmaster

Bandsman

1st (Tartar) Sq. 13 L.

37th Inf. Regt.

40th

43rd/44th

58th

H.Q. 16th Inf.Div.

63rd

64th

65th

66th

74th

82nd

84th

85th

PLATE 22

MONOGRAMS AND BADGES FOR INFANTRY SHOULDER STRAPS

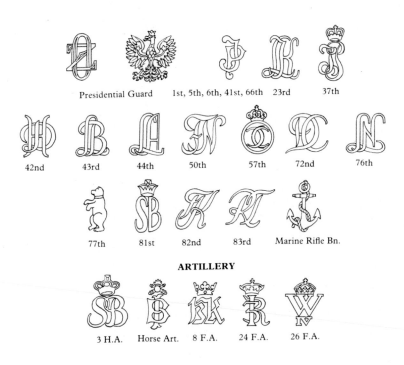

Presidential Guard   1st, 5th, 6th, 41st, 66th   23rd   37th

42nd   43rd   44th   50th   57th   72nd   76th

77th   81st   82nd   83rd   Marine Rifle Bn.

ARTILLERY

3 H.A.   Horse Art.   8 F.A.   24 F.A.   26 F.A.

ENGINEERS

Radiotelegraphic Regt.   Bridging   Electro-technical   Narrow gauge railways

1 2 3 4 5 6 7 8 9 0

PLATE 23

POLAND

INFANTRY REGIMENTAL BADGES

Officers School
(Reg.Army)

Officers School
(Reserve)

Officers School
for N.C.O.

Training Centre

1st Regt.

2nd

3rd

4th

5th

6th

7th

8th

9th

10th

11th

12th

13th

14th

15th

16th

17th

18th

19th

20th

21st

22nd

23rd

24th

25th

PLATE 24

INFANTRY REGIMENTAL BADGES

26th   27th   28th   29th   30th

31st   32nd   33rd   34th   35th

36th   37th   38th   39th   40th

41st   42nd   43rd   44th   45th

48th   49th   50th   51st   52nd

53rd   54th   55th   56th   57th

PLATE 25

POLAND

INFANTRY REGIMENTAL BADGES

58th

59th

60th

61st

62nd

63rd

64th

65th

66th

67th

68th

69th

70th

71st

72nd

73rd

74th

75th

76th

77th

78th

79th

80th

81st

82nd

83rd

84th

85th

86th

PLATE 26

HIGHLAND RIFLE REGIMENTS AND RIFLE BATTALIONS

1st. H.R. Regt	2nd	3rd	4th	5th

6th	1st. Rifle Bn.	2nd	3rd	Marine Rifle Bn.

CAVALRY

School	1st Light Horse Regt.	2nd	3rd

1st Lancers	2nd	3rd	4th	5th

6th	7th	8th	9th	10th

PLATE 27

POLAND

CAVALRY

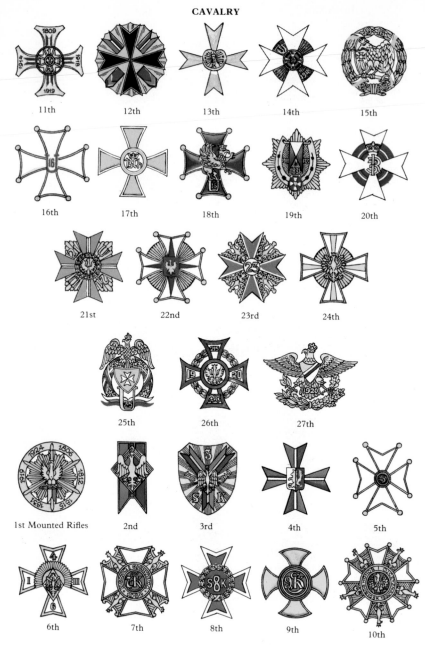

11th

12th

13th

14th

15th

16th

17th

18th

19th

20th

21st

22nd

23rd

24th

25th

26th

27th

1st Mounted Rifles

2nd

3rd

4th

5th

6th

7th

8th

9th

10th

PLATE 28

FIELD ARTILLERY

1st F.A. Regt. 2nd 3rd 4th 5th

6th 7th 8th 9th 10th

11th 12th 13th 14th 15th

16th 17th 18th 19th 20th

21st 22nd 23rd 24th 25th

26th 27th 28th 29th 30th

PLATE 29

POLAND

ARTILLERY

1st Medium Art. Regt.

2nd

3rd

4th

5th

6th

7th

8th

9th

10th

1st Heavy Art. Regt.

Horse Art.

Art. Officers Sch.

Survey Art.

1st Motorised Art. Regt.

31st F.A. Regt.

1st A.A. Art. Regt.

A.A. Artillery

Cadet Force Instr.

PROFICIENCY BADGES

Sword-Lance

Rifle Association

Marksman

National Sport badge

Riding

PLATE 30

ENGINEERS AND SIGNALS

Eng. School

Fortifications

Training Centre

Officers' School

Regular Army

Reserve

1st Bn.

2nd

3rd

4th

7th

8th

9th—6th

1st Railway Bn.

Mounted Pioneers

Bridging Bn.

Signals Corps

Signals School

Signals Officers' School

Signals Tr. Centre

Radio Tr. Signals

1st Telegraphic Bn.

5th

7th

1st Signals Regt.

Electro-Techn. Bn.

PLATE 31

POLAND

ARMOURED TROOPS

Armd. Corps

A.C. Training Centre

1st Armd. Bn.

2nd

3rd

4th

5th

6th

7th

8th

9th

10th

12th

1st Armd. Train. Group

2nd

SERVICES, SCHOOLS, ETC.

Inspectorate General of the Armed Forces

Staff College

F.D.C.

N.C.O. Training School

Geographical Institute

Medical Officers School

Army Chemical Inst.

Military Police

1st Cadet Corps

PLATE 32

NATIONAL COCKADE

CAP BANDS

Generals   Colonel-brigadier

COLLAR PATCHES AND SHOULDER STRAPS

Colonel-brigadier (Infantry)

Lieutenant-general   Major-general

General's badge for
shoulder cords

Officers' belt buckle

PLATE 33

BELGIUM

RANK BADGES

Officers

Senior officers
Chass. of the Ardennes

Junior officers
Grenadiers

Corps and Services

Colonel
Gen. Staff (Inf.)

Colonel
Chasseurs-on-Foot

Lieutenant-colonel
Engineers-Signals

Major
Grenadiers

Captain-commandant
Chasseurs-on-Horse

Captain
Artillery

Lieutenant
Carabiniers

2nd Lieutenant
Transport Corps

Warrant Officers

W.O. 1st Class
Frontier Cyclists Regt.

Lancers

W.O.
Carab. Cyclists

PLATE 34

Sergeants and Corporals

Sergeants
Administrative Service

Corporals and privates
Transport Corps

Chevrons

Sergeant-major   1st Sergeant   Sergeant   Corporal   Private 1st Class

Corps and Services

Guides   Chass. of the
Ardennes   Commissaries   Light Horse   Lancers

Doctors   Pharmacists   Dentists   Veterinaries   Medical Service
(O.R.)

Legal Service   Administrative Service   Military Supplies

PLATE 35

OFFICERS' BADGES ON PEAKED CAP, JACKET AND GREATCOAT

Lieutenant-colonel (Artillery)

Lieutenant (doctor—
Medical Service)

PLATE 36

CORPS AND SERVICE BADGES

Carabiniers

Chasseurs-on-Foot

Grenadiers

Chasseurs of the Ardennes

Fortress units

Cavalry

Chasseurs-on-Horse

Cyclists

Light Horse

Guides

Lancers

Cav. Depot

Art. Depot

Artillery

Horse Artillery

Infantry

Mot. Artillery

A.A. Artillery

Fortress Namur

Regiments Liege

Artillery Repair Service

Military Railways

Pontoon Service

Signals

Transports H.Q.

Transport Corps

River Transport

Camouflage Service

Commissariat (other ranks)

Road-River ways Maintenance

Engineers

Band

Water Suppliers

PLATE 37

BELGIUM

CORPS AND SERVICE BADGES

Chaplains

Catholic, Protestant and Jewish Chaplains

Medical, Veterinary
and Pharmacist Services
(other ranks)

Civilian Personnel

REGIMENTAL, ARMY CORPS NUMERALS

'ATTRIBUTS DES FONCTIONS'

Generals

General Staff

Commissaries

Medical, Veterinary
and Pharmacist officers

Administrative
officers

Officers-N.C.O.
archivist secretaries

Officers
Military Supplies

N.C.O. secretaries
of Commissariat

Officers-N.C.O.
quartermasters

Aerostat
officers

Advocate generals

Judge advocates

Clerks

PLATE 38

GENERALS' RANK BADGES
worn on peaked cap

First Marshal of the Empire   Marshal of Italy and Generals

on field service cap
1934-35

2   3   4   5   6   7

1935-43

1   2   3   4   5   6   7

on both forearms

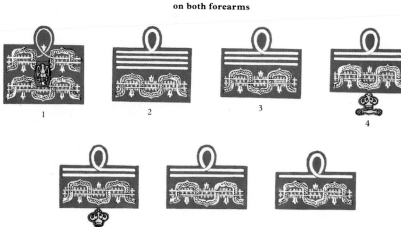

1   2   3   4   5   6   7

1. First Marshal of the Empire   2. Marshal of Italy   3. General of Army   4. General "in command" of an Army   5. General of Army Corps   6. General of Division   7. General of Brigade.

PLATE 39

OFFICERS' RANK BADGES
worn on peaked cap

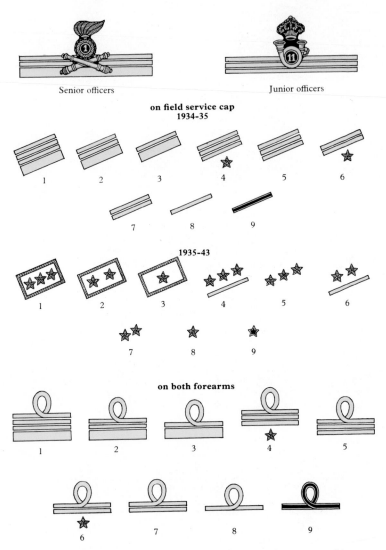

Senior officers   Junior officers

on field service cap
1934-35

1935-43

on both forearms

1. Colonel   2. Lieutenant-colonel   3. Major   4. 1st Captain   5. Captain   6. 1st Lieutenant
7. Lieutenant   8. 2nd Lieutenant   9. Cadet

PLATE 40

WARRANT OFFICERS' RANK BADGES

worn on peaked cap

worn on shoulder straps

| *Aiutante di battaglia* | W.O. Major | Chief W.O. | W.O. |

NON-COMMISSIONED OFFICERS AND OTHER RANKS
worn on both forearms (1909-1939)

| Sergeant-major | Sergeant | Corporal-major | Corporal |

on both upper arms (since 1939)

| Sergeant-major | Sergeant | Corporal-major | Corporal |

PLATE 41

ITALY

COLLAR PATCHES

Infantry

Grenadiers

Cavalry

Commiss.

Unass. Inf.

Art.

Eng.

Admin.

Med.

Vet.

Fencing Instr.

Supply

G.A.F.

M.G.

Mortars

Mot. M.G.

Div. Scout Group

Divisional Art.

Div. Eng.

Mot. Inf.

Tanks

Light Tanks

Motor Transport

Mot. Artillery

Alpine Art.

Bersaglieri

10th Assault Regt.

Alpini

Alpine Eng.

Guastatori

Chemical Centre

Parachutists

Para-*Guast.*

General Staff

M.V.S.N.

'M' Bns.

Adjutant

PLATE 42

CAP BADGES

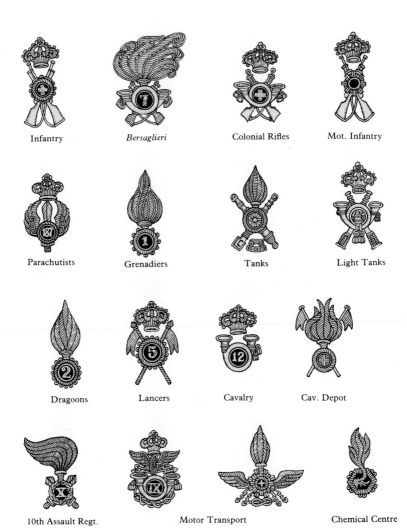

Infantry   *Bersaglieri*   Colonial Rifles   Mot. Infantry

Parachutists   Grenadiers   Tanks   Light Tanks

Dragoons   Lancers   Cavalry   Cav. Depot

10th Assault Regt.   Motor Transport   Chemical Centre

PLATE 43

CAP BADGES

Divisional Artillery   Army Corps Art.   Army Art.   Coast Art.

Light A.A. Art.   Heavy A.A. Art.   Light Art. Regt.   Horse Art.

Mot. Art.   Train Art.   Sappers   Bridging Engineers

Signals (Radio)   Signals   Railway Engineers   Miners

PLATE 44

CAP BADGES

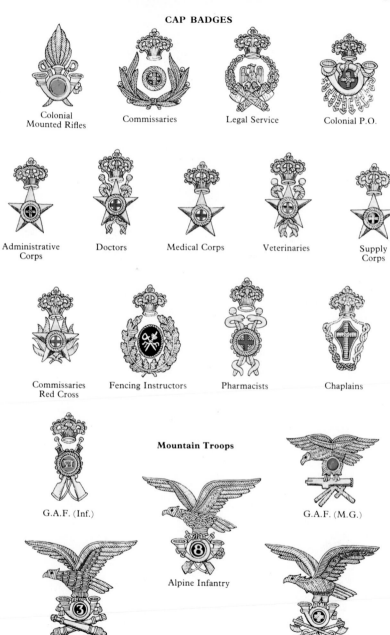

Colonial
Mounted Rifles

Commissaries

Legal Service

Colonial P.O.

Administrative
Corps

Doctors

Medical Corps

Veterinaries

Supply
Corps

Commissaries
Red Cross

Fencing Instructors

Pharmacists

Chaplains

Mountain Troops

G.A.F. (Inf.)

G.A.F. (M.G.)

Alpine Infantry

Alpine Artillery

Alpine Engineers

PLATE 45

ITALY

DIVISIONAL ARM SHIELDS

Infantry Divisions

Motorised Divisions

Alpine Division

ARM AND BREAST BADGES

G.A.F.

Guastatori

Parachutists

1

2

Assault

CAP BADGES

Alpini

Medical Corps

3

4

Bersaglieri

OTHER BADGES

Gilded pioneer badge

Silvered Infantry badge

Brass shoulder plate
(Sergeants, corporals & privates)

Grenadiers' plate worn
on ammunition pouch

PLATE 46

EARLY FASCIST CAP BADGES

Officers   Generals   Black Shirts

MILIZIA VOLONTARIA SICUREZZA NAZIONALE
1923-38

Officers   Generals   Doctors

Chaplains   N.C.O.s   Black Shirts

1938-43

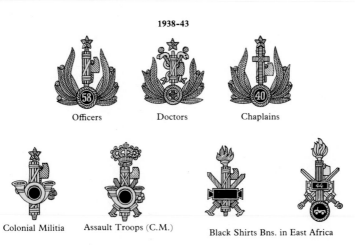

Officers   Doctors   Chaplains

Colonial Militia   Assault Troops (C.M.)

Black Shirts Bns. in East Africa

PLATE 47

ITALY

M.V.S.N. RANK BADGES

worn on both forearms
1923-35

1   2   3   4

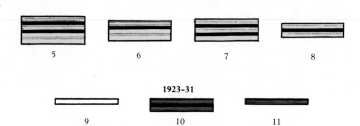

5   6   7   8

1923-31

9   10   11

worn on headgear
1923-35

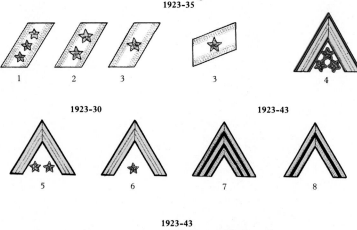

1   2   3   3   4

1923-30   **1923-43**

5   6   7   8

1923-43

9   10   11

1. Comandante generale   2. Luogotenente generale   3. Console generale   4. Console
5. Primo seniore   6. Seniore   7. Centurione .   8. Capo manipolo   9. Capo squadra   10. Vice
capo squadra   11. Camicia Nera scelta

PLATE 48

worn on both forearms
1935-38

1938-43

1935-43

1931-38

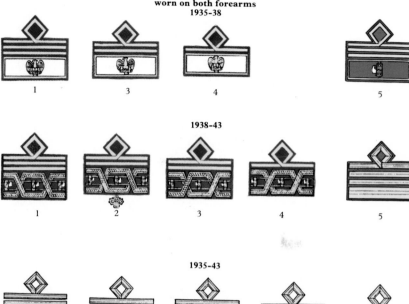

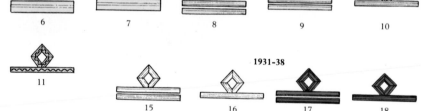

shoulder straps

on both upper arms
1938-43

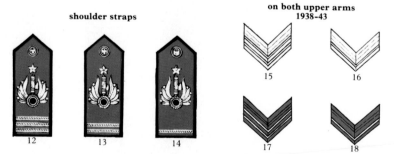

1. Comandante generale   2. Luogotenente generale (Chief of Staff)   3. Luogotenente generale
4. Console generale   5. Console   6. Primo seniore   7. Seniore   8. Centurione   9. Capo
manipolo   10. Sottocapo manipolo   11. Aspirante   12. Primo aiutante   13. Aiutante capo
14. Aiutante   15. Primo capo squadra   16. Capo squadra   17. Vice capo squadra   18. Camicia
Nera scelta

PLATE 49

ITALY

M.V.S.N. RANK BADGES
worn on the headgear
1935-38

1

3

4

5

1930-43

6

7

11

15

1. Comandante generale 3. Luogotenente generale 4. Console generale 5. Console
6. Primo seniore 7. Seniore 11. Aspirante 15. Primo capo squadra

on the peaked cap 1938-43

1st Honorary corporal

Honorary corporal

ARM SHIELDS

Black Shirts zones

M.V.S.N. H.Q.

B.S. Divisions (1935)

Indep. Legion

B.S. Div. (1940)

PLATE 50

CAP BADGES

Generals

COLOURED CAP BANDS

Staff College

Infantry   Cavalry   Artillery   Engineers   Chemical Warfare   Services

COLLAR PATCHES

Tunic

Jacket

Major, Artillery

Greatcoat

RANK BADGES WORN ON COLLAR PATCHES

Generals   Senior commanders   Commanders   Junior commanders

PLATE 51

U.S.S.R.

ARMY RANK BADGES (1935-40)

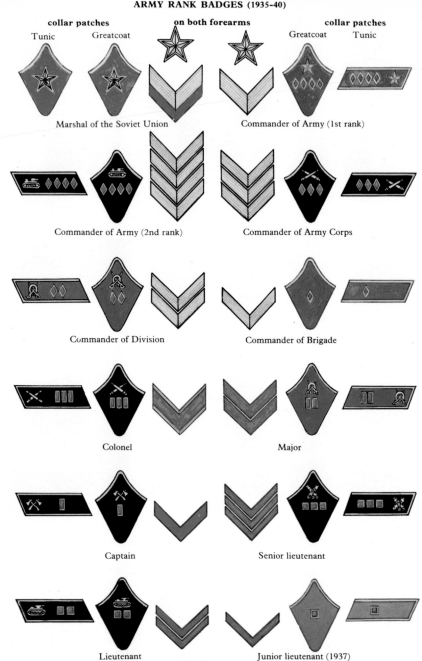

collar patches — on both forearms — collar patches
Tunic — Greatcoat — Greatcoat — Tunic

Marshal of the Soviet Union

Commander of Army (1st rank)

Commander of Army (2nd rank)

Commander of Army Corps

Commander of Division

Commander of Brigade

Colonel

Major

Captain

Senior lieutenant

Lieutenant

Junior lieutenant (1937)

PLATE 52

Political Personnel

Commissar of Army (1st rank)

Commissar of Army (2nd rank)

Commissar of Army Corps

Commissar of Division

Sleeve

Commissar of Brigade

Commissar of Regiment

Commissar of Battalion

Senior Politruk

Politruk

Junior politruk (1937)

PLATE 53

U.S.S.R.

Administrative Personnel

Intendant of Army

Intendant of Army Corps

Intendant of Division

Intendant of Brigade

Intendant 1st Class

Intendant 2nd Class

Intendant 3rd Class

Technician 1st Class

Technician 3rd Class (1937)

Technician 2nd class (1937)

Junior Commanders

Sergeant-major

Junior Platoon Co.

Section Co.

Private

PLATE 54

COLLAR BADGES
before 1936

Infantry   Border Guards   Cavalry   Machine Gunners   Artillery   Medical Dept.

Engineers

Camouflage   Signals   Veterinaries

Railways   Drivers   Railways (Stations-Harbours)   Armd. Trains   Tanks   Armd. Cars

added in 1936

Medical   Band   Veterinaries   Commissariat

Armd. Troops   Legal   Administrative   Chemical   Technical Troops   Signals

PLATE 55

ARMY RANK BADGES (1940-43)

Generals' cap badge

Marshal of the Soviet Union

General of the Army

Colonel-general

Lieutenant-general

Major-general

Colonel

Lieutenant-colonel

Major

Captain

PLATE 56

ARMY RANK BADGES (1940-43)

Senior lieutenant   Lieutenant

Junior lieutenant

Junior Commanders

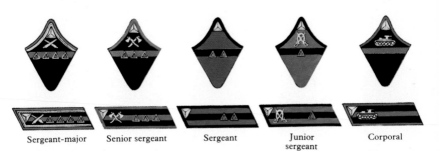

Sergeant-major   Senior sergeant   Sergeant   Junior sergeant   Corporal

Kiev Tank School

Guards

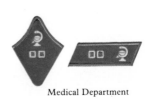

Medical Department

PLATE 57

MARSHAL OF THE SOVIET UNION AND GENERALS

Parade Uniform (15.1.1943)

Marshal

Generals

Collars

Cuffs

Generals' shoulder boards
(All uniforms except Field)

Marshal
of the Soviet Union

General of Army

Colonel-general

Lieutenant-general

Major-general

Greatcoat collar patches for Parade and Ordinary Uniforms

Marshal

Generals

PLATE 58

SENIOR COMMANDERS AND COMMANDERS
Collar Patches

Army (except Eng./Techn. staff)

Engineer/Technical staff

Senior commanders

Commanders

Cuff Patches

Senior commanders
Commanders

Shoulder Boards

Colonel

Lieutenant-colonel

Major

Captain

Senior lieutenant

Lieutenant

Junior lieutenant

ALL OTHER RANKS
Greatcoat Collar Patches

PLATE 59

U.S.S.R.

MEDICAL, VETERINARY AND LEGAL SERVICES

Lawyer of Army Corps

Major-general

Lawyer 2nd Class

Lieutenant

Junior Commanders and Private

Sergeant-
major

Senior
sergeant

Sergeant

Junior
sergeant

Corporal

Private

Army

Eng./Techn. Staff

Junior commanders

Private

Cadets

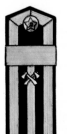

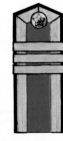

PLATE 60

FIELD UNIFORM

Colonel

Lieutenant-colonel

Major

Junior lieutenant

Captain

Senior lieutenant

Lieutenant

Junior lieutenant

Sergeant-major

Senior sergeant

Sergeant

Junior sergeant

Corporal

Private

O.R.'s belt buckle

wounded stripes

PLATE 61

U.S.S.R.

MARSHALS

Collar and cuff   4.2.1943

4.2.1943

Marshal of the Soviet Union   Artillery   Armour

SUPREME MARSHALS 27.10.1943

Artillery   Engineers   Signals   Armour

MARSHALS 27.10.1943

Engineers   Signals

PLATE 62

JUNIOR SOLDIERS SCHOOL
21.9.1943

Kalinski   Orlov   Stalingrad   Novo-Cherkask

ARTILLERY SPECIALISTS' SCHOOL
27.10.1943

MILITARY TRANSPORT

Cap band   Arm badge

PLATE 63

U.S.A.

CAP BADGES

Army Officers

West Point Academy

Transport Service

Harbour Boat Service

W.A.C.

Warrant Officers

U.S. Army Band

U.S. ARMY DIVERS' BREAST BADGES

Enlisted Men and W.A.C.

Master

1st Class

2nd Class

Salvage

RANK BADGES

General of the Army

General

Lieut. general

Maj. general

Brigadier

Colonel

Lieut. colonel

Major

Captain

1st Lieut.

2nd Lieut.

Chief warrant officer

Warrant officer

PLATE 64

NON-COMMISSIONED OFFICERS

Master sergeant

First sergeant

Technical sergeant

Staff sergeant

Technician
3rd grade

Sergeant

Technician
4th grade

Corporal

Technician 5th grade

Private 1st Class

Three-year
service stripe

U.S. ARMY MINE PLANTER SERVICE

Engineer

Master mine planter
or
Chief engineer

1st mate mine planter
or
Assistant engineer

2nd mate mine planter
or
2nd assistant engineer

Mine planter

PLATE 65

U.S.A.

OFFICERS' COLLAR BADGES

Officer's U.S.   Engineers   Special Service   Signal C.   Unassigned Officer   Field Artillery

Infantry   Military Police   Armd. Force   Tank Destroyer Force   Coast Art.   Cavalry

Band   Nat. Guard Bur.   General's Aide   Transp. Corps   Gen. Staff   Warrant Officer   W.A.C.

Ordnance   Intelligence   A.F.N.   Quartermaster   Chemical Corps   Adjutant Corps   Finance

Physio-Therapy   Judge Advocate   Chaplains   Inspector G.S.   Hospital Dietitian

Medical Corps   Contract Surgeon   Sanitary Corps   Nurses Corps   Dental Corps   Pharmacy Corps   Vet. Corps   Med. Administrati

BREAST BADGES

Gen. Staff

Combat Infantryman   Expert Infantryman

Paratroops   Glider badge

PLATE 66

SHOULDER SLEEVE INSIGNIA
Army Groups

6th

12th

15th

Armies

1st

2nd

3rd

4th

5th

6th

7th

8th

9th

10th

15th

Army Corps

1st

2nd

3rd

4th

5th

6th

7th

8th

9th

10th

11th

12th

13th

14th

15th

16th

18th

19th

20th

21st

22nd

23rd

24th

36th

PLATE 67

U.S.A.

SHOULDER SLEEVE INSIGNIA
Infantry and Airborne Divisions

1st

2nd

3rd

4th

5th

6th

7th

8th

9th

10th

11th

13th

17th

24th

25th

26th

27th

28th

29th

30th

31st

32nd

33rd

34th

35th

36th

37th

38th

39th

40th

41st

42nd

43rd

44th

45th

63rd

65th

66th

69th

70th

71st

75th

PLATE 68

SHOULDER SLEEVE INSIGNIA
Infantry and Airborne Division

 76th
 77th
 78th
 79th
 80th
 81st
 82nd

 83rd
 84th
 85th
 86th
 87th
 88th
89th

 90th
 91st
 92nd
 93rd
 94th
 95th
 96th

 97th
 98th
 99th
 100th
 101st
 102nd
 103rd

 104th
 106th
 Americal

 1st

 2nd

Cavalry Divisions

 3rd
 21st
 24th
 56th

PLATE 69

U.S.A.

SHOULDER SLEEVE INSIGNIA

Cavalry Division

61st   62nd   63rd   64th   65th   66th

ARMY GROUND FORCES

Army Ground Forces   Replacement and School Command   General Hqs. Reserve   A.G.F. Replacement Depot   Army Service Forces   A.S.F. Training Center

Armd. Center   Airborne Command   A.A. Command   Amphibious Units   Ports of Embarkation

Engineer Amphibious Command   Army Specialized Training Program   A.S.T.P. (Reserve)   Tank Destroyer Units   Bomb Disposal personnel

Theaters

Pacific Ocean Area   European   European (Advance Base)   North African

South Atlantic   China-Burma-India   Middle East

PLATE 70

SHOULDER SLEEVE INSIGNIA
Headquarters

Allied Force Hqs.

S.H.A.E.F.

Hqs. South East Asia
Command

Base Commands

Iceland

Greenland

GHQ S.W. Pacific

Defense Commands

Southern

Eastern

London

Labrador, North-East
and Central Canada Command

Caribbean

Bermuda

Atlantic

Military District
of Washington

A.A. Art. Command
Western D.C.

A.A. Art. Command
Eastern D.C.

Pacific Coastal
F.D.S.

Chesapeake Bay
F.D.S.

Frontier Defense Sectors

A.A. Art. Command
Central D.C.

A.A. Art. Command
Southern D.C.

New England

N.Y.-Philadelphia   Southern Coastal

PLATE 71

U.S.A.

SHOULDER SLEEVE INSIGNIA
Service Commands

1st

North West

Persian Gulf

2nd

3rd

4th

5th

6th

7th

8th

9th

Departments

Alaskan

Antilles

Panama

Philippine

Hawaiian

MISCELLANEOUS U.S. UNITS

Combat Team
442

1st S.S.F.

Merrill's Marauders

Rangers

Task Force

Chinese Combat
Training Command

French Forces
Training with
U.S. Troops

Allied Airborne

U.S. Military
Mission to Moscow

Veterans
Administration

Rangers

PLATE 72

SHOULDER SLEEVE INSIGNIA
Miscellaneous U.S. Units

Panama Hellgate

Hawaiian Separate
Coast Art. Bde.

Hawaiian Division

Hawaiian
Coastal
Defense

Philippine
Division

Amphib.
Training
Force 9

Aleutian
Islands

Officer's
Candidate School

Excellence
in
Artillery

Hawaiian
Nat'l guard

Filipino
Bn.

Army Hostesses

U.S. Military Academy
West Point

U.S.O. Camp Shows

Airborne Troops

Glider Borne Paratroops

Glider Borne Troops

Paratroops

PARATROOPS IDENTITY BACKGROUND OVALS

SLEEVE BADGES

W.W.1. Overseas
Chevrons—wounds

Meritorious
Service

Meritorious Awards

Overseas
Service Stripes

PLATE 73

GERMANY

OFFICERS' CAP BADGES (1, 2, 3) COLLAR (4, 5, 6, 7) AND CUFF (8, 9, 10) PATCHES

4

2

6

5

1

7

8

9

3

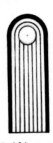
10

OFFICERS' RANK BADGES

| Field-marshal | Colonel-general | General | Lieutenant-general | Major-general |

| Colonel | Lieutenant-colonel | Major | Captain | Lieutenant | 2nd Lieutenant |

PLATE 74

NON-COMMISSIONED OFFICERS AND OTHER RANKS

1. Cap badge   2, 3, 4. Collar patches   5. Cuff patch

| Staff-sergeant | Sergeant-major | Sergeant | Lance-sergeant | N.C.O. |

| Staff-corporal | Corporal-major *(over 6 years' service)* | Corporal-major | Corporal | Senior private |

Privates' shoulder straps

PLATE 75

GERMANY

ARM BADGES (Except Mountain Guide)

Sniper   *Jäger*   Standard-bearer   Mountain Troops   Mountain Guide

Helmsman   Signaller   Gunlayer   Smoke Troops operator

Defence Works   Medical Corps   Farriers   Artificer   radio-operator   Ordnance

Motor Maintenance   Pigeoneer   Fortification Construction   Saddler cadet   Paymaster cadet   Fortification Maintenance

CUFF TITLES

PLATE 76

SHOULDER STRAPS BADGES

 Legal

 Anti-Tank

 Technical

 Reconnaissance

 Veterinary

 Administration

 Doctor

 Guards

 Ordnance

 Band

 Mot. Cyclist

 Mounted

 M.G. Bns.

 Observation

 Schools

 Art. Sch.

 Army Mot. Sch.

 Ord. Sch.

 War Sch.

 Physical Tr. Sch.

 Trainer Units

 Fortifications

 Tank Research

 N.C.O. Sch.

 Divisional H.Q.

 Frontier Defence

Experimental Stations

 N.C.O. Sch.

 Army Group H.Q.

 Observer Trainer

 O.R.'s belt buckle

 A.T. Trainer

PLATE 77

GERMANY

CLOSE COMBAT CLASP

GENERAL ASSAULT BADGES

General Assault

25–50

75–100

COMBAT BADGES

Infantry Assault

Army Parachutist

Army Balloon Observer

Army Anti-Aircraft

TANK BATTLE BADGES

Tank Battle

25–50

75–100

PLATE 78

TANK BATTLE BADGES

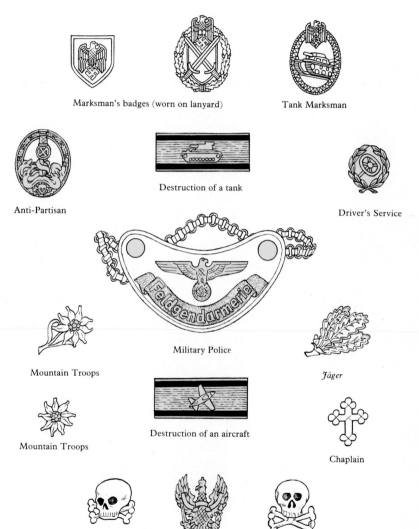

Marksman's badges (worn on lanyard)

Tank Marksman

Anti-Partisan

Destruction of a tank

Driver's Service

Military Police

Mountain Troops

Jäger

Mountain Troops

Destruction of an aircraft

Chaplain

Commemorative regimental badges

PLATE 79

GERMANY

ARM SHIELDS

WOUNDED BADGES

Spanish
Civil War

2nd W.W.

20.7.1944

PLATE 80

SCHUTZSTAFFEL
Cap Badges

Collar Patches

Arm Badge

Standard Bearer's Gorget

Officer's Belt Buckle

O.R.'s Belt Buckle

Cuff Titles

Adolf Hitler   **ϟϟ-Polizei-Division**

Hohenstaufen   **Das Reich**

PLATE 81

Germania

Deutschland

Der Führer

Reichsführer-SS

Totenkopf

30. Januar

Nord

Reinhard Heydrich

Nordland

Westland

Nordland

Westland

Götz von Berlichingen

Prinz Eugen

Florian Geyer

Wallonie

Theodor Eicke

Charlemagne

Frundsberg

PLATE 82

SCHUTZSTAFFEL

Collar Patches

5th

11th

13th

14th

15th

18th

19th

20th

21st

22nd

23rd

23rd–34th

25th

27th

28th

29th (Italian)

33rd

29th–30th (Russian)

36th

Indian

British

PLATE 83

OFFICER'S RANK BADGES

1933-34	1934-42	1942-45

Reichsführer-SS

SS-Oberstgruppenführer

SS-Obergruppenführer

SS-Gruppenführer

SS-Brigadeführer

SS-Oberführer

PLATE 84

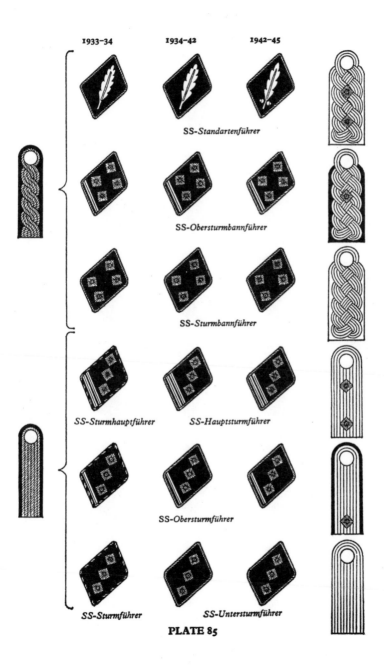

1933-34   1934-42   1942-45

SS-Standartenführer

SS-Obersturmbannführer

SS-Sturmbannführer

SS-Sturmhauptführer   SS-Hauptsturmführer

SS-Obersturmführer

SS-Sturmführer   SS-Untersturmführer

PLATE 85

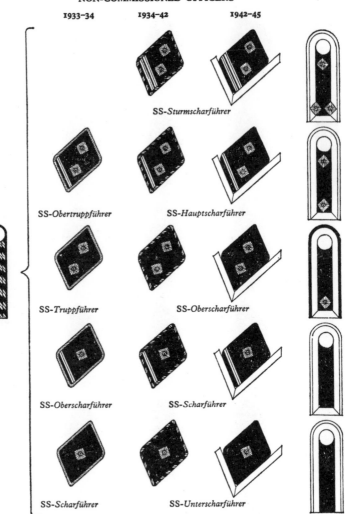

1933–34   1934–42   1942–45

SS-*Sturmscharführer*

SS-*Obertruppführer*   SS-*Hauptscharführer*

SS-*Truppführer*   SS-*Oberscharführer*

SS-*Oberscharführer*   SS-*Scharführer*

SS-*Scharführer*   SS-*Unterscharführer*

PLATE 86

OTHER RANKS

1933-34	1934-42	1942-45

SS-*Rottenführer*

SS-*Sturmmann*

SS-*Mann*   SS-*Oberschütze*

SS-*Leibst.* ADOLF HITLER   DEUTSCHLAND   GERMANIA   DER FÜHRER

SS-*Stabsscharführer*   Alter-*Kämpfer*   ex-Police/ex-Soldier   ex-*Stahlhelm*

PLATE 87

RANK BADGES FOR CAMOUFLAGE UNIFORMS

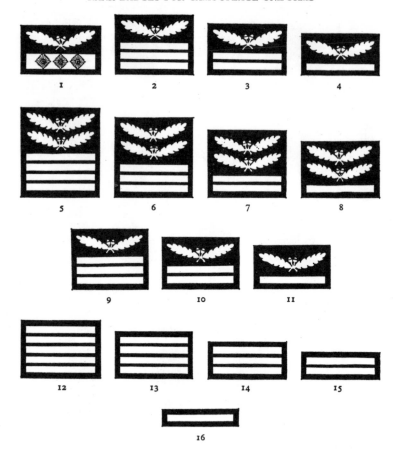

1. SS-*Oberstgruppenführer* 2. SS-*Obergruppenführer* 3. SS-*Gruppenführer* 4. SS-*Brigadeführer*
5. SS-*Oberführer* 6. SS-*Standartenführer* 7. SS-*Obersturmbannführer* 8. SS-*Sturmbannführer*
9. SS-*Hauptsturmführer* 10. SS-*Obersturmführer* 11. SS-*Untersturmführer* 12. SS-*Sturmscharführer*
13. SS-*Hauptscharführer* 14. SS-*Oberscharführer* 15. SS-*Scharführer* 16. SS-*Unterscharführer*.

PLATE 88

Great Britain

In the second half of the seventeenth century, soldiers began to wear uniforms, the 'uniform' at first being confined to the coat, which was predominantly red. The soldier provided his own trousers and shoes, the choice of which was left to his discretion.

At that time the colonel 'owned' the regiment, and his emblem and colours were profusely displayed on the uniforms and standards.

Cromwell's New Model Army came into being in 1645 and was the first organised British Army. After the Restoration in 1661 it became the Standing Army, the forefather of the Regular Army.

Red remained the colour of the infantryman's coat for two centuries, with the exception of the Rifle regiments, when they were eventually formed, who wore 'rifle green'. The Royal Engineers wore red coats, and red or blue coats were worn by the various cavalry regiments. The Royal Artillery and service branches of the Army adopted blue uniforms.

In 1751, a Royal Warrant ended the wearing of the colonels' emblems, and replaced them with proper regimental 'devices', as badges were then called. Some of these 'devices' are still worn nowadays. At the same time uniforms became standardised, and the above was the first of a long series of royal warrants and precise 'Dress' regulations.

Khaki uniforms were worn for the first time during the Indian Mutiny and were then white uniforms, roughly dyed, in order to make the soldiers less conspicuous. The word 'khaki' is derived from Urdu and means 'dusty'.

In later campaigns, for instance during the Afghan War, uniforms were again dyed, but it was only during the Boer wars that the adoption of a camouflaged uniform became imperative, because of the guerrilla nature of the war. Khaki was adopted as a standard uniform, to be worn at all stations abroad, except Canada. In 1902, a khaki service dress for all ranks was introduced and its colour proved most suitable for the trench warfare of World War 1. During this war the steel helmet, as we know it, was adopted and, though modified, its design is practically the same today.

World War 1 marked the end of an era, and with it the coloured uniforms also disappeared. Khaki service dress became standard issue, although a blue 'walking out' uniform was chosen in 1936 for the Coronation. The year after, the famous khaki battledress was introduced, together with its appropriate webbing equipment. The headdress was a helmet or the khaki field cap, the latter later being substituted with a beret. The black beret was already worn by the regiments of the Royal Armoured Corps, with the exception of the 11th Hussars who wore a brown beret with a scarlet band. The Airborne Forces wore maroon berets and Commandos and Reconnaissance Corps wore green berets. The rest of the Army was issued with khaki berets.

Battledress was made of khaki serge, and was composed of a tunic or blouse buttoned onto the trousers, the trousers being tucked into the webbing anklets. Variations of battledress tunics can be divided into two types: a smart lined tunic, with all buttons hidden by flaps, and another type with all the buttons showing and normally of a shabbier appearance.

Collar badges were worn on the service dress together with metal shoulder titles on the shoulder straps. New types of identification badges were introduced for the battledress.

In 1940 some coloured felt strips (2 in. $\times$ $\frac{1}{4}$ in.) were adopted on the sleeves, to be worn below the formation sign. Nineteen in all, the colours of these strips were as follows:

scarlet	Infantry (except Rifle regiments)
rifle green	Rifle regiments
purple	Royal Army Chaplains Department
red	Corps of Military Police
green	Intelligence Corps
yellow	Royal Army Pay Corps
Cambridge blue	Army Educational Corps
dull cherry	Royal Army Medical Corps
red–blue	Royal Artillery
blue–red	Royal Engineers
yellow–red	Royal Armoured Corps
yellow–blue	Royal Army Service Corps
blue–white	Royal Signals
green–white	Army Dental Corps
red–green	Pioneer Corps
grey–yellow	Army Catering Corps
red–blue–red	Royal Army Ordnance Corps
red–yellow–blue	Royal Electrical and Mechanical Engineers
black–red–black	Army Physical Training Corps

At about the same time, cloth shoulder titles replaced brass ones and were stitched at the top of the sleeves, just below the seam. They were printed, or embroidered, on coloured felts and, as well as showing the corps or regimental title, they also showed the arm or corps colour.

Infantry regiments (with the exception of Rifle regiments) wore shoulder titles with white lettering on scarlet (QUEEN'S, BUFFS, BEDFS. and HERTS., CAMERONIANS, INNISKILLING, LOYALS, NORTH STAFFORD, DURHAM L.I. etc.). Black and red lettering on 'rifle green' were the shoulder titles of the Rifle Brigade and the K.R.R.C. As in the days of full dress, the former wore green jackets with black piping, the latter green jackets with red piping.

Guards regiments wore shoulder titles in their regimental colours. The Royal Artillery title was in red lettering on a blue background. The Royal Army Ordnance Corps wore the letters R.A.O.C. in blue on red, and the Royal Army Medical Corps R.A.M.C. in white on dull cherry background, and so on.

Some regiments had shoulder titles made abroad and they were not made in the correct colours. For instance, the Duke of Wellington's Regiment, whose shoulder titles were made in Italy, are embroidered on 'flame red' instead of on scarlet.

The cavalry regiments formed part of the Royal Armoured Corps and wore its shoulder title. However, regimental cavalry shoulder titles exist, such as that of the 17/21 LANCERS, embroidered in white on black cloth.

The outbreak of World War 2 caught the British soldier in the colonies wearing the khaki drill service dress, the 'summer' version of the service dress worn at home. Regimental patches were worn on the left side of the colonial helmet on the puggree.

Khaki drill shorts were worn with hose and puttees and, although the uniform was basically the same for both officers and other ranks, that of the former was often made with better cloth, was better tailored and the collar was opened to show the shirt and tie.

Plate 1. Cap Badges and Gorget Patches

The cap badge worn by field-marshals was, and still is, composed of crossed batons on a wreath of laurel, surmounted by the Royal Crest. That of general, lieutenant-general and major-general carries a crossed baton and sword in the centre instead of crossed batons. Brigadier-generals wore the Royal Crest, which was also worn by officers belonging to the Extra-Regimentally Employed List, formed by officers of the judge advocate's staff, staff quartermasters and quartermasters employed on staff and administrative duties.

The gorget patches trace their origin to the metal gorget worn on the chest by officers until about 1830. Previously the gorget was that part of the armour meant to protect the upper chest and the throat of the wearer. The armour slowly went into disuse, but the gorget remained as a symbol of rank in the form of a crescent-shaped, embossed plate, hung around the neck by means of ribbons. Gorget patches were later introduced in

India and, as we know them today, were brought in in 1896. They were later applied on the collar of the service dress.

Field-marshals and generals wore scarlet gorget patches with gold leaves and acorns embroidered along the centre. They were substituted by a gold gimp on the patches worn on the battledress or shirt collar.

Gold leaves and acorns used to be the distinctive ornament of field-marshals and general officers, widely embroidered on the collars, cuffs and on the back flaps of the skirts of the red tunic.

The gorget patches of brigadiers and substantive colonels were made of scarlet cloth with a red gimp. Those for battledress were 2 in. long. The gorget patch button is a smaller version of that worn on the tunic.

Officers' Rank Badges

During the present century the British officers' rank badges did not change a great deal, except for the rank of 2nd lieutenant who, at the beginning of the century, had no star: a lieutenant wore only one star, and a captain two stars. The rank badges illustrated are those commonly known during World War 2; worn on the shoulders from the 1880s, they were basically a composition of three different badges, i.e. the crossed baton and sword, the crown and the star.

Subalterns wore stars; majors wore a crown, and a star was added under the crown for each superior rank. Brigadier-generals wore three stars and a crown. A crossed baton and a sword and a star is the distinctive badge of major-generals, the crown replacing the star for that of lieutenant-generals. Generals had both crown and star over a crossed baton and sword. Field-marshals wore the crossed batons on a laurel wreath, with a crown above.

The star is also called a 'pip', and there are several different types, for instance those worn by Guards regiments, and the black stars and crowns worn by Rifle regiments.

A great variety of crowns and pips can be found nowadays, made in wire embroidery, in gilt and enamel, brass, blackened brass, plastic, anodised metal and worsted, or in bronze for service dress. All these types are in different sizes. The crowns, of course, followed the pattern in use at the time: the Victorian crown until 1902; the Imperial or Kings' crown as it was worn in the reigns of Edward VII, George V, Edward VIII and George VI, until in 1953 Elizabeth II adopted St. Edward's crown, commonly known as the Queen's crown.

The rank badges worn on the battledress were normally of the worsted type in buff and brown thread, machine embroidered, flat or protruding, on a cardboard backing.

Though there are types embroidered on khaki material, others have been embroidered on coloured felts and are listed below:

red	General Staff Royal Artillery Royal Army Ordnance Corps Military Police Pioneer Corps Royal Electrical and Mechanical Engineers
scarlet	Infantry (except L.I. and Rifle regiments)
royal blue	Royal Engineers
Cambridge blue	Army Educational Corps
rifle green	Rifle regiments
dark green	Light Infantry regiments
emerald green	Army Dental Corps
yellow	Royal Armoured Corps Royal Army Service Corps Royal Army Pay Corps
dull cherry	Royal Army Medical Corps
beech brown	Women's Royal Army Corps
purple	Royal Army Chaplains Department
maroon	Parachute Regiment Royal Army Veterinary Corps
grey	Army Catering Corps

Plate 2. Warrant Officers' and Non-commissioned Officers' Rank Badges

Warrant officers wore, and still wear, their rank badges on both forearms of the jacket or tunic, over the cuffs.

Regimental sergeant-majors and superintending clerks of the Foot Guards wear a badge depicting the Royal Arms in full colour embroidered on khaki material (1).

Staff sergeant-majors (1st Class) and conductors wear a smaller badge representing the Royal Arms partly surrounded by a wreath of laurel (2).

This and all the following rank badges could either be thread-embroidered or made in brass.

Regimental corporal-majors and farriers corporal-majors of the Household Cavalry and warrant officers (1st Class) wear the Royal Arms surrounded by a coloured border (3).

Regimental quartermaster-corporals and Farriers quartermaster-corporals of the Household Cavalry, regimental quartermaster-sergeants, and Orderly Room quartermaster-sergeants of the Foot Guards wear a crown surrounded by a laurel wreath (4).

Squadron corporal-majors of the Life Guards wear a crown $1\frac{1}{2}$ in. wide (5). Squadron corporal-majors of the Royal Horse Guards and warrant officers (2nd Class) of other corps and regiments wear a crown 2 in. wide (5).

Warrant officers and N.C.O.s of the Household Cavalry did not use the rank title of 'sergeant', because it is derived from the Latin verb 'servire' (to serve). They replaced it with that of 'corporal'.

Warrant officers of the Royal Artillery are called 'master gunner' respectively of the 1st, 2nd and 3rd class, and wear a gun similar to that in the cap badge, on the forearms below the rank badge; a brass gun if the badge is made in brass, worsted if the badge is worsted.

Bandmasters wear a lyre set on a wreath of oak leaves and surmounted by a crown on both forearms. The same badge, but smaller, is worn by non-commissioned officers and musicians of the military bands, over the rank chevrons or on its own on the right upper sleeve.

Squadron quartermaster-corporals and staff corporals of the Household Cavalry wear four chevrons, pointing upward, below a crown on both forearms (6), drum-majors the same chevrons below a drum (7). Following the same pattern, bugle-majors wear a bugle over the chevrons, and trumpet-majors two crossed trumpets. A crown over the trumpets is worn in the case of a trumpet-major of the Household Cavalry. All the chevrons listed below are worn with points downwards on the upper arm of both sleeves.

Corporals-of-horse of the Household Cavalry, Squadron, Battery and Company quartermaster-sergeants, colour sergeants and staff sergeants, all wear three chevrons below a crown (8).

Other badges can be worn above the chevrons: a gun by sergeants of the Royal Artillery, the engineers' grenade by sergeants of the Royal Engineers, a red flaming grenade by sergeants of the Grenadier Guards and the figure of Mercury by sergeants of the Royal Corps of Signals.

Band sergeants wear the lyre above their chevrons, except for band sergeants (and band corporals) of the Foot Guards who do not wear the badge.

Corporals of the Royal Artillery are called 'bombardiers' and, together with corporals and band corporals of the Foot Guards, wear two chevrons (11).

Band bombardiers, band corporals (except Foot Guards) and lance-corporals of the band and bugles of the Durham Light Infantry wear the lyre above the two chevrons.

The Household Cavalry and Foot Guards have no one-chevron rank as their lance-corporals wear two chevrons. The two-chevron rank of the Household Cavalry has a crown above (10). The lance-corporals and lance-bombardiers of the rest of the Army wear only one chevron (12), with a lyre in the case of band lance-corporals or band lance-bombardiers.

Formation Signs *(Pl. 3–4 also Pl. 13–14).*

The British Army adopted formation signs during World War 1 in order to provide an easy form of visual identification of the various units. These signs were worn on the uniform sleeve and painted on vehicles, road signs, etc. As this information was given by a symbol, the formation sign had the advantage of not disclosing its meaning to an outsider. Each unit was proud of its own formation sign and became very attached to it. It went some way to creating an *esprit de corps.*

After World War 1, the use of formation signs was discontinued, although most Territorials continued wearing their divisional signs until, at the beginning of World War 2, their use was officially reintroduced throughout the Army.

The symbolic meaning of a formation sign is usually connected with the unit it represents, although sometimes in rather obscure ways. The symbol was normally chosen by the personnel of the unit.

There are several types of formation sign: mechanically printed in colour on material, mechanically embroidered on coloured felt and, in certain cases, hand embroidered and woven.

Other types in existence were made by the soldiers themselves in occupied countries during World War 1 and World War 2. And there must be many examples made by keen collectors.

Although the design of the badge is always the same there are often variations of colours: the 'HD' of the 51st (Highland) Division, for instance, could be found in red, yellow or brown. Generally speaking, the details of most signs do not necessarily look the same.

Plate 3. Supreme Headquarters, British and Allied Forces

The formation sign of G.H.Q. Home Forces was represented by a winged lion set on a round red and blue background, with two yellow frames. The Star of India, on the same background but rectangular in this case, was the badge of G.H.Q. India. The badges of the Allied Forces H.Q. (Algiers and Naples), Supreme Headquarters Allied Expeditionary Forces (north-western Europe), Supreme Allied Command, south-east Asia, and H.Q. 15th Army Group were worn both by American and British troops, the latter composed of 8th British and 5th U.S. Armies in Italy. The S.H.A.E.F. badge shows the crusader's sword alight in the 'darkness' of German-occupied Europe, the sword pointing to the rainbow of peace.

The sign of Allied Land Forces, South-East Asia, was in fact never issued to U.S. forces. American-issued badges are heavily silk woven and can easily be recognised. H.Q. 21st Army Group commanded the 2nd British Army and the 1st Canadian Army.

At the time of the Ardennes battle, the 1st and 9th U.S. Armies came under the operational command of 21st Army Group, the 1st for only a month (16 December, 1944–16 January, 1945), the 9th until 3 April, 1945.

The Headquarters 21st Army Group was formed from G.H.Q. Home Forces and initially had its quarters at St. Paul's School, West Kensington.

The assault forces who landed in Normandy on 6 June, 1944, were the 2nd British and 1st U.S. Armies, under the command of Field-Marshal Montgomery. Subsequently the British forces were grouped into 21st Army Group, and the Americans into 12th Army Group.

On 1 September, 1944, General Eisenhower established his headquarters (S.H.A.E.F.) in France, taking direct command of all operations in that sector. Thus Field-Marshal Montgomery was the commander of 21st Army Group only.

The sign of Central Mediterranean Force symbolises the 'torch of liberty' being brought from over the sea.

Armies

The 1st and 2nd Armies wore a similar formation sign: the crusader's shield and sword, with a red cross on the shield for the 1st and a blue cross for the 2nd Army. The 1st Army invaded North Africa during the winter 1942–43, while the 2nd Army, formed in England in the summer of 1943, landed in Normandy and took part in the whole north-western European campaign.

The 8th Army was formed in Egypt in 1941 from the existing Army of the Nile. The first occasion its name appeared in print was when General Sir Alan Cunningham was appointed as its commander, on 18 November, 1941, although it was officially known as such from about 26 September.

It fought in the North African campaign, from El Alamein to Tunis, took part in the invasion of Sicily and, together with the 5th U.S. Army, slowly crept up the Italian peninsula, reaching Austria by the beginning of May, 1945.

The 9th Army was formed in the Levant, at the rear of the 8th Army, and was commanded by General Sir Henry M. Wilson. He was nicknamed 'Jumbo', a fact which influenced the design of the Army's badge.

A yellow Assyrian lion was adopted as the sign of the 10th Army that was formed in Iraq in 1941 at the time of the rebellion and controlled Syria, Iraq and Persia.

The Burmese dragon was the symbolic animal chosen for the badge of the 12th Army, raised in Burma on 28 May, 1945, that together with the 14th Army was to retake Burma and Malaya from the Japanese. The 14th Army was the formation that for years withstood the Japanese armies.

Army Corps

In September, 1939, the British Expeditionary Force was sent to France. Originally it was composed of the 1st and 2nd Corps deployed between the 1st and the 7th French Armies, the latter supporting the Belgians who were supposed to defend the area between Louvain and Antwerp in case of retreat. The spearhead design of the 1st Corps was adopted because it was the 'first' Corps of the Army. The formation sign of the 2nd Corps was chosen after the name of its commander, Lieutenant-General Sir Alan Brooke. In March, 1940, the B.E.F. had been strengthened by an additional Corps, the 3rd, whose badge was a fig leaf, after the name of its commander, Lieutenant-General Sir Ronald Adam.

The 4th Corps was part of the 14th Army, together with the 15th, the 33rd and later the 34th Indian Corps.

The 5th Corps took part in the Norwegian expedition in 1940, hence the choice of a Viking ship as its badge. Later it joined the 1st Army and took part in the North African campaign. It landed in Sicily and, as part of the 8th Army, fought its way all along the Italian peninsula.

The charging knight of the 8th Corps was adopted in February, 1943 as it was composed of two armoured divisions. It landed in Normandy and subsequently took part in the operations, reaching the River Elbe in the spring of 1945.

The 9th Corps saw active service in North Africa with the 1st Army. It wore two formation signs: the black cat in connection with the cat's reputed nine lives and a white trumpet with nine white squares on its banner.

The 8th Army was originally formed by the 13th and 30th Corps, the gazelle becoming the badge of the former during its connection with the desert. The 13th Corps remained with the 8th Army and, at the end of the war, occupied north-east Italy, while early in 1944, the 30th Corps, then formed by the 50th (Northumbrian), 51st (Highland) and 7th (Armoured) Divisions, returned to Britain to join the 2nd Army in training for the invasion of Europe.

The 10th Corps was formed before the battle of El Alamein. Heavily armoured, it had been concentrated behind the lines and was employed in the breakthrough operation in the sector of the 30th Corps.

The 11th Corps served as part of the Home Forces and was later disbanded in Britain before it had seen active service overseas.

The 12th Corps, together with the 1st, 8th and 30th Corps, belonged to the 2nd Army and fought in France, Belgium, Holland and Germany. Its formation sign with an oak, an ash and a thorn in an oval on a black background was chosen as a link with the name of its commander, Major-General Sir A. F. A. N. Thorne and with 'the Oak, the Ash and the Thorn', in *Puck of Pook's Hill* by Rudyard Kipling, the Corps having been raised in the Pook's Hill country.

The 25th Corps had a red lion on a yellow rectangular background, formerly the badge of the Headquarters of British Troops in Cyprus.

Plate 4. Armoured Divisions

The Guards Armoured Division was raised in September, 1941, and it adopted the formation sign of the Guards Division of World War 1. It landed in Normandy and took an active part in the campaign in north-western Europe.

The 1st Armoured Division fought with the B.E.F. in France in 1940 and, after refitting in Britain, it was sent to the Middle East towards the end of 1941. Later, during the same campaign, together with the 10th Armoured Division, it formed the 10th Army Corps, which drove from El Alamein to Tunisia. As part of the 8th Army it fought in the Italian campaign and in 1945 it was broken up, although its 2nd Armoured Brigade continued wearing its formation sign. The rhinoceros was an appropriate divisional badge and a variation of it, a charging rhinoceros, was worn during the latter campaign.

A fox's mask was the sign of the 10th Armoured Division, as it was originally formed of mechanised cavalry and yeomanry units.

The 2nd Armoured Division was sent to the Middle East in November, 1940; a plumed white knight's helmet on a red background was its badge.

The 6th Armoured Division, with the clenched mailed gauntlet sign, served in North Africa with the 1st Army and was later assigned to the 8th Army. It fought in the Italian campaign and reached Gorizia in the north-east by the beginning of May, 1945.

The 7th is the best known of the armoured divisions. It was formed in Egypt in 1938 as a mobile division based near Mersa Matruh. In December, 1939, the division became known as the 7th Armoured Division and its commander, Major-General O'Moore Creagh, adopted the well-known jerboa divisional sign. When later the division was employed in north-western Europe a new sign was adopted, the red jerboa, now picked out in white, on a black rectangular background.

The formation sign of the 8th Armoured Division depicted a traffic light set on the word 'GO' on a green background. This division was sent to the Middle East but was split up soon after its arrival.

The 9th Armoured Division was formed in 1941 and was employed as a training formation until it was disbanded in 1944. Its badge was a black and white panda's head. It is said that this badge was chosen with reference to the division's training role, as the panda, although a species of bear, is not a fierce animal.

Another division raised in 1941 was the 11th Armoured which chose the badge of a charging bull; it landed in Normandy and subsequently fought through France, Belgium, Holland and Germany.

The 42nd Armoured Division was formed by the conversion to armour of the 42nd (East Lancashire) Division. It did not see active service and was disbanded in 1943, its engineers later becoming part of the 79th Armoured Division. As an infantry formation, the 42nd (East Lancashire) Division joined the B.E.F. in France, and took part in the retreat from Dunkirk.

Major-General Sir Percy C. S. Hobart dedicated his life to the assertion of armour as the strength of a modern army. He was the creator of the 7th Armoured Division, later of the 11th Armoured Division, and perhaps his masterpiece was the 76th Armoured Division that he actually commanded until its disbandment in 1945. Initially it was raised as a normal armoured division, but soon after it was trained to handle all sorts of armoured implements, such as amphibious tanks, mine-sweeping tanks and bridging tanks. Other machines laid flexible carpets over soft ground, others carried projectors capable of illuminating the battlefield. Churchill VII tanks were fitted with flame-thrower equipment called 'Crocodile'. They became known as Churchill Crocodile tanks and were extensively used in the north-west European campaign. All these strange-looking tanks became collectively known as 'Funnies'.

Armoured Brigades

The 4th and 7th Armoured Brigades, together with a support group, initially formed the 7th Armoured Division, and were thus entitled to wear the jerboa badge.

The 4th Armoured Brigade was later transferred to Britain and took part in the invasion of Europe, while the 7th was transferred to Burma in 1942 where it adopted the green 'Jungle rat' as its badge. By 1944 the 7th Armoured Brigade was again part of the 8th Army, now on the Italian front.

The fox's mask of the 8th Armoured Brigade obviously originates from the formation sign of the 10th Armoured Division. The Brigade was employed in north-western Europe and so was the 6th Guards Tank Brigade, that was originally part of the Guards Armoured Division.

A white horse on a rectangular or semi-circular green background was the badge of the 9th Armoured Brigade; the horse was chosen because the brigade was formed by cavalry and yeomanry regiments.

The armour-clad horse's head, in white on a black background, served as the badge of the 20th Armoured Brigade. A red devil seen peeping from behind two blue triangles was that of the 16th Armoured Brigade.

The 22nd Armoured Brigade, with the stag's head sign, was composed of yeomanry regiments and served initially with the 8th Army, moving later to north-western Europe.

The 23rd Armoured Brigade was raised in Liverpool and naturally chose the liver bird for its badge. It fought in North Africa and Italy with the 8th Army and later it was despatched to Greece to quell the E.L.A.S. rising. The badge could be either round or square.

The 25th Armoured Engineer Brigade was a special unit for tank support; it took part in the Italian campaign.

The badge of the 27th Armoured Brigade depicted a sea-horse and, together with the 34th Armoured Brigade, it belonged to the 21st Army Group.

Two triangles, one inverted above the other, was a common emblem among armoured and tank units and was called a 'diabolo'. The 31st Independent Armoured Brigade wore a pale green diabolo. The 33rd and 35th Armoured Brigades instead wore equilateral triangles: the former green and black, the latter brown and green.

Army Tank Brigades

Army Tank Brigades wore diabolos composed of isosceles triangles. The 21st Army Tank Brigade initially wore a yellow diabolo, later changing to a black one on a yellow-red shield.

The 23rd Army Tank Brigade wore a green diabolo, the 24th blue and the 25th black with a small white maple leaf to commemorate its association with the 1st Canadian Division.

The 36th Tank Brigade's badge was a red and a black triangle.

The 1st Armoured Replacement Group C.M.F. supplied and refitted all armoured units of the 8th Army in Italy.

Its badge showed the head of Mars on a background of R.A.C. colours: yellow and red.

Cap Badges (*Pl. 5–12*)

Traditionally the headdress of the British soldier always displays the emblem of the unit to which he belongs: battalion badges were even issued to the Volunteer and Territorial units. The metal cap badge, as we know it, is derived from the helmet plate and was brought into general use towards the end of the last century.

Different cap badges were worn on different headdresses and although the officers and 'other ranks' badges were generally similar, those of the former were made of superior metals, i.e. gilt instead of brass, silver plate or silver instead of white metal. In some cases coloured enamels embellished the officer's cap badge. Officers have also worn bronzed badges with 'service dress' and, in the cavalry regiments particularly, many wore gold and silver embroidered badges as well.

In 1941 plastic badges were issued to most of the army with the exception of the cavalry regiments. They were in three colours: grey, pale fawn and brown.

Only 'other ranks' cap badges of the Regular Army, as worn during World War 2, are illustrated in this volume. When the officer's badge differs in design from that of the 'other ranks' a full description is given.

Plate 5. Cavalry and Armoured Regiments
The titles should be read from left to right and from top to bottom:

The Life Guards
Royal Horse Guards (The Blues)
1st King's Dragoon Guards
The Queen's Bays (2nd Dragoon Guards)
3rd Carabiniers (Prince of Wales's Dragoon Guards)
4th/7th Royal Dragoon Guards
5th Royal Inniskilling Dragoon Guards
1st The Royal Dragoons
The Royal Scots Greys (2nd Dragoons)
3rd The King's Own Hussars
4th Queen's Own Hussars
7th Queen's Own Hussars
8th King's Royal Irish Hussars
    Officers had the Harp between the Royal Crest and the roman
    numeral VIII. A scroll below reads: *Pristinae Virtutis Memores.*
9th Queen's Royal Lancers
10th Royal Hussars (Prince of Wales's Own)
11th Hussars (Prince Albert's Own)

Plate 6. Cavalry and Armoured Regiments
12th Royal Lancers (Prince of Wales's)
13th/18th Royal Hussars (Queen Mary's Own)
14th/20th King's Hussars
15th/19th The King's Royal Hussars
16th/5th The Queen's Royal Lancers
17th/21st Lancers
22nd Dragoons
23rd Hussars
24th Lancers
25th Dragoons
26th Hussars
27th Lancers
Royal Tank Regiment
Royal Armoured Corps
Reconnaissance Corps

Before April, 1939, the Royal Tank Regiment was called the Royal Tank Corps and, in that month, together with the mechanised cavalry regiments, it became part of the Royal Armoured Corps. The latter initially wore a cap badge depicting the letters 'RAC' within a laurel wreath; the badge illustrated was adopted in 1941.

The Reconnaissance Corps was raised in January, 1941, and in December, 1943, it also became part of the R.A.C. The Reconnaissance units of the 49th (West Riding) Division wore a small, white metal Yorkshire rose superimposed in the centre of the cap badge; Scottish units wore a Scottish lion on a circular tablet in the centre of the badge.

Plate 7. Corps, Administrative Departments, etc.

Royal Regiment of Artillery
Royal Horse Artillery
Honourable Artillery Company (Artillery and Infantry)
Corps of Royal Engineers
Royal Army Service Corps
Royal Corps of Signals
Royal Army Ordnance Corps
Royal Army Medical Corps
Corps of Military Police
Military Provost Staff Corps
Royal Army Veterinary Corps
Army Air Corps
Army Dental Corps
Royal Electrical and Mechanical Engineers
Intelligence Corps

Plate 8. Corps, Administrative Departments, etc.

Royal Army Pay Corps
Army Physical Training Corps
Pioneer Corps
Army Educational Corps
General Service Corps (unassigned troops)
Army Catering Corps
General Service Corps (training units)
Parachute Regiment

The Intelligence Corps, the Army Physical Training Corps and the Pioneer Corps were formed in 1940, although the latter also existed during World War 1. The Royal Electrical and Mechanical Engineers came into being in 1942, and so did the General Service Corps. The second cap badge of the G.S.C. was adopted in 1944 to be worn by G.S.C. personnel engaged in infantry training.

All ranks of the Parachute Regiment and the Glider Pilot Regiment wore the Army Air Corps badge, of which they were part. In May, 1943, a new cap badge was approved for the Parachute Regiment.

Foot Guards
Grenadier Guards:
> Warrant officers, orderly room sergeants, sergeants, band sergeants and musicians wore a crowned Royal Cypher on the ball of the grenade.

Coldstream Guards:
> The Star of the Order of the Garter in oval shape for officers, round shape for the other ranks.

Scots Guards

Irish Guards

Welsh Guards

The cap badges of the Warrant officers and some N.C.O. ranks of the Foot Guards regiments were often made with different metals to distinguish them from the officers and other ranks.

Plate 9. Infantry of the Line
Hackles and special badges awarded to regiments in Plates 9–12 have been mentioned whenever they were worn.

The Royal Scots (The Royal Regiment)
> The officer's cap badge was diamond-shaped, with the thistle in the centre, in gilt on green enamel, surrounded by a circle inscribed *Nemo Me Impune Lacessit.*

The Queen's Royal Regiment (West Surrey)

The Buffs (Royal East Kent Regiment)

The King's Own Royal Regiment (Lancaster)

The Royal Northumberland Fusiliers—with red hackle

The Royal Warwickshire Regiment

The Royal Fusiliers (City of London Regiment)—white hackle
> Officers: gilt grenade and crown with a silver rose in the centre and a small silver horse below the Garter.

The King's Regiment (Liverpool)

The Royal Norfolk Regiment

The Lincolnshire Regiment
> Officers: a diamond-cut, eight-pointed star in silver with silver sphinx on 'EGYPT', on blue background, surrounded by a gilt circle inscribed: 'Lincolnshire Regiment'.

The Devonshire Regiment

The Suffolk Regiment

The Somerset Light Infantry (Prince Albert's)

The West Yorkshire Regiment (The Prince of Wales's Own)
The East Yorkshire Regiment (The Duke of York's Own)
The Bedfordshire and Hertfordshire Regiment

Plate 10. Infantry of the Line
The Leicestershire Regiment
The Green Howards (Alexandra, Princess of Wales's Own Yorkshire Regiment)
The Lancashire Fusiliers—primrose yellow hackle
The Royal Scots Fusiliers—white hackle
The Cheshire Regiment
The Royal Welch Fusiliers—white hackle
  Officers wore forage cap and beret badges in gold embroidery with a silver dragon on the ball of the grenade.
The South Wales Borderers
The King's Own Scottish Borderers—white and black cock feathers
The Cameronians (Scottish Rifles)—black hackle
The Royal Inniskilling Fusiliers—grey hackle
The Gloucestershire Regiment—back badge
The Worcestershire Regiment—valise star
The East Lancashire Regiment
The East Surrey Regiment
The Duke of Cornwall's Light Infantry—red feathers
The Duke of Wellington's Regiment (West Riding)

Plate 11. Infantry of the Line
The Border Regiment
The Royal Sussex Regiment
  Although the officers' badge is very similar to that of the other ranks, the details of its design are entirely different.
The Hampshire Regiment
  Officers: a silver eight-pointed star with crowned Garter in the centre. The Hampshire red rose within the Garter and the regimental title on a scroll just below.
The South Staffordshire Regiment
The Dorsetshire Regiment
The South Lancashire Regiment (The Prince of Wales's Volunteers)
The Welch Regiment
The Black Watch (Royal Highland Regiment)—red hackle
The Oxfordshire and Buckinghamshire Light Infantry
The Essex Regiment
The Sherwood Foresters (Nottinghamshire and Derbyshire Regiment)
The Loyal Regiment (North Lancashire)

The Northamptonshire Regiment

The Royal Berkshire Regiment (Princess Charlotte of Wales's)
Officers: The China dragon below a crown in silver, on three coils of rope in bronze.

The Queen's Own Royal West Kent Regiment

The King's Own Yorkshire Light Infantry—green pompon

The King's Shropshire Light Infantry

Plate 12. Infantry of the Line

The Middlesex Regiment (The Duke of Cambridge's Own)

The King's Royal Rifle Corps—black badge

The Wiltshire Regiment (Duke of Edinburgh's)
Officers' badges have no coronet nor scroll, and are in silver with gilt cypher.

The Manchester Regiment

The North Staffordshire Regiment (The Prince of Wales's)

The York and Lancaster Regiment

The Durham Light Infantry

The Highland Light Infantry (City of Glasgow Regiment)

Seaforth Highlanders (Ross-shire Buffs, The Duke of Albany's)
The Officers wore a badge similar to that of the other ranks, but with the cypher 'L' and a coronet between the antlers.

The Gordon Highlanders

The Queen's Own Cameron Highlanders—blue hackle

The Royal Ulster Rifles—pipers wear a black hackle

The Royal Irish Fusiliers (Princess Victoria's)—green hackle

The Argyll and Sutherland Highlanders (Princess Louise's)

The Rifle Brigade (Prince Consort's Own)

The Lowland Regiment

The Highland Regiment

Formation Signs (*Pl. 13–14*)

Plate 13. Infantry Divisions

The formation sign of the 1st Division was a white equilateral triangle, on its own or on a black, square background. The triangle represented the top of the spearhead badge of 1st Corps as this was the first division of the B.E.F. in France. Subsequently, the 1st Division landed in North Africa with the 1st Army, and later took part in the Italian campaign.

The badge of the 2nd Division was chosen in 1940 by its commander, Major-General H. C. Lloyd, who had previously commanded a Guards Brigade with a single key as its sign. The crossed keys were the emblem of the Archbishop of York and used to be carried on the shields and banners of his army. This was also the badge of the 5th Infantry Brigade. The Division fought in France with the B.E.F. and later in the Far East.

The 3rd Division was also in France with the B.E.F. and later with the 21st Army Group.

The 4th Division was sent to France in October, 1939, later taking part in the operations in North Africa, Italy and Greece. Initially its badge was the fourth quadrant of a circle, but later became a circle with the fourth quadrant detached, as illustrated.

The 5th was a Yorkshire division. It served with the B.E.F. and later one of its brigades was sent to Norway. Afterwards the division was sent to Madagascar, and from there to India and Iraq. It was later employed in Italy and finally in north-western Europe.

The 6th Division served with the B.E.F., in the Western Desert, in Syria, and later in Tobruk during the siege, where it was renumbered the 70th and, as such, was sent to India.

The 9th (Scottish) Division was raised in 1939 and amalgamated in 1940 with the 51st Division, the latter having been depleted in France.

The 12th Division took part in the first stage of the war in France and was subsequently disbanded.

The 13th Division re-adopted the sign it had worn during World War 1. It was reformed in Greece in the winter of 1945–46 during the campaign against E.L.A.S., drafting the British units of the 4th Indian Division due to return to India. The sign was chosen as an omen of good luck; the horse-shoe was intended to combat the unlucky number 13.

The 15th (Scottish) Division saw service in north-western Europe.

The formation sign of the 18th Division represents a windmill, in association with East Anglia where it was raised. It was sent to Singapore just before the Japanese invasion.

The rose of the 23rd Division could be found on a blue or green background. This division took part in the first campaign in France and later, back in Britain, was disbanded.

The 36th Division fought against the Japanese. The emblem of its 29th Brigade and that of its 72nd were linked together to form the divisional sign.

The 38th (Welsh) Division carried the yellow cross of St. David in its sign as it was a second-line division made up of Welsh Territorial units. It remained in the Home Forces for the duration of the war.

The 40th Division was formed in Sicily in 1943. The World War 1 sign portrayed a bantam cock, but to commemorate the battle of Bourlon Wood an acorn and an oak leaf on a white diamond was superimposed. In World War 2 only the acorn remained as the sign.

The 42nd (East Lancashire) Division's badge has not been illustrated in this plate because, as early as 1941, it was converted into an armoured division and is included on Plate 4.

The 43rd (Wessex) Division adopted as its badge the arms of the kings of Wessex. It was a division of the 21st Army Group.

The 44th (Home Counties) Division saw active service in France and was then sent to the Middle East. It was disbanded after the battle of El Alamein where it fought in the Southern sector of the front line.

The 45th (Wessex) Division was a second-line territorial division and as such was part of the Home Forces. Its formation sign was Drake's drum.

The 46th (North Midlands) Division served with the B.E.F. and later with the 1st Army in Tunisia. It took part in the Italian campaign and saw a spell of service in Greece.

The 47th (London) Division adopted the 'Bow Bells' as its badge and was part of the Home Forces.

The 48th (South Midlands) Division, like the 47th, did not serve abroad. The badge shows a macaw as, when its commander first entered the divisional headquarters at Littlecote, a macaw kept in the house shouted 'Good luck, good luck!'

The 49th (West Riding) Division initially wore its World War 1 badge, the white rose of York. It was sent to Norway in 1940, and then to Iceland where it adopted the familiar 'polar bear' sign. At first the bear had a bowed head, but this was later raised to make it appear more aggressive. Back in Britain, in 1943, the division joined the 21st Army Group then training for the invasion of Europe.

The double 'T' badge of the 50th (Northumbrian) Division could be seen until a couple of years ago on a large H.Q. sign at Kirklevington, Teesside. The division took part in operations with the B.E.F. and later with the 8th Army in North Africa. It took part in the invasion of north-western Europe and in the liberation of Norway.

The 51st (Highland) Division fought some pitched battles in France and after the Dunkirk evacuation was moved to the Middle East. After the conquest of North Africa and Sicily it was repatriated in time to join the 21st Army Group.

The formation sign of the 52nd (Lowland) Division was St. Andrew's cross on a shield and, as it had been trained for mountain warfare, had the word 'Mountain' on a scroll below the shield. It was in France with the B.E.F. and returned to the continent as part of the 21st Army Group.

The 53rd (Welsh) Division landed in Normandy and subsequently took part in the invasion of north-western Europe.

The 54th (East Anglian) Division adopted the initials of the name of its commander, Major-General J. H. T. Priestman, as its badge. It was drafted into the 'Line of Communications' of the 21st Army Group, its 162nd Independent Brigade still wearing the 'JP' sign.

The 55th (West Lancashire) Division stayed in Britain engaged in a training role. Its badge depicts the red rose of Lancaster with its double set of 5 leaves representing the double 5.

The 56th (London) Division adopted Dick Whittington's cat as its badge. It was posted in the area of Palestine–Syria–Iraq as a security force. Later it took an active part in the Italian campaign.

The 59th Division was part of the 21st Army Group. Pithead machinery against a slag heap was its badge.

The 61st, 76th, 77th and 80th Divisions did not serve overseas, but were employed in a training role as part of the Home Forces.

The 78th Division was part of the 1st Army in North Africa; later taking part in the Italian campaign, it reached Austria in May, 1945.

Plate 14. Independent Infantry Brigades and Brigade Groups

The 1st and 24th Independent Guards Brigade Groups, the 32nd Independent Guards Brigade and the 33rd Guards Brigade all wore formation signs in the colours of the Household Brigade: blue and red. The same colours were also used in the signs of brigades which were converted from artillery units; the 301st and 304th Infantry Brigades' signs even displayed artillery emblems, i.e. the crossed guns and crossed searchlight beams.

The design and colour of some formation signs were borrowed from the traditions of the brigade's battalions, i.e. the Irish shamrock of the 38th Infantry Brigade, the sphinx of the 56th, and the colours in the formation signs of the 70th, 71st, 204th, etc. Independent Infantry Brigades.

Regional associations were shown, e.g. the arms of Cornwall in the sign of the 73rd Independent Infantry Brigade, previously worn by personnel of the Devon and Cornwall County Division. The tulip of the 212th Independent Infantry Brigade was previously worn by the Lincolnshire County Division, and the seaxes of the 223rd marked the Brigade's association with Essex.

The King chessman was the emblem of the 206th Independent Infantry Brigade. The 1st Battalion Dorsetshire Regiment, the 1st Battalion Hampshire Regiment and the 2nd Battalion Devonshire Regiment were brigaded together during the defence of Malta, and adopted the Maltese cross as their brigade's badge.

The 29th and 31st were Independent Brigade Groups.

The Airborne Forces (Pl. 15)

The first British parachute units were born in June, 1940, on the personal instruction of the Prime Minister, Mr. Winston Churchill. As the Commandos were being raised at the same time, No. 2 Commando underwent parachute training. In November, 1940, it became the 11th Special Air Service Battalion, divided into two wings: Parachute Wing and Glider Wing.

The first war action carried out by parachutists was inspired by the commandos. On the night of 10 February, 1941, 'X' Troop of the 11th S.A.S. Battalion landed in the south of Italy and succeeded in blowing up the aqueduct of Tragino.

In September, 1941, the 11th S.A.S. Battalion became the 1st Parachute Battalion, the first of four battalions of the 1st Parachute Brigade.

The 4th Battalion later participated in the formation of the 2nd Parachute Brigade, together with the 5th (Scottish) Battalion and 6th (Welsh) Battalion.

Three battalions were raised in India: the 151st, later transferred to the Middle East and renumbered 156th, the 152nd Indian and 153rd Gurkha Parachute Battalions. The 10th Parachute Battalion was raised in Palestine, and the 11th was formed by a nucleus of parachutists of the 156th.

Thus the 10th, the 11th and the 156th Parachute Battalions formed the 4th Parachute Brigade. The 1st, 2nd and 4th Parachute Brigades and the 1st Air Landing Brigade, by June, 1943, had formed the 1st Airborne Division.

While the 1st Airborne Division was taking part in the North African campaign of General Eisenhower, and later in the Italian campaign, the 6th Airborne Division was being raised in Britain. Eventually it was composed of the 3rd Parachute Brigade, which in its turn was composed of the Canadian Parachute Battalion and the 8th (Midland Counties) and 9th (Home Counties) Battalions.

The 5th Parachute Brigade was formed of the 7th (Light Infantry), 12th (Yorkshire) and 13th (Lancashire) Battalions.

The 6th Air Landing Brigade was composed of the Glider Pilot Regiment and the Airborne Infantry Battalions it carried.

In November, 1943, the 1st Airborne Division (minus the 2nd Brigade) came to Britain to join the Allied Airborne Army in training for the invasion of Europe. The 6th Airborne Division took part in the Normandy landing and the 1st Division later joined in the campaign at Arnhem.

Meanwhile the 2nd Independent Parachute Brigade saw active service in Italy and Greece and took part in operation 'Anvil', the invasion of southern France.

The Army Commandos (*pl. 15 and 16*)

The first Commandos were formed in June 1940, each consisting of five troops, with fifty men to each troop. Later, in 1941, they were reorganised into six troops of sixty-five.

Only three weeks after the idea of raising such a force had been conceived, the first raid on the French coast took place during the night of 23–24 June. Many others followed.

In February, 1941, Nos. 7, 8 and 11 Commandos were sent to the Middle East to join forces with Nos. 50–52, who amalgamated to form the Combined (Middle East) Commando. Nos. 7, 8 and 11 formed respectively 'A', 'B' and 'C' Battalions and the Combined (Middle East) Commando became 'D' Battalion of 'Layforce', a brigade of the 8th Army's 6th Division. The brigade was named after its commander, Lieutenant-Colonel R. E. Laycock, later to become Chief of Combined Operations. After fighting in North Africa, Syria and Crete, Layforce was disbanded and Laycock returned to Britain to command the Special Service Brigade.

Subsequently, four Special Service Brigades were formed grouping together the Army and the Royal Marine Commandos. The first of the R.M. Commandos, No. 40 was raised in February, 1942.

The Special Service Group was made up of the 1st Special Service Brigade (Nos. 3, 4 and 6 Commandos, 45 R.M. Commando and 1st and 8th Troops of the No. 10 (Inter-Allied) Commando) and by the 4th Special Service Brigade composed of R.M. Commandos. It took part in the invasion of north-western Europe.

The 2nd Special Service Brigade was in Italy, composed of Nos. 2 and 3 Commandos, and Nos. 40 and 41 R.M. Commandos. The 3rd Special Service Brigade formed by Nos. 1 and 5 Commandos and Nos. 42 and 44 R.M. Commandos served in the Far East.

Nos. 1 and 6 Commandos took part in the landings in French North Africa, and were used in an infantry role during the following winter campaign.

No. 10 (Inter-Allied) Commando was formed of French, Belgian, Dutch, Norwegian and Polish troops, the 10th ('X') Troop mainly made up of Germans and Austrians. This Commando was then broken up and its troops used in different raids and on different fronts.

Towards the end of 1944 the Special Service Brigades were renamed Commando Brigades.

Plate 15. The Airborne Forces

The Pegasus badge was worn by members of both 1st and 6th Airborne Divisions. The first parachute units adopted the PARACHUTE shoulder title, also with the '1', '2' and '3' battalion figures incorporated below. It should be mentioned that the 1st Parachute Battalion wore a green lanyard, the 2nd a yellow lanyard, the 3rd a red and the 4th a black lanyard. For the duration of the war the 4th painted its equipment black.

The 5th was a Scottish battalion and wore the Balmoral bonnet, with an Army Air Corps badge on a Hunting Stuart tartan patch, until September, 1944. The 6th Parachute Battalion was of Welsh extraction, and its members wore the Welsh black flash at the back of the collar.

The 12th Battalion wore a light blue lanyard.

The Parachute Regiment came into being in 1942 and, together with the Glider Pilot Regiment, adopted appropriate shoulder titles, dark blue lettering on a pale blue background.

The red beret was first worn by the regiment when it went to North Africa in November, 1942.

The 21st and 22nd Independent Parachute Companies were the 'pathfinder' units, respectively belonging to the 1st and 6th Airborne Divisions.

Special Forces Cap Badges

The common feature of the commandos' uniform was the green beret. The commandos raised in the Middle East adopted a 'knuckle-duster' knife as their cap badge and, initially, No. 2 Commando wore a dagger in between two letters 'S', for Special Service. No. 6 Commando wore a roman VI embroidered on a square black patch, and No. 9 Commando a black hackle.

The first recruits of the Special Air Service came from Layforce and initially they operated in the Western Desert in conjunction with the Long Range Desert Group. Later S.A.S. became operationally independent and split into the Special Raiding Squadron and the Special Boat Service; the latter specialised in amphibious warfare in the Aegean.

In time the 1st and 2nd Special Air Service Regiments came into being, and in March, 1944, together with two French parachute battalions and a Belgian parachute company, they formed the Special Air Service Brigade, that was used in north-west Europe before and after D Day.

The Raiding Support Regiment was raised in 1943 and served on both sides of the Adriatic before disbandment in 1945. Like that of the S.A.S., its cap badge was embroidered in coloured thread.

The Long Range Desert Group and Popski's Private Army were units for raiding and reconnaissance operations. Both raised in the Middle East, they followed the 8th Army and were disbanded in 1945. The former wore brass, bronze and white metal cap badges. The cap badges of the P.P.A. were generally made in brass, but some white metal and silver badges were made in Italy.

'V' Force was formed of British servicemen and Indians, many belonging to the hill tribes of Burma, and was employed behind the Japanese lines.

Wings

Glider Pilot and S.A.S. wings were worn on the left breast, above the medal ribbons or above the pocket; all qualified parachutists of the Regular Army wore their badges on the upper right sleeve, below the shoulder title.

Parachutists and Glider Pilots, other than Regular Army, wore a white parachute or a glider embroidered in pale blue on the forearm of the left sleeve.

Plate 16. Commando Shoulder Flashes

The formation sign of Combined Operations symbolically depicted its role and was red on black. Early in 1944 all commando units began to wear the red dagger on a triangular black background.

A number of shoulder flashes have been worn by different units in different periods, and only some are illustrated. Some troops wore a special badge: for instance, the 101st Troop of No. 6 Commando. 'V' Force's badge could be found embroidered on dark green felt or woven on khaki. The Special Boat Service badge was made in metal and enamel.

However, during the war, all units were issued with printed shoulder titles, such as that of No. 6 Commando (illustrated). The set covered No. 1 to No. 12 Commando, plus F.F. (Free French) Commando and Commando S.B.S.

Poland

Poland became a unified nation in the 10th century and, because of its position in the heart of Europe, it fought a succession of wars against the neighbouring states, until, in 1772, its first partition took place.

Another partition of Poland took place in 1793 and yet another two years later. Soon after, the Polish lancers of the Napoleonic Army became well known on the battlefields of Europe. Their headdress was a tall, flat-topped, square-shaped 'czapka' with a spreadeagle clutching an 'Amazon' shield at the front.

Napoleon formed the Duchy of Warsaw, but after his defeat in 1813 the Duchy ceased to exist and Poland once again came under the control of its powerful neighbours: Austria, Prussia and Russia.

The outbreak of World War 1 found the Poles politically divided, although the aim of all parties was to achieve Polish national independence.

Polish units were raised by either contendant and finally, in November, 1918, Poland achieved its independence.

The Polish Army was initially formed from various units which came back to Poland after the war still wearing different uniforms, predominantly Austrian, German and French, although Russian and even Italian uniforms were in use at the time.

The first 'dress' regulations and Polish uniforms appeared in 1919.

Later, in the 1930s, new regulations were issued which gradually changed the uniforms until, in 1939, all the officers wore:

The evening dress, that consisted of a khaki tunic (model 1936) and dark trousers with double lateral stripes and piping within. A special silk evening belt was also worn with this uniform.

The garrison or walking-out uniform, made of khaki material, and consisting of tunic (model 1936) and breeches or long trousers.

The field uniform, exactly the same as the above, but without any patches and badges, except rank insignia that were still present on the shoulder straps. For summer the tunic was made of a light khaki dress linen.

The non-commissioned officers were entitled to the same uniforms. A notable difference was that they had only single stripes on the evening trousers, instead of the double stripes and piping worn by officers.

The other ranks were issued with two basic uniforms: a 'walking-out' dress and the field service uniform, both introduced in 1936. The 1919 tunic, without breast pockets, was no longer manufactured after 1936, although it was still worn by a few regiments during World War 2.

The pattern of the greatcoat was identical for officers and men alike, the only difference being in the quality of the cloth. Officers and senior N.C.O.s also wore ankle-length capes without buttons. All ranks serving in the mountain divisions were also issued with capes, but theirs were shorter and with six buttons. A black leather coat could also be worn by personnel of the tank battalions and motorised units.

The outstanding features of the Polish uniform have always been the square-shaped, peaked cap ('czapka') and the 'zigzag' ornament worn by all ranks on the collar of the tunic.

It should be added that officers and warrant officers wore the 'czapka' with a metal rim around the visor; all ranks of the three Light Horse regiments and of the Frontier Defence Corps wore instead a normal, round-peaked cap with metal-rimmed visor.

All ranks of the 21st and 22nd Mountain Divisions wore a stiff felt 'dress' hat with the Polish eagle and rank badges at the front, and a feather on a cluster of downy feathers was attached onto the side of this hat. The feathers were also worn on the 'czapka'.

Another mountain division, the 11th, was formed before the war but only its band and the 1st Battalion of the 49th Regiment were issued with special hats. The hat of the 11th (Carpathian) Mountain Division was modelled on the hats used by the southern Carpathian mountaineers, called 'Huculi'.

The forage cap was the standard field cap until 1937 when a new head-dress was introduced: it was a square-topped cap with a soft peak and folding sides that could be lowered to cover the ears. However, in 1939, both headdresses were still worn as the forage cap remained very popular, particularly among the cavalry, some units of which also wore a regimental collar pennon on its left side.

Personnel of armoured, motorised and anti-aircraft units wore black berets.

About 1935 a new Polish steel helmet was introduced. However, in the Polish campaign of 1939 the cavalry and horse artillery wore old French helmets and the 10th Cavalry Brigade (motorised) had German World War I helmets.

The colour of the band of the peaked cap and the colour of the stripes on the evening dress trousers showed corps, service or regimental distinctions.

The evening and walking-out dress trousers for generals were khaki. The infantry, cavalry, horse artillery, armoured corps, military police and supply train wore dark blue evening trousers. The artillery (except horse artillery), engineers, signals and ordnance wore dark green evening trousers. The services, except those mentioned above, had black evening trousers.

The officers' trousers had broad double stripes with piping in between; the regular N.C.O.s wore a single stripe, 40 mm wide, instead.

A list of cap bands and evening trousers' stripes colours is given below:

	Cap Band	*Stripes/Piping*
Generals	khaki	dark blue/dark blue
Infantry-Highland Rifles	dark blue	yellow/yellow
Rifle Battalions	dark blue	yellow/yellow
1st Light Horse	crimson	crimson/white
2nd Light Horse	white	white/white
3rd Light Horse	yellow	yellow/yellow
1st Lancers	crimson	crimson/crimson
2nd Lancers	white	white/white
3rd Lancers	yellow	yellow/yellow
4th Lancers	cornflower blue	cornflower blue/ cornflower blue
5th Lancers	cherry red	cherry red/cherry red
6th Lancers	light blue	light blue/light blue
7th Lancers	crimson	crimson/white
8th Lancers	dark yellow	dark yellow/dark yellow
9th Lancers	crimson	crimson/white
10th Lancers	crimson	crimson/crimson
11th Lancers	white	white/white
12th Lancers	crimson	crimson/crimson
13th Lancers	pink	pink/pink
14th Lancers	yellow	yellow/yellow
15th Lancers	scarlet	scarlet/scarlet
16th Lancers	white	white/white
17th Lancers	yellow	yellow/yellow
18th Lancers	cornflower blue	cornflower blue/ cornflower blue
19th Lancers	dark blue	white/white
20th Lancers	crimson	crimson/crimson
21st Lancers	turquoise	turquoise/turquoise
22nd Lancers	white	white/white
23rd Lancers	orange	orange/orange
24th Lancers	white	white/white
25th Lancers	scarlet	scarlet/scarlet
26th Lancers	pink	pink/pink
27th Lancers	yellow	yellow/yellow
1st Mounted Rifles	crimson	crimson/crimson
2nd Mounted Rifles	crimson	crimson/crimson
3rd Mounted Rifles	crimson	crimson/crimson

	Cap Band	Stripes/Piping
4th Mounted Rifles	crimson	crimson/crimson
5th Mounted Rifles	white	white/white
6th Mounted Rifles	white	white/white
7th Mounted Rifles	white	white/white
8th Mounted Rifles	white	white/white
9th Mounted Rifles	yellow	yellow/yellow
10th Mounted Rifles	yellow	yellow/yellow
Mounted Pioneers	scarlet	scarlet/scarlet
Recce (Mot. Bde)	crimson	crimson/green
Anti-Tank (Mot. Bde)	scarlet	scarlet/orange
Field Artillery	*dark green	scarlet/scarlet
Medium Artillery	*dark green	scarlet/scarlet
Heavy Artillery	*dark green	scarlet/scarlet
Motorised Artillery	*dark green	scarlet/scarlet
Horse Artillery	*black	scarlet/scarlet
Anti-Aircraft Artillery	*dark green	scarlet/scarlet
Survey Artillery	*dark green	scarlet/scarlet
Armoured Corps	orange	orange/orange
Engineers	*black	raspberry red/raspberry red
Signals	*black	cornflower blue/ cornflower/blue
Train	sky blue	sky blue/crimson
Military Police	scarlet	scarlet/yellow
Ordnance	*emerald	black/scarlet
Admin./Supply	khaki	royal blue/cherry red
Medical Service	*cherry red	cherry red/dark blue
Legal Service	*raspberry	raspberry/raspberry
Geographical Service	*black	white/white
Commissaries	*black	scarlet/scarlet

* Denotes velvet

Plate 17. Officers' Rank Badges

All ranks of the Polish Army wore the same cap badge on the upper front of the headdress: the cap badge depicting the Polish eagle holding an 'Amazon' shield, was made in white metal or oxidised silver.

A small version of this badge was worn on the forage cap, and a small embroidered badge was worn on the field cap.

The generals wore a large silver-embroidered 'zigzag' ornament on the band of the peaked cap together with a stripe of silver braid and rank stars, the latter at the front under the cap badge.

All the other officers also wore rank stars on the cap band; the senior officers with two stripes of silver braid, the others with one stripe only.

Two stripes of silver braid were carried from corner to corner across the top of the 'czapka' and down the sides, ending under the cap band. The generals wore a khaki cap band while most officers wore the coloured bands which have been described in the previous pages.

Generals had the 'zigzag' ornament embroidered on the outside edges of the collar patches, on the shoulder straps, and also on the cuffs of the tunic. The officers' 'zigzag' was narrower than that of the generals and was the same for senior and junior officers, worn on the collar only.

Marshals wore a silver eagle clutching crossed batons on the collar patches (Plate 18) and on the shoulder straps they had the crossed batons only, embroidered above the 'zigzag' device.

All the generals had a silver embroidered eagle on the collar patches and stars on the shoulder straps.

The same eagle, but in silver metal, was worn on the collar by officers of the General Staff (Plate 18).

Plate 18. Officers' Rank Badges

The basic rank badge of Polish officers and generals alike was the five-pointed star, embroidered in silver wire on the shoulder straps. The senior officers were distinguished by 5-mm double bars embroidered in silver wire on the shoulder straps, at 15 mm from the seam. Regimental numbers and monograms were usually embroidered at 7·5 mm from the seam and, in the case of senior officers, they were evenly embroidered across the double bars.

Monograms for Cavalry Shoulder Straps

The monograms worn on the shoulder straps were usually 30 mm high, made in silver wire embroidery for officers and warrant officers, and in white metal for the other ranks. They were the monograms of illustrious Polish generals and leaders, some of them at one time connected with the regiment; those illustrated in Plate 18 were mostly adopted in the 1930s by regiments of Light Horse, Lancers and Mounted Rifles.

A list of all the cavalry regiments, with number and full regimental title, is given further on in these pages and should be consulted in order to decipher the meaning of the monograms.

Plate 19. Warrant Officers' and N.C.O.s' Rank Badges

The warrant officer of the Polish Army wore one silver star at the front of the cap and on the shoulder straps. He also wore stripes on the 'czapka', as did the officers, but in dark red instead of silver.

The staff-sergeant and sergeant wore chevrons on the cap and on the shoulder straps; the other ranks wore stripes instead.

Chevrons and stripes were embroidered in silver on red felt when used on the cap, and they were made of braid on the shoulder straps. The chevrons were set at a 90° angle. The arms of those on the cap were 25 mm long and the stripes 25 × 4 mm in size.

The warrant officers wore the same 'zigzag' on the collar as officers, while the other N.C.O.s wore a simpler pattern of the same device, embroidered in silver. The 'zigzag' of the soldiers was made of silver braid.

There were two types of braid for use on the shoulder straps. The first was a silver braid with narrow red stripes on the edges that was used by warrant officers and non-commissioned officers of the Army and by cadets of the Reserve. The shoulder straps of the latter had an additional edging made of two twisted cords: one red and one white. The silver and red symbolise the white and red of the Polish national flag.

The cadets of the Regular Army wore different shoulder straps altogether. They had silver piping and all-silver braid and the monogram 'SP' (Szkoła Podchorążych), and their shoulder straps were made of coloured cloth, with coloured piping showing between the silver piping and the silver braid.

The colours of the Regular Army cadets' shoulder straps were:

	Shoulder Strap	Piping
Infantry	yellow	dark blue
Cavalry	crimson	dark blue
Artillery	dark green	black
Anti-Aircraft Artillery	dark green	yellow
Engineers	black	scarlet
Signals	black	cornflower blue
Armoured Corps	orange	black
Medical Service	cherry red	dark blue

Cadets were trained in different army colleges. Medical cadets attended additional lectures at Warsaw University and engineer cadets at Warsaw Polytechnic. The training lasted three years with the exception of the medical and engineering training which lasted on average six and four years respectively.

A Regular Army cadet wore a narrow silver braid stripe around the top and along the seam of the cuff for each year of college training. During the fourth year he wore a thick stripe representing the first three years and a narrow stripe for the additional year. Another narrow stripe was added for each successive year of training.

The training of reserve officers was carried out in Cadet Officers'

Schools and, on completion of the courses, they wore a stripe of red-edged silver braid around the top of the cuffs, but not down the seam.

All cadets were given N.C.O. ranks and wore special white metal badges on the collar, as illustrated, above their corresponding shoulder straps.

Plate 20. Collar Patches

Collar patches were worn on the collar of the tunic, with the 'zigzag' ornament embroidered or stitched along the front and bottom sides. They were usually made in cloth, although officers of certain corps and services had velvet collar patches.

A complete set of collar patches has been illustrated as they were worn on the tunic adopted in 1936, and the officers' collar patches, made in velvet (both patch and piping), have been marked * in the following list.

	Collar Patch	Piping
Generals	*dark blue	crimson
Infantry	dark blue	yellow
Infantry (Frontier Defence Corps)	dark blue	dark green
Rifle Battalions	dark blue	nile green
Field Artillery	*dark green	black
Medium Artillery	*dark green	scarlet
Heavy Artillery	*dark green	raspberry red
Survey Artillery	*dark green	white
Anti-Aircraft Artillery	*dark green	yellow
Engineers	*black	scarlet
Railway Engineers	*black	cherry red
Ordnance	*emerald green	black
Signals	*black	cornflower blue
Military Police	scarlet	light yellow
Legal Service	*raspberry red	black
Geographical Service	*black	white
Commissaries	*black	scarlet
Administrative Service	*royal blue	cherry red
Chaplains	*violet	none
Medical Service—Doctors	*cherry red	dark blue
Pharmacists	*cherry red	cornflower blue
Dentists	*cherry red	light blue
Veterinaries	*cherry red	dark green

Collar patches were worn on the greatcoat collar, in the form of two 5-mm stripes, except by those units which wore pennons. The colour of the patch was represented by the stripe at the bottom, the stripe at the top represented the piping of the normal collar patch.

All Mounted troops wore 'pennons' on the collar of the tunic and great-coat instead of collar patches, and they were miniature replicas of the pennons worn on the cavalry lances.

The 'zigzag' ornament, in this case, was embroidered directly onto the collar of the tunic and the pennon was sewn above it. With the adoption of the 1936 tunic with pointed collar, the pennons also took on a pointed shape.

The correct way to show these badges graphically remains, however, the rectangular shape worn before 1936.

The colours of the Polish cavalry were crimson and dark blue; Horse Artillery wore black and scarlet pennons, and Mounted Pioneers the same colours reversed. The cavalry squadrons of the Frontier Defence Corps had dark blue and dark green pennons, the signal squadrons black and cornflower blue. Light blue with a crimson stripe were the pennon colours of the supply train.

The Armoured units wore a triangular pennon half black and half orange on the tunic's collar and greatcoat collar. The orange, together with crimson and green, were adopted as the colours of the bi-pointed pennons of the Reconnaissance units, and the pennons of the Anti-Tank units of the motorised brigade were in red, black and orange.

Plate 21. Collar Patches

All three regiments of Light Horse wore silver collar pennons, the first two with a crimson stripe in the centre, the 3rd with a yellow stripe. The regiments could be further distinguished one from the other by the differently coloured stripes on the evening dress trousers and cap bands.

The colours of the Lancers' pennons were as follows:

1st Lancers	crimson–white
2nd Lancers	white–dark blue
3rd Lancers	yellow–white
4th Lancers	cornflower blue–white
5th Lancers	cherry red–white–cornflower blue
6th Lancers	light blue–white–light blue
7th Lancers	crimson–white–crimson
8th Lancers	dark yellow
9th Lancers	crimson–white–crimson–white
10th Lancers	crimson–white–dark blue–white
11th Lancers	crimson–white–crimson
12th Lancers	crimson–white–dark blue
13th Lancers	pink–cornflower blue–pink
14th Lancers	yellow–white–yellow
15th Lancers	white–scarlet

16th Lancers	dark blue–scarlet–white
17th Lancers	white–scarlet–yellow
18th Lancers	white–scarlet–cornflower blue
19th Lancers	dark blue–white–dark blue
20th Lancers	crimson–dark blue–white–crimson
21st Lancers	turquoise–yellow–white–turquoise
22nd Lancers	white–crimson–white
23rd Lancers	orange–white–orange–white
24th Lancers	white–yellow–white
25th Lancers	white–cornflower blue–scarlet
26th Lancers	pink–cornflower blue–white
27th Lancers	yellow–white–dark blue–white

The basic colour of the Mounted Rifles was dark green and this was combined with other colours to form the pennons of the Mounted Rifles regiments. They were:

1st Mounted Rifles	dark green–crimson
2nd Mounted Rifles	dark green–blue–crimson
3rd Mounted Rifles	dark green–yellow–crimson
4th Mounted Rifles	dark green–white–crimson
5th Mounted Rifles	dark green–crimson–white
6th Mounted Rifles	dark green–white
7th Mounted Rifles	dark green–yellow–white
8th Mounted Rifles	dark green–blue–white
9th Mounted Rifles	dark green–crimson–yellow
10th Mounted Rifles	dark green–white–yellow

Plate 22. Collar Badges

Metal badges were worn on the collar to indicate a particular branch of service, or as a regimental distinction.

Officers of the General Staff wore an eagle similar to that of generals, but in silver metal instead of silver embroidery. The reason for this difference was that the eagle of the generals represented a permanent rank while that of the staff officers represented an appointment only and, therefore the metal badge could be taken off when necessary.

The Naval Service badge was used by Army officers on duty with the Navy in harbours, coastal defence, etc.

The 48th, 49th and 53rd Infantry Regiments, together with all other units of the 11th (Carpathian) Mountain Division, wore the double cross on mountain pine twigs and oak leaves as collar badge and feather holder. Regiments of the 21st and 22nd Mountain Divisions (from 1st to 6th Highland (Podhale) Regiments, 21st and 22nd Field Artillery and other divisional units) wore the swastika on pine twigs. This design was changed just before World War 2, the swastika being turned anti-clockwise.

There were three branches of Christian chaplains in the Polish Army: Catholic, Protestant and Orthodox, each wearing a different cross (illustrated from left to right on this plate). Rabbis wore plain violet collar patches.

Craftsmen and personnel of N.C.O. schools wore their own badges and bandsmen wore a lyre; the bandmasters wore a lyre over two oak leaves.

The 1st (Tartar) Squadron of the 13th Lancers had collar badges pinned on the collar pennons in pairs with the stars facing inwards.

The 44th Infantry Regiment traces its origin to a World War 1 rifle legion of Polish-American volunteers and wore white metal bugles (22 × 17 mm) on the collar, with the mouthpieces facing inward.

The Headquarters of the 16th Infantry Division (and the 16th Field Artillery Regiment of the same division) wore enamelled collar badges (21 × 25 mm) and differently-designed enamelled badges were also adopted by each of the divisional infantry regiments 64th, 65th and 66th.

The other pairs of collar badges were worn all facing one way; for instance, the lion of the 40th and the mounted knight of the 85th Regiment.

On the collar of the greatcoat, the badges were positioned below the coloured stripes.

Plate 23. Monograms and Badges for Shoulder Straps

The monograms were usually embroidered in silver wire on officers' and warrant officers' shoulder straps and in white metal for the other ranks.

N.C.O.s could also wear embroidered badges on uniforms they had purchased privately.

The badge of the Presidential Guard was initially the letters 'O' and 'Z' interlaced (Oddział Zamkowy), but later a Polish eagle (30 mm tall) was adopted instead.

The 1st, 5th, 6th, 41st and 66th Infantry Regiments wore the initials of Joseph Piłsudski (also worn by the 1st Light Horse) and, when the famous Marshal died in 1935, they adopted black piping around the left shoulder strap.

The 37th Infantry Regiment and the 8th Lancers were named after Prince Joseph Poniatowski, Commander-in-Chief of the army of the Grand Duchy of Warsaw and Marshal of the French Empire.

The list of regiments of the Polish Army (p. 137) will help to clarify the meaning of the monograms.

The bear of the 77th Infantry Regiment was the emblem of Samogatia, the medieval name of part of East Prussia–Lithuania.

All ranks of the Marine Rifle Battalion wore an anchor on the shoulder straps. The Battalion was part of the Army and was detailed for coastal defence.

Engineers wore initials related to their specialisation on the shoulder straps: 'R' was the initial used by the Radiotelegraphic Regiment. An 'M' was worn by the Bridging (Mostowy) Engineers; an 'E' by the Electrotechnical Engineers and an 'S' was worn by Engineers attached to the narrow-gauge railways.

The other units wore regimental numbers, embroidered in silver wire for officers and warrant officers, in white metal for the other ranks.

Commemorative Badges

Special badges were worn by regiments and other formations of the Polish Army, and by colleges and training centres. These were not strictly intended for identification purposes, but were generally awarded on fulfilment of certain conditions, i.e. for serving in the unit for one year during a war, or after three months service at the front. In peacetime they were awarded after one year of active service, or, in the case of the Reserve, for having participated in two army manoeuvres. The badge was generally awarded on the regimental day, or on completion of manoeuvres, and could be withdrawn from deserters or as some other disciplinary punishment.

They were worn on the left breast pocket, 4 cm below the button, only the Staff College badge was worn on the right breast pocket and the badges of the Armoured Corps and Signals were worn above the ribbons. The badges were normally made in enamel for officers and warrant officers and plain metal for the other ranks, but some regiments had the same badge for all ranks. Both types have been illustrated together in this volume.

Some regiments had names taken from geographical locations with which they were historically associated. Some took the name of the most important among their battle honours or they were named after honorary 'chiefs', i.e. former Polish kings, national heroes and famous soldiers and, in certain cases, the regiment was named after late commanding officers or living generals. For instance, 3 Pułk Szwoleżerów Mazowieckich Imienia Pułkownika Jana Kozietulskiego can be translated as: 3rd Regiment of Light Horse of the region of Mazovia, named after Colonel Jan Kozietulski, who led the charge of the Polish Light Horse (Chevau-Lègers) of the Imperial Guard at Somo Sierra in 1807.

A list of regiments as they existed in 1939, with full regimental titles, is given on pages 137–40, together with some information relating to the badges they wore.

Infantry Regimental Badges (*Pl. 24, 25, 26*)

Blue and yellow were the predominant colours of the infantry badges, although other colours were used as well.

Regiments with the word 'Legion' in their title were those raised from the Volunteer Polish Legions of World War I. The centre pieces of the badges of the 1st, 5th and 6th Infantry Regiments were actually replicas of that of the 1st Brigade of Legions. The centre piece of the badge of the 2nd Regiment was a replica of that of the 2nd Brigade and also the badges of the 3rd and 4th Regiments incorporated motifs of World War I badges.

The 14th Infantry was a regiment from the region of Kujawy and the 15th was known as the wolves' regiment and thus had four wolves' heads in its badge. The mermaid with sword was taken from the coat of arms of Warsaw and can be seen in the badges of the 19th and 21st Regiments: the 19th was named after the 'Relief of Lwów'; the 21st after the city of Warsaw.

A monument built in honour of T. Kościuszko and the walls of Kraków are shown in the badge of the 20th and the soldier in the badge of the 23rd is Colonel L. Lis-Kula, to whom the regiment was dedicated.

The ribbon of the *Virtuti Militari* Order and the decoration itself can be seen respectively in the badges of the 22nd and 56th.

The Cross of Kaniów, with an eagle on crossed swords, is depicted in the badges of the 29th, 30th and 31st Infantry Regiments. The four emblems in the badge of the 36th are those of Warsaw University, Warsaw Polytechnic, the Central Agricultural College and the Central College of Commerce. The regiment was called 'Academy Legion'.

The coat of arms of Savoy, or the Italian colours, are part of the badges of the 42nd, 50th, 51st, 52nd and 81st Regiments and the white Cross of Savoy is depicted in the badge of the 53rd. Francesco Nullo, to whom the 50th Regiment was dedicated, was an Italian patriot who fought in Poland during the 1863 revolution.

The words 'Dzieci Lwowskie' which appear in the regimental title of the 40th mean 'Children of Lwów'. The 81st Regiment was raised in Grodno and dedicated to King Stefan Batory.

French emblems or colours were incorporated in the badges of the 42nd, 43rd (Bayonne Legion), 49th and 52nd, the latter a rifle regiment from the eastern region of the Kresy.

The badge of the 58th portrayed King Bolesław Chrobry, the founder of Gniezno, where the regiment was raised. The coat of arms of this town is shown among others in the badge of the 69th.

The badges of the 59th (Greater Poland) and 61st Regiments illustrate allegorically the fall of Prussia in World War I.

The 60th (Greater Poland) was raised in Gostyn and the coat of arms of this town is part of the regimental badge.

The 32nd was a Masovian regiment and a badge similar in shape to that of the 86th was worn; the eagle in the latter holds the coat of arms of Mińsk.

Silesian eagles are present in the badges of the 73rd, 74th (Upper Silesia) and 75th Regiments, while Polish–Lithuanian and Samogitian emblems were part of the badges of the 76th and 77th. The 81st was named after the town of Grodno, and the bow and arrow of Pińsk are shown in the badge of the 84th, a regiment from the region of Polesie. The badge of the 85th carries the Madonna of Ostra Brama (Wilno) in its centre.

Plate 24

1st (Legion) J. Piłsudski's Infantry Regiment
2nd, 3rd and 4th (Legion) Infantry Regiments
5th (Legion) J. Piłsudski's Zuchowatych Infantry Regiment
6th (Legion) J. Piłsudski's Infantry Regiment
7th, 8th and 9th (Legion) Infantry Regiments
10th, 11th, 12th and 13th Infantry Regiments
14th Ziemia Kujawska Infantry Regiment
15th Wilków Infantry Regiment
16th, 17th and 18th Infantry Regiments
19th Odsieczy Lwowa Infantry Regiment
20th Ziemia Krakowska Infantry Regiment
21st Warszawski Infantry Regiment
22nd Infantry Regiment
23rd Colonel L. Lis-Kula's Infantry Regiment
24th and 25th Infantry Regiments

Plate 25

26th and 27th Infantry Regiments
28th, 29th, 30th and 31st Kaniowski Rifle Regiments
32nd, 33rd, 34th and 35th Infantry Regiments
36th Academy Legion Infantry Regiment
37th Prince J. Poniatowski's Łęczyce Infantry Regiment
38th and 39th Lwowski Rifle Regiments
40th Dzieci Lwowskie Infantry Regiment
41st Marshal J. Piłsudski's Suwalski Infantry Regiment
42nd General J. H. Dąbrowski's Infantry Regiment
43rd Bayonne Legion Rifle Regiment
44th American Legion Rifle Regiment
45th and 48th Kresowy Rifles Infantry Regiments
49th Huculski Rifle Regiment

50th Francesco Nullo's Infantry Regiment
51st, 52nd, 53rd and 54th Kresowy Rifles Infantry Regiments
55th Poznański Infantry Regiment
56th Wielkopolski Infantry Regiment
57th King Carol II of Rumania's Infantry Regiment

Plate 26

58th Infantry Regiment
59th and 60th Wielkopolski Infantry Regiments
61st and 62nd Infantry Regiments
63rd Toruński Infantry Regiment
64th (Pomorski) Murmańsk Rifle Regiment
65th Starogardzki Infantry Regiment
66th Marshal J. Piłsudski's Kaszubski Infantry Regiment
67th, 68th and 69th Infantry Regiments
70th Infantry Regiment (12th Wielkopolski Rifle Regiment)
71st Infantry Regiment
72nd Colonel D. Czachowski's Infantry Regiment
73rd Infantry Regiment
74th Górnośląski Infantry Regiment
75th Infantry Regiment
76th L. Narbutt's Lidzki Infantry Regiment
77th, 78th, 79th and 80th Infantry Regiments
81st King Stefan Batory's Grodzieński Infantry Regiment
82nd T. Kościuszko's Syberyjski Rifle Regiment
83rd R. Traugutt's Poleski Rifle Regiment
84th Poleski Rifle Regiment
85th Wileński Rifle Regiment
86th Infantry Regiment

Plate 27. Highland Rifle Regiments and Rifle Battalions

The Highland Rifle Regiments were six in all and they belonged to the 21st and 22nd Mountain Divisions. The motifs in their badges are the swastika, pine twigs and axe heads.

The enamel colours of the badge of the 1st Rifle Battalion were dark blue and nile green, which were the colours of the collar patches of the six rifle battalions. The griffin of Pomerania is depicted in the badge of the 2nd Battalion.

The Marine Rifle Battalion was an Army unit, and thus there is an army sword and the Polish eagle on a marine background in the centre of its badge.

Cavalry (*Pl. 27 and 28*)

The Polish lancers were called Ułans, thus the 'U' is displayed in some badges. The cavalry badges are simpler in design than those of the infantry; most were in the shape of crosses. The officers' badges were made in coloured enamels that showed, in one way or the other, the colours of the regimental pennons. Some badges displayed the monogram worn on the shoulder straps and the majority displayed the Polish eagle. The 18th Lancers had the Pomeranian griffin as its centre and the 13th Lancers had the Madonna of Ostra Brama (centre).

Dark green was present in the pennons of all the Mounted Rifle Regiments and it also appeared in most of their regimental badges.

In 1939 the Polish cavalry was formed of the following regiments:

Plate 27
1st J. Piłsudski's Light Horse Regiment
2nd Rokitniański Light Horse Regiment
3rd Colonel J. Kozietulski's Mazowiecki Light Horse Regiment
1st Colonel B. Mościcki's Krechowiecki Lancers Regiment
2nd General J. Dwernicki's Grochowski Lancers Regiment
3rd Śląski Lancers Regiment
4th Zaniemeński Lancers Regiment
5th Zasławski Lancers Regiment
6th Kaniowski Lancers Regiment
7th General K. Sosnkowski's Lubelski Lancers Regiment
8th Prince J. Poniatowski's Lancers Regiment
9th Małopolski Lancers Regiment
10th Litewski Lancers Regiment

Plate 28
11th (Legion) Marshal E. Śmigły-Rydz's Lancers Regiment
12th Podolski Lancers Regiment
13th Wileński Lancers Regiment
14th Jazłowiecki Lancers Regiment
15th Poznański Lancers Regiment
16th General G. Orlicz-Dreszer's Wielkopolski Lancers Regiment
17th King Bolesław Chrobry's Wielkopolski Lancers Regiment
18th Pomorski Lancers Regiment
19th General E. Różycki's Wołynski Lancers Regiment
20th King Jan III Sobieski's Lancers Regiment
21st Nadwiślańskich Lancers Regiment
22nd Podkarpacki Lancers Regiment
23rd Grodzieński Lancers Regiment

24th Lancers Regiment
25th Wielkopolski Lancers Regiment
26th Hetman K. Chodkiewicz's Wielkopolski Lancers Regiment
27th King Stefan Batory's Lancers Regiment

1st and 2nd Mounted Rifles Regiments
3rd Hetman S. Czarnecki's Mounted Rifles Regiment
4th Ziemia Łęczycka Mounted Rifles Regiment
5th Mounted Rifles Regiment
6th Hetman S. Żółkiewski's Mounted Rifles Regiment
7th Wielkopolski Mounted Rifles Regiment
8th Mounted Rifles Regiment
9th General K. Pulaski's Mounted Rifles Regiment
10th Mounted Rifles Regiment

Plate 29. Field Artillery

The basic colours of the Field Artillery (Artyleria Lekka) badges were green and black. They were also the colours of their collar patches.

The first three were 'Legion' regiments as they were derived from the Polish artillery of World War 1. The 4th F.A. Regiment was named after the Kujawy region and the 5th was from Lwów.

The 8th 'Płocki' F.A. Regiment was dedicated to King Bolesław Krzywousty and the 10th 'Kaniowski' had the Cross of Kaniów in its badge. The 12th and 13th were named after the Kresy region; the 16th was a Pomeranian regiment and the 25th named after the region of Kalisz.

The 24th F.A. Regiment was dedicated to King Jan III Sobieski; the 26th to King Władysław IV.

There were thirty-one regiments of Field Artillery, but the 31st was never part of a division and was used as a training unit.

Plate 30. Artillery

The gunners of the Medium Artillery Regiments (Artyleria Ciężka) wore green and red collar patches, and the same colours are also present in their regimental badges.

The 2nd M.A. Regiment was named after the region of Chełmn and dedicated to Hetman J. Zamoyski. The 3rd was dedicated to King Stefan Batory and the 6th was nicknamed 'The Defenders of Lwów' and had the coat of arms of that town in its badge. The Polish Army included 10 Medium Artillery regiments.

There was one regiment of Heavy Artillery (Artyleria Najcięższa), of which the other ranks' badge is illustrated, and only one commemorative Horse Artillery badge, although each battery had its title and honorary leader.

The badge of the Survey Artillery, which was a specialised service composed of surveyors and rangefinders, was made in its colours of white and green enamel.

1st Marshal E. Śmigły-Rydz's A. A. Artillery Regiment wore a badge made in green and yellow enamel. Just before the outbreak of World War 2 another badge was adopted, made in bronze and worn by all A. A. Artillery units.

The badge of the 1st Motorised Artillery Regiment showed the 'anti-clockwise' swastika which the Polish Army adopted in the early 1930s. The green and black centre is enclosed in a cogwheel, the emblem of motorisation.

The last badge illustrated did not belong to the Artillery. It represents a profile of Marshal J. Piłsudski and was worn by Instructors of the Cadet Force.

Proficiency Badges

Although not strictly Army badges, the National Sports Badge (divided into three classes) and the Rifle Association Badge (which was divided into four classes) were both worn above the right breast pocket at the level of the first button. However, in the case of officers and warrant officers they were worn on the cross belt, just below the shoulder straps. There were also proficiency badges for equestrian skills, ski-ing and motoring.

Plate 31. Engineers and Signals

The breast pocket badges of the Polish Engineers, when made in coloured enamels, were generally in the Corps colours of black and red. Picks, shovels, axes and anchors were the symbols usually shown in the badges.

There were eight battalions in all, numbered 1 to 8, the 6th wearing the badge of the old 9th Battalion.

There were also separate badges for Railway and Bridging Battalions and a different red and black badge was worn by the Mounted Pioneers.

The Signals' officers' badges were made of black and cornflower blue enamels, most of them with the 'lightning' device associated with the Corps.

Personnel of the Electrotechnical Battalion wore a badge with the 'E' initial worn on the shoulder straps and the black and red colours of the Engineers on a background of 'electric' blue.

Plate 32. Armoured Troops

In 1939 the Polish Army had twelve armoured battalions, numbered from 1 to 12. (The 11th was an experimental battalion, attatched to the A.C.

Training Centre, and wore its badge.) Their badges depicted dragons, knights' helmets and other motifs appropriate to armour. The enamel colours were generally black and orange.

The 1st and 2nd Armoured Train Groups wore special badges, both with a knight's plumed helmet in the centre.

Services, Schools, etc.

The badge of the Inspectorate General of the Armed Forces was worn above the left breast pocket and showed the monogram of Marshal Piłsudski and the marshals' crossed batons on a blue background. All the other badges illustrated, with the exception of the grenade badge of the Military Police, were worn on the left breast pocket.

The Frontier Defence Corps garrisoned the eastern borders and was a regular army corps, while the Border Guards were deployed on the other borders. Both were under the Ministry of the Interior. Both infantry and cavalry of the F.D.C. wore the same badge whose motto, 'Za Służbę Graniczną', means 'For Frontier Service'.

The Geographical Institute trained personnel of the Geographical Service who were employed in survey and mapping operations.

The Military Police (Zandarmeria) wore two badges: one badge was worn on the breast pocket and the other was worn only by policemen on actual policing duties. It hung on a chain fixed behind the collar on the left of the greatcoat, but above the medal ribbons on the tunic.

Additional Information

The badge for wounds was a ribbon half the width of that of the *Virtuti Militari* Cross; its ribbon was 4–7 cm long, with each wound represented by a silver star.

Front Service Stripes: they were worn on the upper right sleeve and were represented by inverted silver chevrons, one for each period of six months at the front.

Long Service Stripes (Regular Army): the stripes were normally worn by N.C.O.s on the upper left sleeve. The chevrons, in this case, were in silver braid with red edgings. One chevron was worn for each consecutive period of three years' service. A wider chevron was awarded on the 12th year and two wide chevrons were awarded for twenty-one years of service, together with normal narrower chevrons for the intermediate years of service.

Belgium

The Belgian military tradition goes back far beyond 1830, when national independence was gained.

In fact there were Belgian troops in the Austrian Army and, at the time of Napoleon, many Belgians took to his flag. At Waterloo there were Belgian units on both sides, some within Napoleon's army and others in Wellington's.

The Legion that fought for Napoleon was disbanded in 1815 when the territory of Belgium became part of the Kingdom of the Netherlands, and some infantry units were subsequently raised in the Netherlands, with a Belgian identity.

After the 1830 Revolution, on 14 October of that year, the National Congress proclaimed the Independence and, on 14 July of the following year, Prince Leopold of Saxe-Coburg became the first king of the Belgians. The new state was recognised internationally by the Treaty of London on 19 April, 1839.

After 1830, the new army was formed and there were French instructors who were responsible for the staff, while Polish instructors were mainly responsible for the raising and training of the cavalry units. Therefore, Lancers became part of the Belgian cavalry. The Guides regiment, which was one of the first cavalry units to be formed, originated from Cossack units which occupied Belgium during the Napoleonic wars.

In 1914, the corps and regiments of the Belgian Army wore their traditional uniforms, but later during the war khaki uniforms were introduced, with a steel helmet of French inspiration. The Belgian Lion's head was on the front of this helmet.

The khaki field uniform, although modernised in the 1930s, remained basically the same until World War 2. The rank badges were worn on the collar, in the form of stars and bars for officers and warrant officers, and on the forearms by the other ranks in the form of stripes.

Two different types of collar patches were worn on the jacket by officers and warrant officers. Generals, senior officers and advocates of the Legal Service wore collar patches 35 mm wide at the base, with an angle of 68° at the top; the other officers' and warrant officers' collar patches were 30 mm wide at the base, with a 72° angle at the top corner. The angles between the sides and the base were always of 98°. The height of the patch corresponded to the badges it contained.

Pointed collar patches were also worn on pointed collars as, for instance, on the leather tunic; they were made on an angle of 45°.

The officers wore khaki jackets while soldiers had tunics; all wore collar patches in the colours of their corps and services, and metal badges attached onto them if so required by regulations. The field cap was a characteristic forage cap with piping on the sides and along the top, and a tassel at the front. The piping and tassel were in the colour of the collar patches, and in gold or silver for the officers.

The Chasseurs of the Ardennes wore a dark green beret with the boar's head cap badge and the Border units a black beret with the wheel cap badge. In 1930, a dark blue full dress uniform was adopted for the officers. It consisted basically of a dark blue peaked cap, double-breasted tunic and trousers with large coloured stripes. Its style and piping colours varied according to different units.

Detachable shoulder cords were worn for parade and special duties, mainly on the khaki uniform. There were different types for generals, officers, warrant officers and regular N.C.O.s; the generals wore the Royal Cypher (King Leopold III, 1934–51) on the shoulder cords.

The Royal Cypher was also displayed on the buckle of the silk waist belt.

Plate 33. National Cockade, Cap Bands, Collar Patches and Shoulder Straps

All ranks of the Belgian Army wore a black, yellow and red cockade on the peaked cap.

The corps or service badge was also worn on the peaked cap, embroidered or pinned on the cap band, at the front over the chinstrap and various accoutrements showed the rank of the wearer.

Depending on their employment, generals were divided into three categories:

Generals of the Corps, who wore the badges illustrated here;

Generals of the Services, who kept the badges of their branch of service, adding general's stars and double bars on their particular collar badges;

Generals belonging to the cadre of Engineers of Military Productions (Military Supplies), who wore their badge representing a cogwheel superimposed on crossed hammers, and royal blue collar patches with scarlet piping.

All generals wore rank stars on the shoulder straps and, as already mentioned, the Royal Cypher badge on the shoulder cords.

Generals of the Corps wore the 'thunderbolt' badge (see Plate 38) on the cap and collar. On the peaked cap it was embroidered on an amaranth red band with twin vertical gold bars and gold piping. The chinstrap was formed by two sliding, smooth gold cords, of the pattern worn by all officers. They wore black collar patches with amaranth piping and the 'thunderbolt', stars and double bars embroidered in gold wire.

In 1939 there were two general's ranks as colonel-brigadiers wore colonel's badges with the addition of a scarlet red band on the cap. The gold belt buckle represented at the bottom of this plate was used by all officers, including generals.

Plates 34 and 35. Rank Badges

Officers

The cap band of the senior officers' peaked cap carried two single vertical gold bars and gold piping, while the only accoutrement granted to the junior officers' cap was a gold chinstrap. All cavalry units wore silver instead of gold.

Warrant officers wore silver badges and silver chinstrap cords on the peaked cap.

The rank badges worn on collar patches were represented by six-pointed stars (diam. 12 mm), embroidered or pinned on the patch at a distance of 15 mm one from the other, centre to centre.

One gold bar (30 mm × 7 mm), or two in the case of generals, was applied at the base of the patch in the case of a senior officer. A narrower bar was used as well for the rank badge of 1st captain and warrant officer 1st class and on its own, to denote the rank of 'clerk' of the Legal Service (Plate 35).

Captain-commandant or 1st captain refer to the same rank, some corps using one title, others the other.

The Belgian warrant officer was called 'adjutant', and wore stars and bars of silver.

Badges were worn on the headdress, on the collar of the jacket, tunic and greatcoat, and on the shoulder straps; the collar patches of the jacket and tunic being the common denominator, as they showed rank, colours of the corps or service, and often the corps or service's badge.

No collar patches were worn on the greatcoat collar, only badges embroidered or pinned directly on the collar itself.

Corps and Services

Represented in Plate 34 and Plate 35 are the patches of all Belgian corps and services as they were in 1939. I have illustrated these patches as they can be displayed by the collector. However, I am now going to describe them in the order of precedence applied by Belgian army regulations.

The corps and service badges were always worn, embroidered or pinned, on greatcoat collars but they were not necessarily worn on the collar patches as the colours of these were self-explanatory.

The badge of General Staff officers was, and still is, known as 'demifoudre' and was worn on the cap, collar and shoulder straps. G.S. officers actually serving at the General Staff also wore an amaranth red arm band on the upper left arm, while G.S. officers attached to field units wore the unit's badge on the shoulder straps instead of the 'demi-foudre'.

For instance, a G.S. infantry officer stationed in the fortress of Namur, would be wearing the royal crown and Namur's garrison badge 'N' underneath on the shoulder straps.

§ The remaining patches are as follows:

Infantry of the Line: scarlet red collar patch with royal blue piping. Crown

Grenadiers: scarlet–royal blue. Grenade

Carabiniers: dark green–yellow. Bugle

Chasseurs-on-Foot: dark green–yellow. Crown

Chasseurs of the Ardennes: dark green–scarlet. Boar's head

Carbiniers Cyclists: dark green–yellow. Bicycle wheel

Frontier Cyclists Regiment: scarlet–royal blue. Bicycle wheel

Guides: amaranth red–green. Crown over crossed sabres

Lancers: white–royal blue. Crossed lances

Chasseurs-on-Horse: yellow–royal blue. Sabre across bugle

Light Horse: royal blue–scarlet. Grenade (with open flame)

Artillery		Crossed cannons
VII A. C.		Cogwheel on crossed cannons
Artillery	royal blue–scarlet	
Horse Artillery		Horse shoe and crossed cannons
Anti-Aircraft Artillery		Torch, crossed cannons and wings

Engineers: *black–scarlet. Roman helmet

Transport Corps: ultramarine blue–royal blue. Car wheel

Doctors: *amaranth–amaranth	
Pharmacists: *emerald green–green	Caduceus within wreath
Dentists: *dark violet–amaranth	
Veterinaries: *ultramarine–royal blue	

Medical Service (O.R.): amaranth–royal blue. Caduceus

Commissaries: royal blue–sky blue. Caduceus of Mercury

N.C.O.s Secretaries of Commissariat: royal blue–grey blue. 'S' and 'I' interlaced

as above but attached to Army Corps: royal blue–grey blue. Letter 'I'

* *Denotes velvet; all other patches were in felt*

Officers Administrative
Secretaries, N.C.O. Archivist } royal blue–ultramarine.
and Treasury Secretaries: } 'S' and 'A' interlaced

Administrative Officers: royal blue–grey blue. Letter 'A'

Judge Advocate Generals
Judge Advocates } royal blue–ultramarine (see badges below)
Clerks

Members of the Legal Service did not wear the usual army ranks. There were only two officers' ranks, both represented by a 7 mm gold bar on the collar. Small differences in their badges further distinguished the two ranks, i.e. Judge Advocate Generals were entitled to an oak wreath while Judge Advocates wore a laurel wreath around the badge. Clerks of the Courts wore the *faisceau de licteur* without a wreath (Plate 38).

Officers of the } royal blue–scarlet. Cogwheel on crossed
Military Supplies: } hammers

Officers Supplies
Accountants and } royal blue–grey blue. Letter 'M'
Quartermasters N.C.O.s

Sergeants and Corporals

Sergeants and bandsmen of the regular army wore a peaked cap with white metal badges and a leather chinstrap, while corporals and privates were entitled to wear the peaked cap only after respectively ten and fifteen years of active service. Their chinstrap was faced with khaki material.

The rank stripes were of silver braid for sergeants and red for corporals, worn on the forearms over the cuffs, pointing inwards at a 30° angle. Both sergeants' and corporals' stripes were 50 mm long and 5 mm in depth.

Plate 36. Officers' Badges on Peaked Cap, Jacket and Greatcoat

Officers wore their corps or service badges on the cap and greatcoat collar and often on the collar patches.

The badges on the shoulder straps had not necessarily to be the same, as they represented the unit the officer was attached to at the moment. The same rule applies to all the other ranks.

This plate, for instance, shows the badges worn by a lieutenant-colonel of Artillery attached to the Engineers and Fortifications Headquarters.

He thus wore the Engineer's helmet and the fortress badge on the shoulder straps.

The other set of badges relate to those worn by a lieutenant doctor of the Medical Service attached to the 2nd Grenadier Regiment.

Grenadiers serving in grenadiers regiments did not wear the crown on the shoulder straps.

Infantrymen and Chasseurs of the Ardennes wore only the crown with the regimental number underneath on the shoulder straps; Carabiniers wore the crown, the bugle and the regimental number, while Chasseurs-on-Foot wore the crown and the bugle with the number in its centre.

The crown over the bicycle wheel with regimental number was worn by the Frontier Cyclists Regiment.

Guides wore the crown over the regimental number on the shoulder straps. Grenade and number were worn by cavalrymen of Light Horse regiments. Lancers and Chasseurs-on-Horse wore only the regimental number.

However, if a doctor, for instance, became attached to a regiment of Chasseurs-on-Horse, he would wear the 'bugle and sabre' badge as well as the regimental number on the shoulder straps, because in this case the regimental number would not be enough to identify his unit. Troops of any corps or service attached to the cavalry divisions wore the crossed sabres on the shoulder straps.

Gunners wore only the regimental numbers, except those serving with Army Artillery (Heavy), who also wore the crossed cannons, or those serving with the VII Army Corps (motorised) Anti-Aircraft Depot or in the Artillery Repair Service, who wore the appropriate badges as well as the unit's number.

Artillery units stationed at the Namur and Liège Fortresses wore the 'N' or 'L' badges under the crown.

Sappers generally wore the battalion's number on the shoulder straps but when attached to other units, as they more often are, they wore that unit's badge. For instance, sappers attached to the Chasseurs of the Ardennes Division wore the boar's head and the divisional number. Specialised Engineers units wore their own particular badges.

Troops of the Corps of Transport, with 'car wheel' badge on the cap and Transport's collar patch, wore the badge of the units they were attached to on the shoulder straps while, vice-versa, an officer of the Administrative Service attached to the Corps of Transport would be wearing the 'car wheel' badge on shoulder straps.

Plate 37. Corps and Service Badges

The badges illustrated in this and the following plate could be found embroidered in gold or silver wire, in white metal or brass.

The Belgian infantry was divided into: Infantry of the Line, Grenadiers, Carabiniers, Chasseurs-on-Foot, Chasseurs of the Ardennes. Carabiniers Cyclists, the Frontier Cyclists Regiment and any other unit of cyclists wore a badge representing a bicycle wheel.

The cavalry was composed of regiments of Guides, Lancers, Chasseurs-on-Horse and regiments of Light Horse.

Two crossed cannons were the symbol of artillery, but gunners serving in the Cavalry Corps, or Cavalry Divisions, had a horseshoe added to the crossed guns. The Artillery of the VII Army Corps had a cogwheel superimposed on the cannons; the Anti-Aircraft Artillery and the Artillery Repair Service were entitled to particular badges of their own.

The badge 'R' of the Cavalry Depot stands for *Remonte*, and 'P', an artillery badge, stands for *Parc d'artillerie*. The roman helmet was the badge of the engineers, but specialised engineering units wore different badges on the shoulder straps. The crossed axes was the badge of the *Pontonniers*, the winged wheel that of the Military Railways, the letter 'F', standing for *Fontainiers* the service of water suppliers. Signal troops and the Camouflage Service also wore different badges.

Independent from the Corps of Transport, there was the Headquarters of Transport (*Direction des Transports*). Its badge clearly explains its role by representing, as a whole, the badges of the road, river and railway transportation systems.

'I' stands for *Intendance*, or the Commissariat Service.

Plate 38. Corps and Service Badges and Numerals

Chaplains had three different badges depending which religion they represented. Other ranks of the Medical, Veterinary and Pharmacist Services wore a badge similar to that of the officers, the caduceus, but without wreath.

Civilian personnel attached to the Armed Forces wore the Belgian Lion on the headdress and collar of their uniform. Generals, however, did not wear the amaranth red band on the peaked cap. Civilian personnel also wore a black, yellow and red armband on the left upper arm, with their name, surname and service to which they were attached on the reverse.

Civilian personnel serving in the Military Railway Service, Telegraphic and Telephone Service, wore the metallic letters C.F.T. on a 7 mm × 54 mm patch of green material, stitched on the armband.

Roman numerals represented army corps numbers; arabic numerals were reserved for battalion, regimental and divisional numbers.

'Attributs des Fonctions'

The badges illustrated at the bottom half of plate 38 are badges of 'functions' or duties (*Attributs des Fonctions*). They show the appointment of an officer or N.C.O. and therefore, in the Belgian army regulations, are always shown grouped apart from the others.

They were all worn on the cap, as well as on the collar and shoulder straps.

Auxiliary troops wore the scarlet and royal blue infantry collar patches, the royal crown on the peaked cap and, on the forage cap and shoulder straps, the roman helmet, with regimental number below, in roman numerals.

Personnel of the services not listed above wore the headdress badges of their previous corps or service.

Cap Badges of Regiments in Plate 37 and 38

	Forage Cap and Beret	*Peaked Cap*
Infantry of the Line	crown regimental number	crown
Grenadiers	grenade regimental number	grenade
Carabiniers	bugle regimental number	bugle
Chasseurs-on-Foot	bugle regimental number	bugle
Chasseurs of the Ardennes	boar's head regimental number	boar's head
Carabiniers Cyclists	bicycle wheel regimental number	bicycle wheel
Frontier Cyclists Regt	crown bicycle wheel	bicycle wheel
Guides	crown crossed sabres regimental number	crown crossed sabres
Lancers	crossed lances regimental number	crossed lances
Chasseurs-on-Horse	sabre across bugle regimental number	sabre and bugle
Light Horse	grenade regimental number	grenade

	Forage Cap and Beret	*Peaked Cap*
Artillery	crossed cannons regimental number	crossed cannons
VII Anti-Aircraft Artillery	cogwheel on crossed cannons	
Horse Artillery	horse shoe–crossed cannons regimental number	horse shoe– crossed cannons
Anti-Aircraft Artillery	torch-wings–crossed cannons regimental number	torch-wings– crossed cannons
Fortress Artillery	crown crossed cannons	—
Artillery Repair Service	compass and lightnings	
Engineers	roman helmet	
Engineers Battalions	roman helmet battalion number	roman helmet
Transport Corps	car wheel	
Doctors, Pharmacists, Dentists, Veterinaries	caduceus within wreath	
Medical Service (O.R.)	caduceus	
Commissaries	caduceus of Mercury	
N.C.O.s Secretaries of Commissariat	'S' and 'I' interlaced	
as above but attached to A. C. and field units	letter 'I'	
Officers Administrative Secretaries, N.C.O.s Archivist and Treasury Secretaries	'S' and 'A' interlaced	
Administrative Officers	letter 'A'	
Judge Advocate Generals	*faisceau de licteur* within oak wreath	
Judge Advocates	*faisceau de licteur* within laurel wreath	
Clerks	*faisceau de licteur*	
Catholic Chaplains	Latin cross	
Protestant Chaplains	Maltese cross	
Jewish Rabbis	Star of David	

	Forage Cap and Beret	*Peaked Cap*
Officers of the Military Supplies		cogwheel on crossed hammers
Officers Supplies Accountants and Quartermaster N.C.O.s		letter 'M'
Civilian personnel attached to the Armed Forces		Belgian lion

Italy

For centuries, Italy was divided into several independent states. It was finally united in 1861 by the House of Savoy, whose kings, through war and diplomacy, succeeded in taking over all the remainder of the Italian peninsula.

The origins of the House of Savoy are lost in the past. At the beginning of the eleventh century, Umberto Biancamano, Count of Aosta, ruled over Savoy, Maurienne, Belley and, of course, Aosta. Having control of the Alpine passes between France and Italy, the Savoy rulers were constantly involved in the wars between neighbouring countries. In 1416, Emperor Sigismund made Amedeus VIII a duke. At the Peace of Utrecht, the House of Savoy obtained the island of Sicily, and became a monarchy. But in 1720, King Victor Amedeus II exchanged Sicily for Sardinia, and henceforth the rulers became Kings of Sardinia.

In 1557, Duke Emmanuel Philibert (known as 'Ironhead') began to organise his feudal militias into a number of companies, under the command of captains, with 400 men to each company. A regiment was made up of six companies, commanded by a colonel appointed by the Duke.

By Royal Decree of 19 October, 1664, the infantry regiments adopted the name of the province in which they were recruited, instead of, as formerly, being referred to by their colonel's name or by French titles of Savoyard derivation.

As early as 1626, barracks were built and in 1671 troops were given their first uniforms, a blue sash having been the only common distinguishing feature of the Army since 1572.

The uniforms of the Sardinian Army, and later those of the Italian Army, tended to follow the pattern of those of neighbouring France.

The region of Savoy and Nice were lost to France after the French Revolution, and in 1801 Piedmont also was annexed by France. It became the 27th French Territorial Division, recruiting for the 111th Infantry Regiment, 31st Light Infantry, 21st Dragoons and 26th Light Horse of the Imperial Army. Several legions of Italian volunteers also followed the fortunes of Napoleon, with the green, white and red cockade as their national emblem.

The Congress of Vienna re-established the Kingdom of Sardinia to the status it had had before the French Revolution, and the remainder of Italy came under the Austrian sphere of influence.

King Charles Albert (1831–49) waged war with Austria but was defeated in both the 1848 and 1849 campaigns. His successor, Victor

Emmanuel II (1849–78), conducted the Second and Third Wars of Independence and successfully unified all the Italian States under the Savoy crown. In 1861 the Kingdom of Sardinia became the Kingdom of Italy and, in 1870, Rome became its capital.

The grey-green field uniform was adopted in 1909 and consisted basically of a soft cap (*kepi*) and a tunic with a high collar and four pockets for the officers (pocketless for the other ranks). Officers and mounted troops wore breeches with boots or leggings; the remainder of the army wore trousers and puttees.

After World War 1, in 1923, new dress regulations were published by which four patch pockets were added at last to the other ranks' tunics. Stripes were added onto the seams of the officers' breeches. Unfortunately, at the same time, the other ranks' trousers were replaced by ugly plus-fours.

New regulations modified the Italian uniform yet again in 1933. The high collar was replaced by a more comfortable open collar; the peaked cap and a field cap called *bustina* (little envelope) were issued to all ranks.

In 1935 a new type of helmet, initially with a small crest, replaced the French type adopted during World War 1.

Officers were entitled to wear three uniforms: black for special duties; white, ordinarily worn during summer; and grey-green, the only uniform most officers owned. However, alternated with different headdresses (peaked cap, field cap and helmet), with metal decorations or ribbons, different shoulder boards or epaulettes, etc., these three uniforms could be adapted into several forms of dress, depending upon the duties performed by an officer.

Until 1889, the 'colonial' uniform was white for all ranks, but a new khaki uniform was then introduced, redder in tone than British khaki.

Other ranks also wore a grey cotton garrison uniform, the jacket having side pockets only on which no badges were worn, except collar stars and N.C.O.s' chevrons.

The arms and corps of the Italian Army were distinguished from each other by different colours, worn on the uniform in the form of piping or facing on the collar, cuffs, etc.

The colours were:

Infantry, Grenadiers	scarlet
Medical Corps and Pharmacists	amaranth red
Bersaglieri (Rifle regiments), Engineers	crimson
Alpini (Mountain Infantry)	green
Artillery	yellow
Veterinary Corps	light blue
Motor Transport, Administrative and Supply Corps	blue

General Staff	turquoise blue
Commissariat	violet
Fencing Instructors	white

Cavalry regiments had piping and facing in the regimental colours.

On the white and khaki uniforms the coloured piping was around the shoulder boards only.

The tunic of the officers' black uniform was double-breasted with two rows of buttons, pointed cuffs and a folded collar buttoned up to the neck.

The collars and cuffs were generally made of black velvet, edged with coloured piping (Infantry, Artillery, Engineers, Supply and Administrative Corps), but officers of specialised corps (Doctors, Pharmacists, Veterinaries, Commissaries and General Staff Officers) wore collars made entirely of coloured velvets.

Alpini and *Bersaglieri* had coloured cuffs and wore their flames on a black velvet collar. Grenadiers wore silver 'double bars' on both the red cloth collar and the cuffs.

The officers of the Tank Corps wore red 'flames' on a black collar, and the Motor Transport Corps black 'flames' on a blue collar.

Coloured stripes were also worn on the trousers.

The headdress of the grey-green uniform for officers and other ranks alike was a peaked cap, a field cap or a steel helmet. Special troops were issued with different types of headdress as well.

Bersaglieri wore a wide-brimmed black hat with a cluster of cockerel feathers, or a crimson felt fez with a blue tassel, the latter taking the place of the field cap.

All mountain troops wore the traditional feathered hat: officers wore a gilded feather holder; other ranks had an oval woollen pompon instead, each battalion having a different colour. Senior officers wore a white goose feather, junior officers an eagle feather and other ranks a crow feather.

Dragoons wore their own traditional crested helmet, while Lancers and the rest of the Cavalry wore sealskin caps.

All ranks of the Horse Artillery were issued with a stiff grey-green kepi with a black leather visor.

The officers' tunic was grey-green with open collar and four patch pockets. The shoulder boards and the cuffs were edged with coloured piping and the upper part of the collar was faced or piped in much the same way as the collar of the black uniform. An exception was made for the infantry where all ranks wore the regimental patch instead of red piping on the collar. The collar itself was made of black velvet for officers and that of other ranks was faced with black felt.

Officers had grey-green breeches with 2 cm black double stripes and coloured central piping; warrant officers also wore breeches but they had only a narrow coloured piping along the seams. The other ranks wore facings only on the upper part of the collar, under the patch or 'flame', without any pipings.

The *Guardia alla Frontiera* (Frontier Guard) was raised in 1934. All ranks wore a green cap band on the peaked cap and green facing on the upper part of the collar. The infantry of the Border Guard wore additional red piping, the engineers, crimson, and the artillery, yellow.

In the late 1930s, a number of armoured and motorised divisions were formed and all troops attached to these wore the upper part of the collar faced with blue felt and the collar patches and 'flames' superimposed onto it.

Plate 39. Generals' Rank Badges

Owing to the great numbers of World War I officers reaching higher ranks, and to the enormous numerical expansion of the Army, it became necessary, in the mid-thirties, to adopt new ranks for generals. The rank of general 'in command' of an army denotes that the wearer was an Army Corps general, detailed to command an army.

After the conquest of Ethiopia, King Victor Emmanuel III became Emperor and, together with Mussolini, his military rank became that of First Marshal of the Empire. The title of an Italian field general always referred to the unit he was in command of, i.e. General of Army, General of Army Corps, etc. Generals of army services who did not command field units had titled ranks (major general, etc.).

The generals' cap badge was the crowned eagle of Savoy, that centuries before had been used on the regimental banners; it was embroidered in gold wire for marshals, generals of army and generals of Army Corps, and in silver for all the others.

The generals' cap badge was embroidered on red felt; General Staff officers wore the same cap badge, but embroidered in gold on grey-green.

Generals of the Medical Corps and of the Commissariat wore their cap badges embroidered on the colour of the Corps, and generals of the Legal Corps wore all their badges on grey-green instead of red.

The typical ornament of the generals' rank badge was called a *greca*, a simplification of the traditional embroideries worn by Piedmontese generals in the Sardinian Army.

It was embroidered on the band of the peaked cap with one additional silver stripe for brigadiers, two for Division and Army Corps generals (the latter with gold cap badge). There were three silver stripes for generals of Army and four for marshals of Italy. The First Marshal of the Empire wore two *greche* on the cap band.

The same pattern was followed for rank badges worn on the jacket or greatcoat, with additional crowns and batons in gold for certain ranks. As these rank badges were rather cumbersome on the field cap, in 1935 stars were adopted as rank badges, for generals and all other officers alike.

The rank badges on the sleeves were worn over the cuffs, and were embroidered on cherry red for medical generals, on violet for commissariat generals and on grey-green for all other generals.

Shoulder boards and metal epaulettes are not illustrated in this book because they are considered parts of the uniform, rather than badges. Epaulettes were in silver and shoulder boards in silver braid, with red backing; gold stars, and a smaller replica of the cap badge, were embroidered in the centre. Generals of the three Army Corps mentioned above wore a small replica of the corps' cap badge instead.

Plate 40. Officers' Rank Badges

Officers also had their rank badges on the headdress and, normally, on both forearms of the jacket. In the case of the black uniform, white summer uniform and colonial uniform, such badges were worn on the shoulder boards instead of on the forearms. Gold embroidered stars (with a small bar at the outside end of the shoulder board in the case of 1st Lieutenant or 1st Captain) were worn by junior officers; the same by senior officers but with an additional 6 mm gold braid stripe (called *millerighe*) around the edges. A small replica of the cap badge was also attached in the centre of the shoulder board. Black shoulder boards were worn with black and colonial uniforms, and grey-green shoulder boards with grey-green and white uniforms.

Colonel regimental commanders wore all badges on red (a brick red called *robbio*) backing; unassigned colonels wore them on grey-green, as did other officers. A colonel 'in command' of a Brigade wore colonel's badges (on red) on the forearms and on the band of the peaked cap, and a silver general's cap badge and small silver eagle on the shoulder boards in place of stars.

The officers' badges were gold braid stripes, 10 mm in depth, on the forearms, the top stripe being adapted into a loop. A 17 mm gold stripe was the basic insignia of senior rank, a thin black woven gold-edged stripe, that of cadets.

Any officer 'in charge' of a superior command had a red patch inside the loop of the rank badges; a gold star inside the loop showed that the officer, of any rank, was an adjutant.

The rank of 1st captain, or 1st lieutenant, was given to officers after twelve years' service as a captain or lieutenant, or after twenty years' commission. They wore a small gold star under the rank badges, stitched onto the cuffs.

During the war, all rank badges became smaller and later, instead of gold, they were made in yellow silk.

The rank badges of medical officers and commissaries are stitched onto a rectangular backing felt which was in the colour of their particular service. Chaplains wore their badges on purple backing.

Plate 41. Warrant Officers' Rank Badges

The Italian warrant officer was, and is still, called a *maresciallo*. There were three ranks which were represented by stripes of a special gold braid which, in one, two or three stripes, were stitched onto the shoulder boards as illustrated.

From September, 1917, for the duration of the war, a new warrant officer's rank was granted for exceptional acts of valour performed by other ranks. Indeed, any warrant officer, N.C.O. or soldier could be granted the rank of *Aiutante di battaglia* on the field. At the end of the war each of them was given a premium of 200 lire for each month of service with such a rank. The sum could not exceed 1,400 lire. During World War 2 the rank consisted of three stripes of warrant officers' braid on red backing, forming a loop around the button. No *Aiutanti di battaglia* were made during World War 2, so nowadays this rank could be considered defunct.

All warrant officers, regardless of their rank, wore, and still wear, one stripe of W.O.'s braid, slightly larger than that mentioned above, around the band of the peaked cap, or a 60 mm stripe on the field cap.

Non-commissioned Officers and Other Ranks

In the Italian Army, only sergeants and sergeant-majors are termed N.C.O.s; they wore gold chevrons, while corporals wore black woven chevrons on both forearms, over the cuffs. Before World War 2 these chevrons were adopted, in shorter, inverted form, on the upper sleeves, and later, during the war, corporals and corporal-majors were issued with red chevrons.

Such chevrons were all woven as a ribbon, then cut and sewn in 'V' form on grey-green material, ready to be stitched onto the sleeves of the wearer. During World War 2 they became smaller and smaller, the gold ones being replaced by yellow woven chevrons.

Sergeants and corporals did not wear any rank badges other than those on the sleeves.

Plate 42. Collar Patches

Italian collar patches are specifically those of rectangular shape while the pointed patches are called 'flames'. They originated from the coloured facings and trimmings worn on the uniforms of the old Sardinian Army.

In the mid-1930s these colours once again became part of the uniform but, when all linings, facings and pipings were abolished in 1940, the 'colours' were restricted to the actual patches. They were worn by all ranks on the collar of the jacket.

According to regulations, the infantry collar patches should have been 60 mm long but as the war went on they became smaller and smaller. The patch illustrated was that of the 291st/292nd *Zara* Infantry Brigade.

By the Royal Warrant of 3 October, 1815, the infantry regiments of the Sardinian Army were 'brigaded' in twos under the same title. The Brigade remained the basic infantry formation ever after. In 1935, a field artillery regiment and support services were attached to each brigade, thus creating an infantry division. From about 1940 the divisional artillery, engineers, medical, administrative and supply units wore their 'flames' sewn onto the collar patch of the divisional infantry.

The cavalry regiments had three-pointed flames, often with coloured edgings; in the case of cavalry Scout Groups attached to infantry divisions, the flames were sewn on the collar patch of the divisional infantry.

The grenadiers of the *Granatieri di Sardegna* Division wore silver or white 'double bars' on a red patch; those of the *Granatieri di Savoia* wore the bars on a royal blue patch, red and royal blue having been the colours of their collars and cuffs during the 1930s.

In the same period all the troops belonging to armoured and motorised divisions were wearing their flames on blue collars: and so in 1940 they adopted their own collar patches by sewing the flames on rectangular blue backgrounds. For a short time in 1940 the armoured artillery wore a blue flame with yellow edging.

The infantry of the *Trento* and *Trieste* (illustrated) Motorised Divisions wore a half infantry patch sewn on a rectangular blue background. Machine-gunners wore two types of patches, both on blue backgrounds.

The first units of Light Tanks were raised on the 19th (Guides) Cavalry Regiment which had three-pointed flames on their blue collar. To commemorate this association, a similar collar patch was adopted, but with two-pointed flames on a blue rectangular background.

Personnel of the Transport Corps wore one-pointed orange flames, but for the newly-formed Motor Transport Corps black flames on blue collar were adopted and subsequently, black flames on blue patches.

In the 1930s, the officers of the Alpine artillery and engineers had worn artillery or engineers' uniforms and were distinguished as mountain troops only by the badges on the headdress and shoulder boards. In 1940 they adopted the flames previously worn by the other ranks, now on rectangular green patches. However, the artillery of the *Julia* Division temporarily adopted green flames with yellow edging, and they were still wearing them during the Greek campaign.

Parachutists of the parachute divisions, personnel of the Chemical Centre and *Guastatori* (Assault engineers) had large, embroidered collar patches, the latter replacing them in 1940 with normal engineers' flames; the sword and flaming grenade was, by then, worn as an arm badge.

The patch of general staff officers could be worn stitched on other collar patches when the officer was posted to a unit. Adjutants wore crowned stars on the collar instead of the usual stars.

All personnel of the Fascist Militia wore two-pointed black flames: the *fascio* was made of gilt for officers; in silver or white metal for N.C.O.s and brass for the other ranks. Personnel of the 'M' (Mussolini's) Battalions, raised in the early 1940s, wore a red 'M' on the flames across the *fascio*.

Cap Badges (*Pl. 43, 44, 45*)

Traditionally the infantry, cavalry and service corps connected with them, wore silver badges, except for the *Bersaglieri* who wore gold. Artillery and engineers, in the old days known as 'skilled' corps, also wore gold.

With the introduction of the 1933 army regulations, gold was granted to all the Army, except, as we have seen, the generals, who kept to their traditional silver badges.

Officers, warrant officers and non-commissioned officers wore gold wire, hand-embroidered cap badges; corporals and soldiers brass or machine embroidered badges in black rayon.

There were two sizes of embroidered badges: a large size worn by officers (W.O. and N.C.O.) on the peaked cap, embroidered on grey-green, black or brick red felt, and on khaki material for colonial uniform. A cap badge embroidered on grey-green was also worn on the white summer cap as the band was grey-green.

The field cap badge was smaller and should not be confused with the badges worn on the shoulder boards which were generally smaller still. It was embroidered in gold for officers (W.O. and N.C.O.) and black rayon for other ranks.

Some large brass cap badges were worn on the other rank's peaked cap before World War 2. These same badges were previously worn on the tricolor cockade of the nineteenth century blue *kepi*, and had always been worn on the colonial helmet.

Plate 43
The cap badges in this and the two following plates are those worn by officers (W.O. and N.C.O.), embroidered in gold and used during the period 1933–43.

Cap badges of corps that were divided into regiments had a black velvet centre where the regimental number was applied or, in the case of un-assigned officers, a cross.

The infantry cap badge was adopted by officers around 1907 and by other ranks in the early twenties. The former was at that time in silver, the latter the same size as that of the officers, but embroidered in black wool.

Officers' cap badges with red centres and other ranks' metal cap badges with red numerals belonged to regiments stationed in the colonies.

The first companies of *Bersaglieri* were raised in 1836 for light infantry duties and until 1870 they wore the battalion number in the cap badge (from 1 to 50). During World War 1, twenty-one regiments of *Bersaglieri* were raised.

The Colonial Rifles were raised in July, 1887 in Eritrea under the name *Cacciatori d'Africa*; their cap badge, a mixture of infantry and *Bersaglieri* designs, could also be found with a green or red centre.

The infantry of the *Trento* and the *Trieste* Motorised Divisions wore a particular cap badge with a cogwheel around the centre. Paratroopers were granted the winged dagger cap badge just before World War 2, the blade of the dagger often being embroidered in silver.

In 1936 light tanks and armoured cars were detached from the Tank Corps to form three groups (S. Marco, S. Giusto and S. Martino) of so-called 'fast' tanks, each group later joining one of the three *Celere* Divisions.

The first four regiments of the Italian cavalry have always traditionally been Dragoons. During World War 1 there also existed eight regiments of Lancers and eighteen regiments of Cavalry, but after the war, most were disbanded. Thus only representative regiments of dragoons, lancers and cavalry saw service during World War 2 still wearing their traditional cap badges.

The 10th Assault Regiment was an independent parachute unit whose members underwent special training for 'commando' type operations.

The Motor Transport Corps changed its cap badge in the mid-1930s as the badge initially adopted symbolised railway transport instead of motor transport. Nevertheless the former badge was kept in use, worn by transport units without motorisation.

Plate 44
In the mid-thirties the old Heavy, Medium and Field Artillery were renamed Army, Army Corps and Divisional Artillery and, at the same time, Motorised Artillery came into being, as part of the Motorised Divisions.

Coast Artillery and most of the Anti-Aircraft Artillery batteries were taken over by the Fascist Territorial Militia while Light Artillery and Train Artillery were disbanded.

The Royal Corps of Engineers was established in 1752, fortification works and engineering previously having been carried out by artillery units. The first Pioneer battalion, of six companies of pioneers and one of miners, was formed in 1816, and the first regiment in 1859. The Regiment (4th) of Bridging Engineers was formed by companies of bridging specialists and the so-called *lagunari*, who were trained for amphibious engineering and stationed near Venice.

The first signal units were part of the Corps of the Engineers and, before World War 1, they were granted the sappers' cap badge with the addition of small lightnings around the grenade, as a symbol of electric sparks.

Railway Engineers and Miners have always been highly specialised sections of the Corps and, although they possessed their independent training depots, were not regimented but, usually at company strength, were attached to the larger formations.

Plate 45

The Colonial Mounted Rifles were raised together with the *Cacciatori d'Africa* in 1887, of which they were the supporting cavalry.

In 1873, the Corps of Military Intendance became the Corps of Commissaries or Commissariat, formed only of officers, with the duty of superintending the supply and administration of the Army. Doctors of the Medical Corps, veterinaries, pharmacists, commissaries of the Red Cross, chaplains and lawyers of the Legal Corps were all officers. Fencing instructors, however, were all 2nd Lieutenants.

The first fifteen companies of *Alpini* were formed by Army Order of 15 October, 1872 and by 1882 there already existed six regiments which by 1909 became eight, totalling twenty-six battalions.

In the meantime, regiments of mountain gunners and companies of pioneers, miners and signalmen were also raised in support of the infantry. The Alpine battalions were never numbered but named instead after the town, mountain, village or valley in the battalion's recruiting area.

A small enamel badge, a different one for each battalion, was also worn on the hat near the feather holder.

Infantry, Artillery and Engineers wore different cap badges, adopted before World War 1. They are still in use today. The *Alpini* cap badge, like the other soldiers' cap badges, was black rayon on worsted. The pattern worn during World War 2 is illustrated in Plate 46.

The Frontier Guard (*Guardia alla Frontiera*) was raised in 1934 and its members wore the mountain troops' hat, with coloured feather holder but without a feather. Divided into infantry, artillery and engineers, they wore the corresponding badges, but with a green centre and roman, instead of arabic, numerals. The Frontier Guard was divided into 'sectors' and not regiments. Machine-gunners wore the special badge of an eagle clutching a machine-gun.

Italian Divisions of World War 2

A list of World War 2 divisions is given in the following pages. A number of these took part in the Abyssinian campaign under a different name or number.

It should be noted that most of the infantry divisions were named after their infantry brigade; in other cases both titles are given. Although this is an official list, by 1943 the greater part of these infantry divisions were only partially formed, others existed only on paper.

The armoured and motorised divisions were all destroyed in North Africa and so was the *Folgore* Parachute Division. The Alpine divisions were employed on all fronts except the North African and the *Celere* divisions were split up and eventually their units were destroyed on the North African and Russian fronts.

Infantry Divisions

No.	Title	Infantry Regiments	Artillery Regiment
13th	RE	1st–2nd	23rd
29th	PIEMONTE	3rd–4th	24th
28th	AOSTA	5th–6th	22nd
6th	CUNEO	7th–8th	27th
50th	REGINA	9th–10th	50th
56th	CASALE	11th–12th	56th
24th	PINEROLO	13th–14th	18th
55th	SAVONA	15th–16th	12th
33rd	ACQUI	17th–18th	33rd
27th	BRESCIA	19th–20th	55th
44th	CREMONA	21st–22nd	7th
14th	ISONZO	23rd–24th (COMO Bde)	6th
15th	BERGAMO	25th–26th	4th
17th	PAVIA	27th–28th	26th
26th	ASSIETTA	29th–30th (PISA Bde)	25th
51st	SIENA	31st–32nd	51st
4th	LIVORNO	33rd–34th	28th
16th	PISTOIA	35th–36th	3rd
3rd	RAVENNA	37th–38th	121st
25th	BOLOGNA	39th–40th	205th
37th	MODENA	41st–42nd	29th
36th	FORLI'	43rd–44th	36th

No.	Title	Infantry Regiments	Artillery Regiment	
30th	SABAUDA	45th–46th (REGGIO Bde)	16th	
23rd	FERRARA	47th–48th	14th	
49th	PARMA	49th–50th	49th	
22nd	CACCIATORI DELLE ALPI	51st–52nd	1st	
2nd	SFORZESCA	53rd–54th (UMBRIA Bde)	17th	
32nd	MARCHE	55th–56th	32nd	
10th	PIAVE	57th–58th (ABBRUZZI Bde)	20th	
102nd	TRENTO (Mot.)	61st–62nd (SICILIA Bde)	46th	7th Bersaglieri Regt.
59th	CAGLIARI	63rd–64th	59th	
101st	TRIESTE (Mot.)	65th–66th (VALTELLINA Bde)	21st	9th Bersaglieri Regt.
58th	LEGNANO	67th–68th (PALERMO Bde)	58th	
61st	SIRTE	69th–70th (ANCONA Bde)	43rd	
38th	PUGLIE	71st–72nd	15th	
57th	LOMBARDIA	73rd–74th	57th	
54th	NAPOLI	75th–76th	54th	
7th	LUPI DI TOSCANA	77th–78th	30th	
9th	PASUBIO	79th–80th (ROMA Bde)	8th	
52nd	TORINO	81st–82nd	52nd	
19th	VENEZIA	83rd–84th	19th	
60th	SABRATHA	85th–86th (VERONA Bde)	42nd	
20th	FRIULI	87th–88th	35th	
5th	COSSERIA	89th–90th (SALERNO Bde)	29th	
1st	SUPERGA	91st–92nd (BASILICATA Bde)	5th	
18th	MESSINA	93rd–94th	2nd	
103rd	PIACENZA	111th–112th	37th	
104th	MANTOVA	113th–114th	11th	
62nd	MARMARICA	115th–116th (TREVISO Bde)	44th	
155th	EMILIA	119th–120th	155th	

No.	Title	Infantry Regiments	Artillery Regiment
153rd	MACERATA	121st–122nd	153rd
80th	SPEZIA (Airborne)	125th–126th	80th
41st	FIRENZE	127th–128th	41st
151st	PERUGIA	129th–130th	151st
47th	BARI	139th–140th	47th
64th	CATANZARO	141st–142nd	203rd
12th	SASSARI	151st–152nd	34th
63rd	CIRENE	157th–158th (LIGURIA Bde)	45th
48th	TARO	207th–208th	
53rd	AREZZO	225th–226th	53rd
105th	ROVIGO	227th–228th	117th
11th	BRENNERO	231st–232nd (AVELLINO Bde)	9th
152nd	PICENO	235th–236th	152nd
154th	MURGE	259th–260th	154th
156th	VICENZA	277th–278th–279th	
158th	ZARA	291st–292nd	
	AFRICA	formed by units stationed in East Africa	
21st	GRANATIERI DI SARDEGNA	1st–2nd–3rd Gren.	13th
	GRANATIERI DI SAVOIA	10th–11th–12th Gren.	

Parachute Divisions

No.	Title	Parachute Regiments	Artillery Regiment
184th	NEMBO	183rd–184th–185th	184th
185th	FOLGORE	186th–187th	185th

Armoured Divisions

No.	Title	Tank Regiment	Armd Regt Artillery	Bersaglieri Regt
132nd	ARIETE	32nd	132nd	8th
133rd	LITTORIO	33rd	133rd	12th
134th	CENTAURO	31st	131st	5th
136th	GIOVANI FASCISTI	3 bns	1 regt	3 bns

'Celere' Divisions

No.	Title	Cavalry Regiments	Celere Art. Regt	Bersaglieri Regt
1st	EUGENIO DI SAVOIA	14th ALESSANDRIA 12th SALUZZO	1st	11th
2nd	EMANUELE FILIBERTO	9th Lanc. FIRENZE 10th Lanc. VITTORIO EMANUELE II	2nd	6th
3rd	PRINCIPE AMEDEO DI AOSTA	3rd Drag. SAVOIA 5th Lanc. NOVARA	3rd	3rd

Alpine Divisions

No.	Title	Alpini Regiment	Mountain Artillery Regt
1st	TAURINENSE	3rd–4th	1st
2nd	TRIDENTINA	5th–6th	2nd
3rd	JULIA	8th–9th	3rd
4th	CUNEENSE	1st–2nd	4th
5th	PUSTERIA	7th–11th	5th
6th	ALPI GRAIE	III–IV Groups 'Valle'	6th

Plate 46. Divisional Arm Shields

Divisional arm shields were adopted in the mid-1930s for the newly formed divisions. They were of identical design, but had different background colour and divisional titles.

Infantry divisions were on a blue background if in enamel, black if on a painted background. Some others were woven and some embroidered.

The badge illustrated, that of the 27th *Sila* Infantry Division, was used during the Abyssinian campaign. Later, the 27th Division was renamed *Brescia* and took part in the North African campaign. The Italian infantry divisions were not motorised. The 61st *Sirte* Infantry Division wore a red embroidered divisional badge and was one of the nine infantry divisions called *Autotrasportabile tipo Africa Settentrionale*. Theoretically, they could be mechanically transported by Army Corps, which was in charge of transport.

The 1st *Trento* Motorised Infantry Division, later numbered 102nd, together with the *Trieste* Division, were the only fully motorised infantry divisions and wore the divisional badge on red backgrounds.

Celere means fast or swift, and the three divisions so named were an amalgamation of motorised units, cavalry units, cyclist and light tank units, with divisional badges on the red motorisation background.

It is worth noting that the traditional colours seem inverted; red had always been the colour of the infantry, while blue was the colour of motorisation.

Alpine divisions wore green badges with roman or arabic numerals, and the Frontier Guard also wore green with the sector number in the centre. Represented here is a woven badge for other ranks.

Arm and Breast Badges

Guastatori were special battalions of assault engineers, trained in laying and lifting minefields, and handling explosives.

The large badge numbered '1' was worn on the breast by parachutists of the Libyan Battalion, which existed between 1938 and 1941. The breast badge numbered '4' was that of a parachute battalion formed in Libya by Italian volunteers in 1938 and disbanded in 1941. Badge No. '3' was the breast badge worn by the first units of parachutists raised in Italy and the badge No. '2' was the arm badge later adopted by all parachute units and worn until recent years.

The 'assault' arm badge was introduced during World War 1. It was in metal or worsted or wire embroidered.

Cap Badges

During World War 2 a number of cap badges were hand-embroidered in black rayon instead of gold wire. They were different from the other rank cap badges in size and appearance, as they were embroidered on a raised cardboard backing (e.g. Medical Corps) while the other ranks' cap badges were always flat. The *Alpini* badge illustrated is that worn during World War 2; another pattern was worn before then and yet another pattern was adopted in the 1950s.

Bersaglieri wore brass badges on the feathered hat. The officer's cap badge is that of the 7th Regiment, illustrated; that of the 5th is the cap badge for other ranks.

Other Badges

Other badges not yet dealt with are the two badges at the bottom left. They are: 1. gilded pioneer badge (40 × 50 mm), for gilded brass shoulder boards, as worn on grey-green full dress uniform in use from 1934; 2. silvered infantry badge worn on metal epaulettes; 3. brass shoulder plates, issued in 1934 to sergeants, corporals and privates and worn on the shoulder straps for guard, parade and special duties. The grenadiers also wore another brass plate (4) attached on each of the ammunition pouches.

The Fascist Militia

The first Fascist squads were raised in 1919 and, in the summer of 1922, they were grouped and organised as a national militia.

After the 'March on Rome' on 28 October, 1922, Benito Mussolini became Prime Minister and, as President of the Fascist Grand Council, one of his first tasks was the reorganisation of the militia which, by a Royal Decree of 1 February, 1923, became the *Milizia Volontaria Sicurezza Nazionale* (M.V.S.N.).

Originally, the M.V.S.N. was divided into fifteen 'Zones', plus an independent Group in Calabria. The Fascist 'Zone' represented the recruiting area of an M.V.S.N. division.

The Fascist Militia was organised on the pattern of the old Roman Army; its units and rank titles were basically as follows:

Unit	*Rank*
Zona—Division	*Luogotenente Generale*—Major General
Gruppo—Brigade	*Console Generale*—Brigadier
Legione—Regiment	*Console*—Colonel
Coorte—Battalion	*Seniore*—Major
Centuria—Company	*Centurione*—Captain
Manipolo—Platoon	*Capo Manipolo*—Lieutenant
Squadra—Section	*Capo Squadra*—Sergeant
	Camicia Nera—Private

The Legion was made up of three cohorts, a cohort of three centuries, and so on. The following is a complete list of the legions as they stood in 1928:

1st Zone (*Piemonte*) H.Q. Torino

1st SABAUDA—Torino
2nd ALPINA—Torino
3rd SUBALPINA—Cuneo
4th MARENGO—Alessandria
5th VALLE SCRIVIA—Tortona
11th MONFERRATO—Casale

12th MONTE BIANCO—Aosta
28th RANDACCIO—Vercelli
29th ALPINA—Pallanza
30th ODDONE—Novara
37th P. PRESTINARI—Torino
38th N. ALFIERI—Asti

2nd Zone (*Lombardia*) H.Q. Milano

6th LOMELLINA—Mortara
7th CAIROLI—Pavia
8th CACCIATORI DELLE ALPI—Varese
9th CACC. DI VALTELLINA—Sondrio

17th CREMONA—Cremona
18th COSTANTISSIMA—Crema
19th FEDELISSIMA—Casalmaggiore
20th PO—Mantova
21st VIRGILIO—Mantova
23rd MINCIO—Mantova

10th MONTEBELLO—Voghera
14th GARIBALDINA—Bergamo
15th LEONESSA—Brescia
16th ALPINA—Como

24th CARROCCIO—Milano
25th FERREA—Monza
26th A. DA GIUSSANO—Gallarate
27th FANFULLA—Lodi

3rd Zone (*Liguria*) **H.Q. Genova**

31st SAN GIORGIO—Genova
32nd GEN. A. CANTORE—
    Sanpierdarena

33rd GEN. A. GANDOLFO—Imperia
34th PREMUDA—Savona
35th LUNEENSE—La Spezia

4th Zone (*Venezia Tridentina*) **H.Q. Verona**

40th SCALIGERA—Verona
41st C. BATTISTI—Trento
42nd BERICA—Vicenza

43rd ALPINA PIAVE—Belluno
44th PASUBIO—Schio
45th ALTO ADIGE—Bolzano

5th Zone (*Veneto*) **H.Q. Venezia**

49th SAN MARCO—Venezia
50th TREVIGIANA—Treviso
51st POLESANA—Adria
52nd POLESANA (2nd)—Lendinara

53rd PATAVINA—Padova
54th EUGANEA—Este
55th ALPINA FRIULANA—Gemona
63rd TAGLIAMENTO—Udine

6th Zone (*Venezia Giulia*) **H.Q. Trieste**

58th SAN GIUSTO—Trieste
59th CARSO—Trieste
60th ISTRIA—Pola

61st CARNARO—Fiume
62nd ISONZO—Gorizia

7th Zone (*Emilia-Romagna*) **H.Q. Bologna**

67th VOLONTARI DEL RENO—
    Bologna
68th R. SFORZA—Imola
69th FOSSALTA—Bologna
70th APPENNINO—Bologna
71st MANFREDA—Faenza
72nd FARINI—Modena
73rd BOIARDO—Mirandola
74th TARO—Fidenza

75th XX DICEMBRE—Ferrara
76th ESTENSE—Ferrara
77th E. TOTI—Portomaggiore
79th CISPADANA—Reggio Emilia
80th FARNESE—Parma
81st A. DA BARBIANO—Ravenna
82nd B. MUSSOLINO—Forli'
83rd S. ANTONINO—Piacenza

8th Zone (*Toscana*) **H.Q. Firenze**

85th APUANA—Massa
86th INTREPIDA—Lucca

88th CAPPELLINI—Livorno
89th ETRUSCA—Volterra

90th PISA—Pisa
92nd F. FERRUCCI—Firenze
93rd GIGLIO ROSSO—Empoli
94th FEDELE—Pis toia

95th MARZOCCO—Firenze
96th PETRARCA—Arezzo
97th SENESE—Siena
98th MAREMMANA—Grosseto

9th Zone (*Umbria-Marche*) H.Q. Perugia

102nd CACC. DEL TEVERE—Perugia
103rd CLITUNNO—Foligno
104th S. TROTTI—Terni
105th B. MOGIONI—Orvieto

108th STAMURA—Ancona
109th F. CORRIDONI—Macerata
110th PICENA—Ascoli Piceno
111th F. MICHELINI TOCCI—Pesaro

10th Zone (*Lazio*) H.Q. Roma

112th DELL'URBE—Roma
113th G. VEROLI—Tivoli
115th DEL CIMINO—Viterbo
116th SABINA—Rieti

117th DEL MARE—Civitavecchia
118th VOLSCA—Velletri
119th N. RICCIOTTI—Frosinone

11th Zone (*Abbrusso–Molise*) H.Q. Pescara

129th ADRIATICA—Pescara
130th MONTE SIRENTE—Aquila
131st M. MORRONE-G. PAOLINI—
    Sulmona
132nd M. VELINO—Avezzano

133rd M. MATESE—Campobasso
134th M. MAURO—Larino
135th GRAN SASSO—Teramo
136th TRE MONTI—Chieti
137th M. MAJELLA—Lanciano

12th Zone (*Campania*) H.Q. Napoli

138th PARTENOPEA—Napoli
139th PISACANE—Napoli
140th AQUILIA—Salerno
141st CAPUANA—Caserta
142nd CAIO MARIO—Cassino

143rd C. RICCI—Benevento
144th IRPINA—Avellino
145th SORRENTINA—Castellamare
146th ALBORNINA—S. Consilina

13th Zone (*Puglie*) H.Q. Bari

148th TAVOGLIERE—Foggia
150th G. CARLI—Barletta
151st D. PICCA—Bari
152nd SALENTINA—Lecce

153rd SALENTINA (2nd)—Brindisi
154th D. MASTRONUZZI—Taranto
155th MATERA—Matera
156th LUCANA—Potenza

14th Zone (*Sicilia*) H.Q. Palermo

166th PELORO—Messina
167th ETNA—Catania
168th IBLA—Ragusa
169th SIRACUSAE—Siracusa
170th AGRIGENTUM—Agrigento

171st VESPRI—Palermo
172nd ENNA—Enna
173rd SALSO—Caltanisetta
174th SEGESTA—Trapani

15th Zone (*Sardegna*) H.Q. Cagliari

175th SALVATERRA—Iglesias
176th S. EFISIO—Cagliari
177th LOGUDORO—Sassari

178th GENNARGENTU—Nuoro
180th BARBAGIA—Isili
181st ARBOREA—Oristano

Independent Group (*Calabria*) H.Q. Reggio

162nd L. SETTIMO—Cosenza
163rd T. GULLI—Reggio
164th E. SCALFARO—Catanzaro

From September, 1929, the militia was reorganised into four Groups (*Raggruppamenti*) with headquarters in Milan, Bologna, Rome and Naples.

After the Abyssinian campaign, from October, 1936, yet another reorganisation took place, once again dividing the Kingdom into zones. There were fourteen Zone Headquarters, with a total of 133 legions. In addition, several independent legions were formed, such as the '18 Novembre' in Turin, and M.V.S.N. units with different duties in Rome, the island of Ponza, etc. At the same time the *Moschettieri del Duce* (Mussolini's bodyguard) was set up.

(As they were territorial units, the Territorial Militias and Anti-Aircraft and Coastal batteries, the legions in Libya and the Fascist Albanian Militia are excluded from this book.)

In the early thirties, the militia was given effective military duties, exceeding the public security purpose it had fulfilled up till then. As, obviously, not all the men were up to the standard that the newly formed Black Shirts battalions demanded, complementary legions were formed which later became territorial Black Shirts battalions.

The Black Shirts battalions served as part of the Black Shirts divisions, or in independent groups, or as assault battalions attached to the regular army divisions.

From December, 1930, the M.V.S.N. recruited new members from the Fascist Youth, by a method known as 'Fascist Conscription'.

The Fascist Youth was divided into different branches according to the age of its members. Boys and girls, on reaching the required age, on April 21st of each year, graduated to the next branch. For instance, all *Avanguardisti* on reaching the age of 15 became *Avanguardisti Moschettieri*; on attaining the age of 17 they became *Giovani Fascisti*. At 21, the *Giovane Fascista* became a member of the Fascist Party and, being in the age of conscription, if he did not join the Army on 21 April, of that year, he was recruited by the M.V.S.N. There was a similar party system for girls and young women.

In 1939, the M.V.S.N. legion was composed of two battalions of Black Shirts: one was formed of men between the ages of 21 and 36, the other was a Territorial battalion with members up to the age of 55.

The average strength of a battalion was twenty officers and 650 other ranks although, particularly in peacetime, all units were under strength due to the fact that most members followed their normal civilian occupations.

The uniforms of the Fascist Militia were similar to those worn by the Army, except that the former, from 1923, had jackets with an open collar, which was worn during World War I only by assault troops. The two pointed black collar patches of the assault troops (with a *fascio* instead of the national star) were also adopted (see Plate 42) together with their black fez. The *Alpini* hat, initially worn with ordinary uniform, was later discontinued.

Plate 47. Fascist Cap Badges

The *fascio* (bundle) was the emblem of the Fascist Party. It is meant to symbolise the unity of the people and demonstrate that unity is strength. The axe was added to symbolise power.

Originally, the axe protruded from the top of the bundle. The badge with the lateral axe was introduced after the formation of the M.V.S.N. and used until 1943. After the Armistice of 8 September, 1943, the Republican Fascist Party, formed in the north of Italy, readopted the old *fascio* with an axe at the top.

Generals wore a badge showing a gold-embroidered eagle clutching the *fascio* and, before the introduction of written regulations, several different patterns were worn. For instance, generals of the Medical Corps, M.V.S.N., had a roundel added to their cap badge with the red cross on a white field.

From 1925 to 1938 officers wore a star over the *fascio*, with a roundel at the bottom for the legion's number, embroidered in gold; doctors wore a different cap badge, with silver snakes and a red cross in the centre. Chaplains had a silver cross superimposed on the normal officer's badge. Chaplains of the militia did not need to be members of the Fascist Party.

Non-commissioned officers wore silver-embroidered cap badges with or without a star. Black Shirts wore brass cap badges.

In 1938 new cap badges were introduced, embroidered in gold for officers, silver and gold for doctors and chaplains, and silver for N.C.O.s. A smaller embroidered version in black rayon was issued for Black Shirts. By then the army-type forage cap was worn by all ranks of M.V.S.N., hence small, wire-embroidered badges can also be found as well as large ones.

In 1923, three legions—the 132nd, 171st and 176th—were sent to Libya for territorial duties. In the following year, instead of replacing them with three more national legions, it was decided to form two legions in Libya from local Italian volunteers and volunteers from Italy. These legions were named *Oea* and *Berenice* and were disbanded in 1934. The following year, some of their members were drafted into the 101st Legion of the 4th *3 Gennaio* Division.

These Libyan units (Colonial Militia) were entitled to wear different cap badges.

Before the Abyssinian campaign a new badge was introduced for the battalions in East Africa, made either in gold and silver embroidery, or in brass. The latter had an interchangeable battalion number and an interchangeable disc in the roundel at the bottom. Drivers were represented by a car, gunners by crossed cannons, and so on.

Plate 48. M.V.S.N. Rank Badges

In 1923 the militia wore the badges that were previously worn by the fascist squads. The rank of *Comandante Generale* was granted to Mussolini only in 1926. Those corresponding to lieutenant-colonel and 2nd lieutenant were used solely by the Colonial Militia. The rank badges were worn on the cuffs of the grey-green jackets. They were rectangular; those for generals being embroidered in gold on a background of silver lace. Some of these badges could be found embroidered on red, the red protruding to form a narrow edging all around the gold frame. Colonels wore a rectangular badge embroidered on brick red. Various types of *fascio*, with an axe at the top or at the side, and with or without a star, could be found.

Officers wore horizontal stripes of gold braid, then in use only in the Navy. Later, as we have seen, with the addition of a loop, they were also adopted by the Army. *Capo squadra* wore one stripe of silver braid; *Vice Capo squadra* wore two stripes of red braid and the *Camicia Nera Scelta* one.

Rank badges were also worn on the left side of the black fascist fez and of the *Alpini* hat. A general's rank was represented by gold stars, stitched on silver lace. The badge was worn at different angles, as illustrated.

Officers wore stripes of gold braid in the form of an inverted V; senior officers a large stripe and stars corresponding to their rank. In 1930 (see Plate 50) narrow stripes of gold braid replaced the stars. It is noteworthy that the Legion Commander always wore his rank badges on brick red backing felt.

N.C.O.s and other ranks respectively had silver and red braid.

Plate 49. M.V.S.N. Rank Badges

In 1935 the M.V.S.N. adopted new rank badges on the sleeves to be worn over the cuffs. These new badges, embroidered in gold for generals and colonels, and in gold braid for other officers, were introduced in order to conform to the newly adopted Army rank badges. Although the militia's rank badges had no oval loop they adopted a diamond-shaped loop over the stripes. New ranks were adopted for the same reason; the rank of cadet (*aspirante*), the three warrant officer ranks, and the new two sergeants and two corporals system in use in the Army.

The sleeve rank badges for generals and colonels were short-lived, as only three years later a new pattern of rank badges was introduced, with the Army's *greca* and diamond-shaped loop embroidered in gold. Obviously they were the same as the Air Force rank badges, although embroidered on grey-green instead of on Air Force blue. After a few months a new type was devised and they remained in use until September, 1943. Colonels changed rank badges in 1935 with the adoption of gold braid stripes on the usual brick red backing felt.

Warrant officers wore their stripes on the shoulder boards, together with smaller replicas of the cap badge. The other ranks adopted the diamond-shaped loop over the sleeve rank badges as early as 1931, e.g. Nos. 16, 17, 18. Later, Army-style rank badges were adopted on the upper sleeve.

Plate 50. M.V.S.N. Rank Badges

In 1935, together with sleeve badges, new rank badges were adopted for wearing on headgear, which consisted at that time of the black fez and the grey-green forage cap.

The generals' and colonels' badges were similar to those worn on the forearms. They were all abolished in 1938. A smaller rectangular replica of the sleeve badge, but without the diamond, was brought into use for headgear. Peaked caps were also adopted in 1938 for officers and warrant officers and, initially, generals wore a gold cord chin strap which was afterwards replaced by a black leather one. In conformity with the Army regulations, generals' ranks were transferred onto the band. The illustrations represent the embroidery worn on the cap band by the *Comandante Generale*.

Benito Mussolini was granted the title of First Honorary Corporal of the M.V.S.N. and later, in 1937, Hitler was made an Honorary Corporal. Badges of this honorary rank were worn on the left of the black fez and on the left upper sleeve. Mussolini's badge was initially made with corporal's red chevrons on black, with a small fascist gold eagle in the centre. In later years it was completely embroidered in gold, losing its simplicity and original meaning. As Italy was still a monarchy, on some occasions Mussolini, who was the Chief of State, wore a crowned fascist eagle.

Arm Shields

The fascist armed forces wore a number of different arm shields out of which I have selected those used by the M.V.S.N.

There are various types, in metal and enamel, painted brass, and painted aluminium, wire-embroidered, and printed on cloth.

Members of a 'Zone's' headquarters wore arm shields with roman numerals, often painted in different colours. The General Headquarters of the M.V.S.N. had one made in brass and black enamel, and each division had its own arm shield with number and divisional title.

Six Black Shirts divisions were raised for the Abyssinian campaign.

1st *23 Marzo* Division
2nd *28 Ottobre* Division
3rd *21 Aprile* Division
4th *3 Gennaio* Division
5th *1 Febbraio* Division
6th *Tevere* Division

Their arm shield was of the design illustrated for the *23 Marzo* and *Tevere*. Later, some divisions were disbanded and others were formed for the Spanish Civil War, which drained the strength of the Fascist Militia.

As a result, the outbreak of World War 2 caught the M.S.V.N. in a period of reorganisation, and only three divisions seem to have existed at that time. They were:

No.	Title	Legions	Artillery Regiment
1st	23 Marzo	102nd–233rd	201st
2nd	28 Ottobre	231st–202nd	202nd
4th	3 Gennaio	270th–240th	204th

An arm shield of the *3 Gennaio* made in light aluminium is illustrated at the bottom right of the plate. Attached to army divisions, M.V.S.N. legions took part in the war and others were rushed to the fronts as independent units as, for instance, the 63rd *Tagliamento* which was sent to Russia. After July, 1943, the M.V.S.N. was disbanded and its units partially absorbed by the Italian regular army.

U.S.S.R.

The Red Army of Workers and Peasants

World War 1 left Russia impoverished. Millions of men had died during the actual war and famine and epidemics followed in the strife of civil war.

The Army was reorganised on a revolutionary basis, with 23 February, 1918, becoming the official birthdate of the newly-formed Red Army of Workers and Peasants.

Officers' titles were replaced by a direct title of command; for instance, a colonel was referred to as a regimental commander and, at the lowest end of the scale, the rank of corporal became that of section commander. The same applied to generals who, by the first Red Army regulations of 1919, became commanders of brigades, divisions, etc.

The military and industrial resources of the U.S.S.R. have always been linked and the first Five Year Plan was eventually launched on 1 October, 1928, with the industrialisation of the U.S.S.R. as its main object. During the second Five Year Plan the Armed Forces in particular were greatly modernised.

The Army was mechanised and armoured units were organised, divided into tank brigades and mechanised brigades. Units specialised in chemical warfare were formed and paratroopers were already trained on a large scale in the early 1930s.

Before 1927, there were two part-time military organisations intended to promote the interest of the masses in military matters: one was the 'OSO', the Association for Collaboration in National Defence. The other was the 'AVIAKHIM' which was formed by the amalgamation of two organisations: that of the Friends of Aviation and of the Friends of Defence and Chemical Industries.

On 23 January, 1927, the OSO and AVIAKHIM merged into 'OSO-AVIAKHIM', which subsequently gave training to millions of young men.

In 1919 uniforms for both ordinary soldiers and commanders were alike. It is interesting to note that the first red star cap badges had a hammer and a plough in the centre; it was not until later that the well-known sickle replaced the plough as the symbol of agriculture.

There are no regimental badges in the Red Army, but great importance has always been given to the different branches of the Army. Each corps or service was represented by its colour which was then shown on the collar patches, piping and frog fasteners of the greatcoat and tunic; as a backing colour under the rank badges, and as a felt backing under the red star on the field cap.

In 1919 the colours of the services were:

Infantry	raspberry red
Cavalry	blue
Artillery	orange yellow
Engineers	black
Border Guards	pale sage green

The various engineer branches were known as a whole as Technical Troops.

In the early 1920s, new collar patches were adopted as the previous ones were insufficient or inadequate to meet the needs of the growing army. Worn by all ranks, they were:

Infantry	raspberry red with black piping
Cavalry	blue with black piping
Artillery	black with red piping
Engineers	black with blue piping
Administrative Service	dark green with red piping

Coloured piping and bands, which are considered as subsidiaries of the uniform in other armies, take the place of badges in the Red Army. For instance, a sniper would wear an infantry shirt-tunic with normal infantry collar patches, plus a vertical raspberry red stripe of material sewn along the tunic's front overlap.

Each corps or service branch of the Red Army offers an independent career which can lead to the highest rank of Supreme Marshal.

Uniforms were grey and, initially, only summer uniforms were khaki. However, from the 1920s khaki became the colour of all army uniforms, with the exception of the armoured troops who also adopted some steel-grey uniforms, symbolising the metallic colour of the tanks.

Characteristic Russian garments were the pointed field cap called *budionowka* and the shirt-tunic. Cossack troops were entitled to wear their traditional uniforms.

The *budionowka* was named after General Budienny who, during the Revolution, introduced this cap for the cavalry troops under his command.

In 1935, army dress regulations provided Russian officers with a khaki parade and a khaki field uniform. The greatcoats were grey, steel-grey for armoured troops, with two rows of four buttons for officers; the greatcoats of the other ranks did not show the buttons.

The generals' uniform was redesigned in 1940: they were provided with a new grey parade uniform and matching greatcoat, a khaki uniform and also a white summer outfit. The uniforms of the officers and other ranks remained basically the same until 1943 when new uniforms were introduced for all ranks.

The traditional Soviet badges were entirely modified; shoulder boards were adopted to show the rank, the badge and the colour of the branch of service, the latter in the form of stripes and piping. Marshals wore oak leaves and generals, laurel leaves, and cuff patches were introduced as well.

These new uniforms saw the Red Army through the latter stages of World War 2 until the final victory.

Plate 51. Cap Badges and Collar Patches

The red star, made of brass and red enamel, was the cap badge worn by all ranks of the Red Army until 1940, when a different badge was adopted by the generals.

The red star with hammer and sickle was introduced in 1922 and two types of it were initially made for the Red Army. The 'rounded' star which is still in use nowadays was actually adopted on 3 April, 1922, but another pattern with straight points ('sharp') was also adopted on 11 July of the same year. The latter star slowly went into disuse.

The red star was worn on its own on the peaked cap and fur hat, while on the field cap it was worn on a star-shaped coloured cloth backing. The cap badge was worn on the *budionowka* above a very large backing star (illustrated), but on the forage cap the backing just protruded below the metal star. The colours were: red for generals, raspberry red for the infantry, blue for the cavalry and black for the artillery, engineers, armoured troops and chemical service. Personnel of the non-combatant services wore dark green backing under the red star.

On the peaked cap, the red star was worn on the cap band, over the chinstrap. Coloured cap bands distinguished the different branches of the Red Army and in 1935 they were as follows:

Generals	red
Infantry	raspberry red
Staff College	raspberry red, white piping
Cavalry	blue, black piping
Artillery and Armour	black (velvet), red piping
Engineers	black, blue piping
Chemical Warfare	black, black piping
Services	dark green, red piping

Basically, the colours of the collar patches were the same.

Army Rank Badges (*Pl. 52–54, also Pl. 56–57*)

All officers' titles had disappeared during the Revolution and new rank symbols were devised for the new 'commanders' in the field. In 1919, the junior commanders' (N.C.O.s') badge was a red equilateral triangle (3 ranks), the commanders' (officers') badge was a red square (4 ranks) and that for senior commanders (generals) was a red diamond (4 ranks). These triangles, squares and diamonds were made of red felt and were worn in a line, one for each rank, below a red star on both forearms, above the cuffs.

On the 31 January, 1922, a new type of rank badge was introduced. It continued to be worn on the forearms and had an additional rank, that of chief commander, represented by a gold triangle below a red star with gold edgings.

The triangles, squares or diamonds were now set one over the other; red for field army commanders, blue for those of the Administrative Services.

By Army Order of 20 June, 1924, the red triangles, squares and diamonds, now made in metal and red enamel, were moved onto the collar patches, and by an army regulation of the following October, the order of the ranks was rearranged. The commanders were divided into four classes:

Supreme commanders (generals) with 1–4 red diamonds
Senior or superior commanders (senior officers), 1–3 red rectangles
(middle) commanders (junior officers), 1–4 red squares
Junior commanders (N.C.O.s), 1–4 red triangles

All ranks of the Red Army wore the same collar patches until the publication of the new, 1935 regulations, brought in on 3 December, which granted gold piping for all officers' collar patches, together with many other changes and improvements to the Soviet military establishment.

The Army was basically divided into three branches: the Field Army, the Political Organisation and the non-combatant Administrative Services. They all wore different badges, illustrated in the three following plates.

The collar patches remained the main feature of the uniform, showing the colour of the arm or service as well as the rank. Three types of officers' collar patch are illustrated on Plate 51: those worn on the khaki tunic, the steel-grey jacket of the armoured troops, and the greatcoat, respectively.

Plate 52. Army Rank Badges
The rank badges adopted in December, 1935, remained in use until July, 1940, when new dress regulations were approved.

The ranks should be read from left to right and from top to bottom.

In 1935 the rank of Marshal of the Soviet Union was instituted. Five generals were promoted to this rank: they were Voroshilov, the Commissar for Defence, Blyukher, the Commander of the Far-Eastern Army, the Chief of Staff, General Tukhachevsky, General Yegorov and Budienny, the Director of Cavalry.

The generals kept to their commander titles while the ordinary rank title was re-introduced for all the other officers, from colonel to lieutenant. The rank of junior lieutenant was instituted only in 1937, and that of lieutenant-colonel in 1940. The Soviet Army nowadays still retains the three lieutenants' ranks.

The 1935 regulations also prescribed the wearing of officers' rank badges on the forearms of the tunic, jacket and greatcoat, in the form of a chevron. These chevrons were 'V' shaped at an angle of 90° and were 6 cm wide at the sides.

The generals' chevrons were made of 15 mm gold braid; those for Commander of Army (1st rank) and Marshal of the Soviet Union consisted of a wider chevron (30 mm), that of the latter in gold and red (15 mm). They also wore a five-pointed gold embroidered 'sharp' star above each chevron, the same for both ranks. The star worn on the greatcoat had a diameter of 60 mm, that on the tunic and jacket 50 mm.

The chevrons of all the other officers, except colonels, were red: lieutenants wore chevrons made of 7·5 mm stripes of red braid. The other officers had 15 mm braid, while colonels also had 15 mm wide braid but with additional gold edgings.

The collar patches of tunics and jackets were 10 cm long and 32·5 mm wide, including the piping. The greatcoat collar patches were 11 cm long and 9 cm wide. Marshals wore only the latter type of patch, both on the tunics and greatcoat, with a large gold star embroidered in the centre of it. The star was similar to that worn on the cuffs.

The commanders of Army wore four red diamonds on their collar patches and the Commander of Army (1st rank) wore the diamonds and a 22 mm, gold-embroidered star, as well as a different type of chevron on the forearms.

By the new regulations, gold piping was adopted on all army officers' collar patches. The coloured piping previously worn only around the patches was then transferred to the edges of tunic and jacket collar and cuffs, and also as a piping along the seams of the officers' trousers.

Plate 53. Army Rank Badges
Political Personnel
The political personnel consisted of the commissars and *politruks* attached to all the different formations of the Army.

They wore collar patches with coloured piping as did the other ranks, with the usual enamel badges of rank pinned onto them. Political personnel was also distinguished from Army personnel by the star that both commissars and *politruks* wore on the forearms. Commissars of Army (1st rank) wore a 'sharp', gold-embroidered star the same as that worn by the corresponding army rank, but without chevron. All the other commissars and *politruks* had a red worsted star with a gold hammer and sickle in the centre instead. The star was 55 mm diameter and was sewn onto the sleeve with red silk 80 mm above the cuff on the tunic, 100 mm above the cuff on the greatcoat.

The rank of junior *politruk* was instituted in 1937. It was shown by two red enamelled squares, corresponding to the army rank of lieutenant. No rank inferior to that was ever instituted

The colours of the collar patches and pipings were as follows:

	Collar Patch	Piping
Infantry	raspberry red	black
Cavalry	blue	black
Artillery	black	red
Armoured Corps	black (velvet)	red
Engineers	black	blue
Chemical Service	black	black
Military Economic Administration, Medical and Veterinary Services	dark green	red

Plate 54. Army Rank Badges
Administrative Personnel and Junior Commanders

The same collar patch and piping colours as those above were worn by junior commanders and soldiers of the army.

Personnel of the Military Economic and Administrative Department, together with medical and veterinary personnel wore dark green collar patches with red piping. The different services were distinguished by additional metal badges, and the officers' titles also differed from those of the combatant or political personnel of the Army.

Illustrated here are the collar patches as worn on the field uniform.

Plate 55. Collar Badges

Metal collar badges were worn by all ranks on the collar patches. They were intended further to identify the branch of service of the wearer, as often the colours of the collar patch and piping were inadequate for this purpose. This was particularly so in the case of officers, who all wore gold piping on the collar patches.

The first Red Army dress regulations to mention collar badges were those of 31 January, 1922, in which about forty badges received official approval. In the following years many badges were changed and others discontinued. For this reason the badges illustrated have been divided into two sections: those worn before the publication of the 1936 regulatons and those badges adopted in 1936 and in later years. Badges from both sections were worn by various units during World War 2.

All ranks wore brass badges on the collar, with the exception of Veterinaries, who had the same badges as the Medical Department, but made of white metal instead of brass.

In 1943, when the badges were transferred onto the shoulder boards, those of officers were of silver when worn on gold shoulder boards, of gold when worn on silver shoulder boards. Other ranks' badges were made in brass.

As the distinctive raspberry red collar patch was quite adequate to identify the infantry, the badge was already discontinued in the mid-1920s. The badge of the border guards and machine-gunners still appeared in the 1924 regulations, but not in the 1936 regulations.

A special regulation of 19 August, 1924, issued a proper badge, instead of the red cross which was used previously, to the medical personnel. It was not a new badge as it had been in use some years before. Subsequently, the badge worn by the Veterinary Service was replaced by one of the same design as the Medical Service, but made in silver instead of gold.

The Chemical Service badge, together with the black collar patch, was instituted by a special regulation of 2 December, 1926, and was initially on a round metal disc. It appears on its own in the regulations of 10 March, 1936.

The armoured troops went through a substantial reorganisation in the 1930s, and finally in 1936 the 'tank badge' was instituted for the tank units of the armoured troops. Armoured artillery and other service branches wore their own badges on the black collar patches of the armoured troops.

Railways, road and river transport communications have always been extremely important in a country as vast as the Soviet Union, and special services were instituted for the running and maintenance of communication routes.

The Commissariat badge was adopted only in 1942 by a special regulation of 30 March.

Plate 56. Army Rank Badges (1940-43)

The regulations of July, 1940 considerably modified the existing badges, although no drastic changes took place as yet. The regulations of 13 July dealt with the marshals and generals who were issued with a new smart grey parade uniform and grey greatcoats, both with red pipings. They were also issued with new khaki and white uniforms, the latter for summer wear. Twin gold cords were granted to marshals and generals, to be worn on the grey, peaked cap of the parade uniform and also on the khaki and white peaked caps of the ordinary uniforms. The black leather chinstrap was still worn on the peaked cap of the field uniform.

A new cap badge was also issued in order to distinguish the highest ranks. It depicted the usual red star in brass and enamel, set on a gilded raised roundel, 30 mm in diameter.

Command appointments were replaced by the appropriate general's titles, starting from major-general, and the appointment of brigade commander thus disappeared.

Although the rank badges remained basically the same, and were still worn on the collar patches and on the forearms, they changed entirely in detail. Gold stars replaced the enamel diamonds in the collar patches of the generals and a gold star above a wreath of laurel now distinguished the rank of Marshal.

New rank badges were adopted on the sleeves as well. The Marshal of the Soviet Union now wore a large gold embroidered star above two chevrons, one above and one below a laurel wreath on a red background. The General of the Army wore a smaller gold star and all the other generals a still smaller star, above a gold chevron with red edging at the bottom. The gold chevron was the same for all generals; only the red backing distinguished the General of the Army from the others.

On the 26 July, 1940, the rank badges of the other officers were also changed. The officers were divided into field officers and subalterns (the individual officer was still addressed as 'commander'), the former distinguished by rectangular red enamel badges, the subalterns wearing square enamel badges (Plate 57).

The sleeve badges were also changed. New chevrons were devised, formed of alternate stripes of red and gold braid.

Plate 57. Army Rank Badges (1940–43)

The three ranks of lieutenant, traditional in the Russian Army, had red enamel squares as rank badges.

The collar patches were those adopted in 1935, with gold piping for all the Army, with the exception of the service branches who wore dark green collar patches with red piping. Collar patches of the latter are illustrated at the bottom right of this plate. They belong to a lieutenant of the Medical Department.

Junior Commanders

The junior commanders' ranks were dealt with by new regulations on 2 November, 1940. Sergeant and corporal's rank replaced the individual commander's appointments, and only the sergeant's ranks were represented by red enamel triangles. Corporals wore junior commander's collar patches without any triangle.

These collar patches were made in the appropriate colours of the branch of the army to which they belonged. Both tunic and greatcoat patches carried a triangular device designed to mark the angle on which the patch was to be set.

The greatcoat collar patches were 8·5 cm wide and 11 cm in length; the upper sides measured 6·5 cm on a straight line. The piping was 2·5 mm wide and the central stripe 10 mm wide.

The tunic's patches were 10 cm long and 3·25 cm wide, with a 5 mm stripe along the centre.

Sergeant-majors wore an additional 3 mm stripe of gold braid, parallel to the piping.

Different collar patches were worn by cadets of the Kiev Tank School; they were made in black velvet and red felt, with a brass badge and the school's monogram.

The Guards badge was instituted on 28 March, 1942. It was an award given to units which had gained particular distinction on the battlefield.

It was an old Russian tradition to give 'Guards' status to meritorious units. Thus such a title was granted on 18 September, 1941 to the 100th, 127th, 153rd and 161st Rifle Divisions, which were renamed 1st, 2nd, 3rd and 4th Guards Rifle Divisions. The title carried several privileges, such as pay and a half for commanders, double pay for soldiers, quicker promotion, and priority in armament and supplies.

The Guards formations were always the spearhead of the Red Army. By the end of the war a 'Guards' title was conferred upon 148 infantry and 20 cavalry divisions and 6 tank armies.

When, on 5 August, 1943, the Red Army took Orel and Belgorod, STAVKA (Headquarters of the Supreme Commander of the Armed Forces) conceived the idea of saluting the liberation of each town with salvos by the Kremlin guns, preceded by the reading of an official message by every broadcasting station in the Soviet Union.

Units received honorary titles in the names of the town they liberated and therefore the 5th, 129th and 380th Rifle Divisions became the 'Orel' Divisions, the 89th and 305th the 'Belgorod' Divisions.

However, as the Soviet advance went on, it was decided to give to each formation only two official titles, and further achievements were rewarded by conferring 'Guards' status.

The gun salutes, depending upon the importance of the town captured, were of 24 salvos from 324 guns, 20 salvos from 224 guns or 12 salvos from 124 guns.

The 1943 Dress Regulations

A number of regulations, published in 1943, changed the entire structure of the Red Army, as well as drastically modifying its uniforms.

The most important change took place in January when the traditional collar patches were abolished and all rank badges were transferred onto piped shoulder boards. Other badges were introduced to replace the collar patches.

The Marshal of the Soviet Union and the generals retained the uniforms adopted in 1940, although some alterations were made to the collar and cuffs of the tunics.

In January, 1943, the commanders were provided with a khaki parade uniform consisting of a peaked cap and a single-breasted tunic with five brass buttons and straight collar. This tunic had no pocket at the front but had two false pockets at the back. They were also provided with a khaki ordinary uniform and a white summer jacket. They were both the same as those adopted by the generals in 1940.

The field uniform was substantially modified also. The patch pockets on the breast of the shirt-tunic were changed to slit pockets with the usual shaped flaps. The folded collar was replaced by a straight collar fastened by two buttons, and three other buttons fastened the tunic.

Junior commanders and privates were issued with ordinary and field uniforms; the former was also used for parade and ceremonial occasions.

The ordinary uniform consisted of peaked cap and pocketless tunic with straight collar and false pockets at the back. Both the summer and the winter field uniforms consisted of a forage cap or steel helmet, the shirt-tunic described above, breeches and high boots.

Greatcoats were worn together with a fur hat or steel helmet.

Plate 58. Marshal of the Soviet Union and Generals

By the regulations of 15 January, 1943, the marshal's grey parade uniform had gold oak leaves embroidered on the cap band, collar and cuffs. The generals had laurel leaves embroidered on the cap band and on the collar of the tunic. On each cuff they had three gold-embroidered double bars.

The marshal wore a red cap band and red piping while the generals' cap bands and piping were in the service branch colours.

	Cap Band	Piping
Infantry	red	red
Artillery	black (velvet)	red
Armoured Troops	black (velvet)	red
Technical Troops	raspberry red	raspberry red
Commissariat	raspberry red	raspberry red

	Cap Band	Piping
Medical–Veterinary Services	dark green	red
Legal Service	red	red

Generals of the Commissariat, Medical, Veterinary and Legal Services were distinguished by silver chinstraps. All the other generals wore the gold chinstraps adopted in 1940.

The shoulder boards were made of gold braid, 14–16 cm in length and 6·5 cm wide, with piping as listed above. The exceptions were the generals of the non-combatant services who wore altogether different shoulder boards.

The Marshal of the Soviet Union wore a large, silver-embroidered star, 50 mm in diameter, on the shoulder boards, while the stars of the generals were 22 mm in diameter. Those for generals of the services were smaller still, and embroidered in gold (Plate 60).

Marshals, generals and commanders were all issued with two great-coats; one for parade uniform, the other for ordinary wear.

All the greatcoat collar patches of both marshal and generals were piped in gold, and were khaki on the ordinary greatcoat. The collar patches of the parade greatcoat were red for a marshal; those for generals were the same colour as their cap band.

The buttons of marshal and generals depicted the emblem of the U.S.S.R., while those of all the other ranks had the five-pointed star with the hammer and sickle in its centre.

Plate 59. Senior Commanders and Commanders

Collar patches, Cuff patches and Shoulder boards

The same peaked cap was worn both with the parade and ordinary uni-forms and, as previously, the coloured cap band identified the branch of service of the wearer. Coloured collar patches on the collar of the parade dress tunic served the same purpose and, at the same time, they displayed the class of rank of the wearer: senior commanders wore two bars and commanders only one on each patch.

Engineers/technical Staff wore silver embroidered bars with a single, gold-wire ornament. The rest of the Army wore gold bars with a silver ornament, thus distinguishing the technical personnel from artillery and armoured troops who also wore black collar patches.

The same regulations (15 January, 1943) also issued all officers with cuff patches which were gold-embroidered double bars. They were worn on the cuffs of the parade uniform: three for each cuff by generals, two by senior commanders and one on each cuff by commanders.

Shoulder boards on the tunic of the ordinary khaki uniform and the white summer uniform were worn to identify both the rank and branch of service of the wearer. There were two types of shoulder board: those made in gold or silver braid, and the field uniform ones made of khaki material (Plate 61). However, as they were detachable, the gold shoulder boards were worn also on the shirt-tunic for special duties.

The shoulder boards illustrated were 6 cm wide, with piping and stripes in the colours listed below:

Infantry	raspberry red
Artillery	red
Armoured Troops	red
Cavalry	blue
Engineers/Technical Staff	black
Commissariat	raspberry red
Medical, Veterinary and Legal Services	red

Officers of the Commissariat were called 'intendants' and they had silver shoulder boards with gold stars and the badge of the service made of brass and enamel. Personnel of the Medical, Veterinary and Legal Services wore shoulder boards that were altogether different (Plate 60).

Senior commanders had shoulder boards with two coloured stripes and rank stars 20 mm in diameter; commanders had only one stripe and smaller stars, 13 mm in diameter. Braid and stripes were woven in one piece, cut at the right length (14–16 cm) and sewn on coloured material that, protruding around the edges, formed the piping. Rank stars and badges were always made of silver when the braid was gold and vice-versa.

All commanders wore patches on the greatcoat collar: the colour of the patch and piping of the parade-ordinary greatcoat corresponded to the colour of the band and piping worn on the peaked cap. The collar patches of the field greatcoat were khaki with coloured piping.

The colours of commanders' cap bands and greatcoat collar patches were:

	Colour	Piping
Infantry	raspberry red	raspberry red
Artillery	black (velvet)	red
Armoured Troops	black (velvet)	red
Cavalry	blue	black
Engineers/Technical Staff	black	black
Commissariat	raspberry red	raspberry red
Medical and Veterinary Services	dark green	red
Legal Service	red	red

Junior commanders and privates wore the same collar patches on the greatcoat.

Plate 60. Medical, Veterinary and Legal Services

Officers of these services had narrow shoulder boards, 4–4·5 cm wide, made of silver braid and edged with red piping. Similar to the boards we have already seen, those for generals, senior officers and junior officers differed one from the other. Generals wore rank stars 20 mm in diameter, while the stars of the other two ranks were respectively 16 mm and 13 mm.

The three services were distinguished by the usual badges, that of the Veterinary Service in silver, the other two in gold.

Junior Commanders and Privates

In 1943 by the regulations of 15 January, the ranks of the junior commanders were also modified.

The red enamel triangles and the old collar patches were abolished and stripes on the shoulder boards were adopted instead. The shoulder boards of the ordinary uniform were made of coloured cloth edged with coloured piping. The rank stripes were of gold braid (silver for the services) with additional badges, numbers and letters to identify the unit of the wearer.

The colours of junior officers' shoulder boards and piping were as follows:

	Shoulder Board	Piping
Infantry	raspberry red	black
Artillery	black	red
Armoured Troops	black	red
Cavalry	blue	black
Engineer/Technical Troops	black	black
Veterinary and Medical Services	dark green	red

The shoulder boards of the field uniforms are illustrated in Plate 61.

Junior commanders and privates also wore coloured patches on the collar of the ordinary uniform. The former had a 6 mm wide stripe of gold or silver braid; privates wore plain cloth patches.

Gold braid was worn by all Army junior commanders except those belonging to the Engineer/Technical Staff, who wore silver braid instead.

Cadets

Cadet junior commanders and cadets were identified by a stripe of gold (or silver) braid stitched around the edges of the shoulder boards.

Plate 61. Field Uniform

The shoulder boards worn on the shirt-tunic were all khaki with red stripes and piping in the colours of the branch of service. Two red stripes distinguished the senior commanders, while commanders had only one stripe along the centre of the shoulder board. Rank stars and badges were also displayed in the usual manner.

Officers of the commissariat had shoulder boards with raspberry red stripes and piping, and officers of the Medical, Veterinary and Legal Services had narrower boards with raspberry red stripes and red piping.

The shoulder boards of junior commanders and privates were edged with coloured piping and the former also wore their rank stripes in the colour of the service branch. Their badges were made of brass.

In 1943, a brown leather belt was issued to the junior ranks and soldiers of the Red Army. It had a rectangular brass buckle with the hammer and sickle within the star in the centre. This belt was worn with all uniforms and also on the greatcoat.

Wound stripes were instituted on 14 July, 1942, and were awarded in two classes represented by gold and red braid respectively. They were sewn above the left-hand side of the right breast pocket.

Plate 62. Marshals

In 1943 a number of regulations entirely modified the structure of the top ranks of the Red Army by creating a new class of officers: the marshals. On 4 February, the rank of Marshal was introduced as well as the existing rank of Marshal of the Soviet Union. Therefore Marshals of Artillery and Armour were created and they wore the silver star, with their service branch badge above, on the shoulder boards. The same large silver star, together with the emblem of the U.S.S.R embroidered in gold and coloured silk, distinguished the rank of Marshal of the Soviet Union.

The stars were 50 mm in diameter.

The new marshals wore gold laurel leaves embroidered on the cap band, collar and cuffs, faced with black velvet and red piping.

On 27 October, 1943, the rank of Supreme Marshal was instituted above that of Marshal and all branches of the Red Army were made eligible for both.

Although the shoulder boards remained the same, made of the same gold braid adopted in the previous January, the size of the silver star was now reduced to 40 mm in diameter to make room for a silver laurel wreath which distinguished the Supreme Marshals.

Infantry and all rifle units, artillery and armour had red piping; all technical troops had raspberry red piping instead.

Plate 63. Junior Soldiers' School

On 21 September, 1943, regulations were issued regarding the uniforms and badges of the students at the Junior Soldiers' School.

They wore grey uniforms of army other ranks' pattern with black leather belt and brass belt buckle. The headdress was the peaked cap, with red band and white piping. In winter, a fur cap was worn with the greatcoat. The collar patches were red with white piping, but without the button.

The junior soldiers wore red shoulder boards with white piping on the greatcoat and all tunics and the monogram 'CBY' (meaning Suvorov's Military School). The smaller monogram referred to the town in which the school was located. They were:

Кд	Krasnorodsk
Нч	Novo-Cherkask
Сп	Stavropol
Ст	Stalingrad
Вж	Voronesko
Кс	Kursko
Хр	Harkov
Ор	Orlov
Кл	Kalinski

Special ranks were given to students of special merit and they were shown in the form of gold braid stripes on the shoulder boards.

Artillery Specialists' School
The shoulder boards worn at this school were particularly narrow, 4 cm wide. They were made in the colours of the service, black with red piping, and the rank of the trainees was shown by stripes of gold braid.

Military Transport
Personnel of Railway Military Transport wore black cap bands and collars, both with green piping. The crown of their peaked cap was faced with red cloth and an additional badge, the winged wheel, was worn on it. The red star was worn as usual, on the cap band above the chinstrap. The arm badge illustrated was worn on the left sleeve above the elbow.

The United States of America

The United States, as we know them now, originate from the colonial territories of North America and, before the Revolution of 1776, the uniforms followed the contemporary British pattern. Subsequently, during the War for Independence and in later years, the new American uniforms followed the French pattern, although a great deal of individuality was displayed in the uniforms of the various state militias, which later became the National Guard.

On 19 October, 1781, Cornwallis surrendered to Washington at Yorktown and a formal peace treaty dividing North America was signed in Paris on 3 September, 1783.

Many badges, even today, show the influence of the thirteen original states by having the thirteen stars representing them included in their designs.

In 1861, at the outbreak of the Civil War, a great number of different uniforms were worn by both the Union and the Confederate forces. Some regiments, for instance, adopted uniforms similar to those of the French Zouaves, and several such regiments fought on either side. The most renowned among these were the Louisiana Tigers of the Confederate Army and the Fire Zouaves of the New York Volunteer Infantry. Some regiments were then known by the colour of their uniforms: for instance, the 'Richmond Blues' and the 'Grays' of New York.

However, the expansion of both armies made necessary by the war led to the simplification and uniformity of the soldiers' dress and, finally, the Union forces adopted dark blue and the Confederates grey clothing. Whenever possible, regimental distinctions were kept alive in various ways. For instance, the soldiers of the 22nd Regiment, New York State Militia, retained their traditional red in the cap band and pipings. They were also issued with red blankets which they proudly sported, rolled above the haversack.

In 1862, the first actual badges were adopted as a result of an everyday incident. General P. Kearny rebuked some officers, assuming that they belonged to his troops and, when he learned that they did not, he decided that all the officers under his command should be identified by a red patch on the front of their cap. Soon the same patch was also worn by all the other ranks of Kearny's Corps, as well as by the officers. The idea subsequently was taken on by other corps and patches of all shapes and colours, in cloth and metal, were adopted by the Union Army.

They were called Corps badges. The emblem was in the shape, not the colour, of the badge; divisions within the corps wore the same shaped badge, but of different colours.

Some of these emblems basically remained with the U.S. Corps until World War 2, for example the round shoulder patch of 1st Corps or the heart-shaped patch of 24th Corps. Some others were taken on by different units; for instance, the red diamond shoulder patch of the 5th Infantry Division, which during the Civil War used to be the patch of the 1st Division of the 5th Corps.

The different branches of the Army were identified by coloured pipings and trimmings worn on the uniform. They were light blue for the infantry, yellow for the cavalry, red for the artillery, red and white for the engineers, etc. The same colours were still worn, in the form of piping on the forage cap, during World War 2.

It was not until 1898, during the Spanish-American war, that the Regular Army adopted khaki field uniform and only during World War 1 did the field uniform (model 1916) become general issue. New webbing equipment and a steel helmet, shaped like the British helmet, was also adopted. The latter was only changed to the familiar American pattern during World War 2.

The uniforms worn by American servicemen during this war can be basically divided into service uniform, field uniform and fatigue uniform, although different clothing was also worn in different climates, and by special troops. Airborne troops, for instance, wore field uniforms differing from the rest of the Army, and they were issued with high-laced boots, while the rest of the army were still wearing gaiters. During the war, gaiters were replaced by boots with attached leather anklets, which fastened with two brass buckles.

The peaked cap and the jacket of the officers' service dress were dark brown and the trousers grey; the O.R.'s service uniform was similar but made entirely of khaki material. During the war, and in later years, a khaki blouse with open collar supplanted the jacket and was worn with the khaki forage cap by both officers and other ranks.

Officers wore a dark brown forage cap and blouse with grey trousers.

The summer uniform was sandy yellow, and consisted of a forage cap, shirt and tie, and trousers. The belt was of the same colour, with a plain rectangular buckle. The tie was tucked under the shirt's overlap between the second and third button.

The field uniform and fatigue uniform were technically the same. Shirt and trousers were olive green, with large patch pockets on both, and without any badges except those of rank.

However, in north-western Europe and Italy during the winter, the American soldiers generally wore waterproof olive green jackets over khaki shirt and trousers. Even the sight of G.I.s with helmet and all the combat webbing being worn over the greatcoat was not uncommon.

Plate 64. Cap Badges

The coat of arms of the United States of America is the badge of the U.S. Army and it is worn by all ranks, on the peaked cap.

It depicts the American eagle, with the stars and stripes set on a shield on the eagle's chest. In its right claw it holds a sprig of laurel, in the other a bundle of arrows. On a scroll, spread above the wings, is the motto '*E Pluribus Unum*' and, above it, there is a round cloud with thirteen stars in the centre.

The officers' cap badge was made of brass or gilded brass, about 75 × 65 mm in size, although much smaller badges can also be found. The other ranks wore the same eagle, attached on a brass disc, 40 mm in diameter.

Officers of the Woman's Army Corps wore a different eagle, on its own, without any embellishments, and the other ranks' cap badge of the W.A.C. was also set on a round disc.

A special cap badge was worn by cadets of the West Point Academy. It depicts the Academy's coat of arms and it is also worn as a collar badge by its permanent staff.

This brass badge shows the helmet and sword of the greek goddess Pallas Athene on the United States shield. There is an eagle above the shield, clutching sprigs of oak and laurel, together with arrows. The motto in the scroll reads: 'Duty, Honour, Country—West Point, MDCCCII, USMA'.

Army warrant officers wore badges different from those of the rest of the army on the headdress and on the collar. The badge depicted an eagle standing on two arrows and a laurel wreath, the ends of which overlap the eagle's wings.

The American eagle was once again in the badge of the Transport Service officers, in this case with the shield on its chest, standing on two crossed anchors.

The cap badge of the Harbour Boat Service has the emblem of the Transportation Corps superimposed on an anchor. It is all in one piece and made in brass. As the U.S. Army went to fight overseas, specialised personnel were employed to transport and ferry the troops onto the ships.

Members of the military bands wore different badges both on the headdress and on the collar. The collar badges were similar to the badge illustrated on the left, but without the wreath.

U.S. Army personnel who qualified as deep sea salvage divers were entitled to wear special badges on the left breast pocket. The diver's badge was awarded in four classes: Master Diver, 1st and 2nd class Divers and Salvage Diver. These badges were made of silver, or white metal, and were instituted on 15 February, 1944.

Rank Badges

From 1780 the rank of American generals was denoted by a number of silver stars, at that time embroidered on the epaulettes. Initially, generals had two ranks; that of brigadier and major-general. The rank of lieutenant-general was instituted in 1799. On 3rd March of the same year the rank of General of the Armies of the United States was conferred on George Washington. However, it ceased to exist when it was excluded from the legislative act of 16 March, 1802, which determined the peacetime military establishment.

On 3 September, 1919, Congress re-established the rank and conferred it on General John J. Pershing. After his death, the rank of General of the Armies of the United States once again ceased to exist.

The rank of General of the Army was authorised and conferred on General Ulysses S. Grant on 25 July, 1866, and on General William T. Sherman on 4 March, 1869. It was again established, by Public Law 482, on 14 December, 1944, and conferred on Generals Marshall, MacArthur, Eisenhower and Arnold. General Bradley subsequently received the rank of General of the Army by Private Law on 18 September, 1950.

The badges of U.S. Army officers are unique as their rank is represented by eagles, leaves and bars instead of stars or pips.

Initially, infantry colonels wore gold eagles as their insignia of rank, while all other colonels wore silver ones. In 1851, the silver eagle was prescribed for all colonels.

The rank of major was depicted by oak leaves in gold. When, later, the rank of lieutenant-colonel was instituted in 1832, he wore the same badge as a major, but in silver instead of gold. Consequently, silver rank badges became senior to gold ones. So in 1872, the gold bars of captains and lieutenants were also changed to silver. The 2nd lieutenant had worn the rectangular frame without any badge on the shoulders of the blue uniform, but when khaki field uniform was adopted, a small bar in gold became the badge of his rank.

The rank badges of warrant officers were of brass and red or brown enamel.

Plate 65. Non-Commissioned Officers

Non-commissioned officers of the U.S. Army wore chevrons on both upper sleeves. Initially, there were only two ranks: sergeant and corporal. Subsequently, the sergeant's rank was progressively developed into five classes, which have remained more or less the same since the Civil War.

Originally, the chevrons pointed downwards, were twice as wide as those used during World War 2 and were in the colour of the branch of service, i.e. pale blue for the infantry, yellow for the cavalry, red for the artillery, etc.

During World War 2, the American non-commissioned officers were divided into Line N.C.O.s and Technicians, the latter with a small 'T' within the chevrons. Illustrated in this plate is the order of rank as it stood in 1943. In 1940 the chevrons were the same with the exception of that of first sergeant which had five stripes at that time instead of six; the company first sergeant had a diamond in the centre and the field first sergeant had no diamond.

First sergeants and master sergeants (1943–48) had equal rank. The title held, and type of chevron worn, is determined by the individual's assignment. In an infantry company or an artillery battery, for example, the senior sergeant would be a first sergeant, while in a staff position, such as operations sergeant in a Division H.Q., the senior sergeant would be a master sergeant. Both men would be receiving the same pay and holding the same rank.

The rank badges were 80 mm wide, and the chevrons were machine embroidered in light khaki silk, or woven in light yellow silk on a dark blue gabardine material.

U.S. Army Mine Planter Service

Although technically a naval service, the mine planters belonged to the Army. They were divided into Mine Planters and Engineers and wore stripes of braid on the cuffs, with an anchor or a ship's propeller above.

The Arms and Services of the U.S. Army

Arms and Service badges (also called service branch badges) were adopted by the Army only in the 1880s. They were small, coloured badges on blue discs, as the colour of the uniform was then blue.

N.C.O.s wore these badges within or under the chevrons and the other ranks wore them over the cuff.

When khaki field uniforms were adopted during World War I these badges, made of bronze, were transferred onto the collar. They were the predecessors of the brass badges worn by all ranks of the U.S. Army during World War 2. The officers wore the badge itself; the other ranks wore a smaller version of the same badge, but on a brass disc. The discs were generally flat, although convex discs have also been issued, with the badge stamped out of the disc itself, or made separately and attached to the back screw.

Officers wore the collar badges in pairs on the jacket and blouse, the U.S. national insignia at the top, the service branch badges at the bottom.

Other ranks wore them in singles, the U.S. on the right and the service branch badge on the left, on the jacket, blouse and summer shirt collar.

The shirt collar of the officers' summer uniform showed the rank badge on the right and the service branch badge on the other side.

Generals wore only the U.S. national insignia and the rank stars.

Plate 66. Officers' Collar Badges

The Arms of the U.S. Army were the Infantry, Cavalry, Field Artillery, Coast Artillery, Engineers, Signal Corps, Armoured Force and Tank Destroyer Force. The other badges illustrated were those of services.

Many of the former could be found with a regimental number attached above the badge, for both officers and other ranks.

The badge of the Armoured Forces depicted a Mark VIII tank; that of the Tank Destroyer Force an M-3 anti-tank vehicle. Most officers' badges were made of brass, some partly in enamel.

General's aides wore an eagle clutching a shield with the 'stars and stripes' on it in coloured enamels. The number of stars corresponded to the rank of the general in question, from one to four stars in a straight line. In the case of an aide to a General of the Army the shield was entirely of blue enamel, with five white stars in a circle in the centre of the shield.

These badges were worn only by officers. The General Staff, Inspector General's Staff and the Judge Advocate General's Corps were also composed only of officers. Chaplains wore white metal badges.

The Adjutant General's Corps badge was worn by officers and other ranks. The officer's badge was made of blue, white and red enamel, that of the other ranks was made of brass, the shield set on a disc.

The badge of the Medical Corps was the caduceus, an adaptation of the staff of Mercury and of that of Aesculapius, the latter a device long associated with medicine. The two serpents allude to preventive and corrective medicine. Different branches of the Medical Corps were identified by letters of the alphabet superimposed on the badge. The letters were made of brass or maroon enamel, that being the Corps' colour.

The Transportation Corps dealt with all types of land and sea transport, therefore its badge was composed of a ship's steering wheel and the 'winged wheel' normally associated with railway transport.

All ranks of the Woman's Army Corps wore a badge depicting the head of Pallas Athene, the Greek goddess of war, on the collar, facing left.

Breast Badges

Both the Combat Infantryman and Expert Infantryman badges were worn on the left breast, over the pocket and the medal ribbons, and were made of silver and blue enamel. The Expert Infantryman badge was instituted on 11 November, 1943, as an award for good service; the Combat Infantryman badge was instituted on 15 November, 1943, for exemplary behaviour in combat.

The Second, Third and Fourth Award of the Combat Infantry badge are represented by additional stars situated between the ends of the oak wreath.

The Department of the Army General Staff Identification Badge was instituted on 23 August, 1933, for officers who had served at least one year on the General Staff. It was in two sizes: the Chief of Staff's badge 77 mm (3 in.), the badge of the others 51 mm (2 in.) in diameter, and was worn on the right breast pocket.

Qualified Army Parachutists wore the winged parachute on the left breast, above the pocket and the ribbons; the same badge was also worn on field uniform on the oval identity background illustrated on Plate 73. Parachute badges could also be found embroidered in white thread directly onto the oval background. Badges for Senior Parachutist (with a star above the parachute) and Master Parachutist (the star in a laurel wreath) have also appeared since the war. The Army Glider Badge was instituted on 14 March, 1944, to be worn by all airborne troops trained in glider combat. Prior to the introduction of this badge the Glider Troops wore the parachute badge with a glider superimposed in the centre.

The breast badges of the U.S. Army divers are illustrated on Pl. 64.

Plate 67. Shoulder Sleeve Insignia

Coloured patches had already been used for identification purposes during the American Civil War, but the 'shoulder patches' as we know them nowadays, were officially introduced in 1918.

In the summer of that year, members of the 81st Infantry Division embarking for France at Hoboken (New Jersey) wore the 'wild cat' badge on the left upper arm and, when eventually they got to France, other units there adopted their own distinctive patches. Initially they were worn unofficially, but permission to wear shoulder sleeve insignia was given on 19 October, 1918.

As these patches were handmade they often differed one from the other; others remained virtually unknown as the formation wearing them was subsequently disbanded or another design was introduced later.

During World War 2 some different types of patches were in use: there were those embroidered on felt, in coloured threads or in gold and silver wire, and others that were entirely embroidered in coloured silks.

The unprecedented expansion of the U.S. Army during World War 2 introduced a great number of new patches, worn by personnel of the Field Formations, and of Defense and Base Commands, Departments, Theaters of Operations, etc.

The background of many shoulder patches was khaki in order to blend the patch with the uniform; therefore, when the new army green uniforms were introduced in 1957, some new badges had to be made which strictly cannot be considered as World War 2 badges, although they are often mistaken for them.

Army Groups

Three Army Groups were formed overseas during World War 2 and they were:

The 6th Army Group, consisting of the U.S. 7th Army and French 1st Army that landed and fought in the South of France;

The 12th Army Group, consisting only of American Armies, the 1st, 3rd, 9th and later the 15th U.S. Armies. This, together with the British 21st Army Group, operated in north-west Europe;

The 15th Army Group, which was formed by the U.S. 1st and British 8th Armies in Italy.

Armies

The design of these shoulder patches suggested the Army's number, except that of the 3rd Army, which displayed the letters 'A' and 'O', as it was the army of occupation in Germany after World War 1.

A capital 'A' on khaki background was the emblem of the 1st Army as it is the initial letter of army and first letter of the alphabet. The 5th Army was organised at Oujda, Morocco, on 5 January, 1943, and therefore a silhouette of a mosque became part of its patch, the final design being approved by Lieutenant-General Mark W. Clark on 18 February, 1943. A capital 'A' with seven steps on each of its sides was the symbol of the 7th Army, and a Roman 'X' on pentagonal background was that of the 15th Army.

The 6th, 8th and 10th Armies fought against the Japanese; the 2nd and 4th Armies remained in the United States and were never engaged in active operations.

Army Corps

Personnel employed at Corps Headquarters wore the corps shoulder patch, whose design was in most cases a pictorial allusion to its number.

However, the shoulder patch of the 12th Corps shows a windmill of the city of New Amsterdam (New York). The 18th was an airborne corps and its patch symbolises its deployment, while the shoulder patch of the 19th Corps depicts an Indian tomahawk; the '2' arrows and '1' acorn in the patch of 21st Corps stand for the Corps number. An arrowhead was the patch of the 22nd Corps and the hart of the 24th Corps was taken from the 24th Corps badge used during the Civil War.

The 1st, 10th, 11th, 14th and 24th Corps fought against the Japanese in the Pacific Ocean area.

The shoulder patch of the 2nd Corps depicts the American eagle and the British lion. It landed in North Africa and together with the 4th, 6th and 21st, took part in the Italian campaign. The 6th and 21st Corps were later transferred to France, and the former fought all the way to Germany.

The 9th and 36th Corps did not go overseas and the 22nd and 23rd, under the 15th Army, became in 1945 the U.S. Occupation Forces in Germany. All the other Corps, not already mentioned above, took part in the operations in north-western Europe.

Plate 68. Shoulder Sleeve Insignia

Infantry and Airborne Divisions

A great number of divisional shoulder patches were adopted during World War 1, but many were changed or at least simplified in the years between the wars. They were worn on the left upper sleeve, and on the right upper sleeve by personnel temporarily attached to a higher formation, the patch of which was worn on the left sleeve.

The Airborne Force was raised in 1941 at Fort Benning (Georgia), and the 501st and 502nd battalions, later to become regiments, were the first units to be formed.

One year later, in the spring of 1942, the 82nd Airborne Division was formed and it was soon followed by other divisions and independent regiments. The deployment of independent airborne regiments led to the adoption of several regimental shoulder patches as well. Among the airborne divisions, only the 82nd and 101st adopted shoulder patches similar to those they had previously worn as infantry formations.

The divisions are as follows:

1st Infantry Division nicknamed 'The Big Red One': its emblem was a large figure '1'. It fought in Tunisia, Sicily, Normandy, the Battle of the Bulge and Germany.

2nd Infantry Division, 'Indian Head': a self-explanatory large patch 10·5 × 8 cm. Normandy, Ardennes, Leipzig.

3rd Infantry Division, 'Marne': the three white bars stand for the divisional number, the blue is the colour of the infantry. Sicily, Cassino, Anzio, Colmar Pocket, Munich.

4th Infantry Division, 'Ivy': its patch is self-explanatory and at the same time it suggests the divisional number. Cherbourg, Bastogne.

5th Infantry Division, 'Red Diamond': Metz, Luxembourg, Mainz–Worms Bridgehead.

6th Infantry Division: six-pointed red star. New Guinea, Philippines.

7th Infantry Division, 'Sight-Seeing': the patch represents two crossed number '7s', one inverted. Attu, Kwajalein, Leyte, Okinawa.

8th Infantry Division, 'Pathfinder': Brittany, Düren, Cologne.

9th Infantry Division: a nine-petalled flower. North Africa, Sicily, Cotentin Peninsula, Germany.

10th Mountain Division: this was a division trained for mountain warfare. Gothic Line, Po Valley.

11th Airborne Division: the divisional number is carried by wings. Leyte, Manila, Cavite.

13th Airborne Division: the winged unicorn. It did not go overseas.

17th Airborne Division: the eagle's claws. It was parachuted across the Rhine.

24th Infantry Division, 'Victory': a green taro leaf. New Guinea, Philippines.

25th Infantry Division, 'Tropic Lightning': a red taro leaf with a yellow lightning in its centre. Guadalcanal, New Georgia, Philippines.

26th Infantry Division, 'Yankee': the monogram 'YD' stands for Yankee Division. Battle of the Bulge, Siegfried Line.

27th Infantry Division, 'New York': the self-explanatory monogram and the constellation of Orion, in association with the name of its World War I commander, Major-General J. F. O'Ryan. Makin Island, Saipan, Okinawa.

28th Infantry Division, 'Keystone': the red keystone from the State seal of Pennsylvania. Paris, Hürtgen Forest, Colmar Pocket.

29th Infantry Division, 'Blue and Grey': a Korean symbol of good luck the colours stand for the blue and grey uniform of the Civil War. Normandy, Siegfried Line, Aachen.

30th Infantry Division, 'Old Hickory': an 'O' and an 'H' with a roman 'XXX' in the centre. St. Lô, Aachen, Malmedy, Stavelot, Rhine Crossing.

31st Infantry Division, 'Dixie': the two 'Ds' stand for Dixie Division. Philippines.

32nd Infantry Division, 'Red Arrow': New Guinea, Leyte.

33rd Infantry Division, 'Prairie': Northern Luzon.

34th Infantry Division, 'Red Bull': a red bull's skull on the shape of an 'olla' or Mexican flask. Tunisia, Cassino, Gothic Line, Po Valley.

35th Infantry Division, 'Santa Fé': the cross that was used to mark the Santa Fé trail. Metz, Nancy, Ardennes, Ruhr.

36th Infantry Division, 'Texas': a flint arrowhead and the letter 'T'. Salerno, Cassino, France, Germany.

37th Infantry Division, 'Buckeye': a division from Ohio. Munda, Bougainville, Lingayen Gulf, Manilla.

38th Infantry Division, 'Cyclone': Bataan.

39th Infantry Division: the triangle symbolises the three states of the Mississippi delta, Mississippi, Louisiana, Arkansas. This division did not go overseas.

40th Infantry Division, 'Sunshine': the patch depicts the sun on a blue sky. Philippines.

41st Infantry Division, 'Sunset': it depicts a Pacific Ocean sunset. Salamaua, Marshalls, Mindanao, Palawan.

42nd Infantry Division, 'Rainbow': Schweinfurt, Munich, Dachau.

43rd Infantry Division, 'Red Wing': its patch symbolises the four States of New England, with a black grape leaf. New Georgia, New Guinea, Luzon.

44th Infantry Division: two '4s' back to back, forming an arrowhead. The Saar, Ulm, Danube River.

45th Infantry Division, 'Thunderbird': a yellow thunderbird. Sicily, Salerno, Cassino, Anzio, Belfort Gap.

63rd Infantry Division, 'Blood and Fire': a drop-shaped patch with burning flames inside and a blood-stained bayonet. Bavaria, Danube River.

65th Infantry Division: a halberd. Saarlautern, Regensburg, Danube River.

66th Infantry Division, 'Black Panther': Lorient, St. Nazaire.

69th Infantry Division: the interlocked divisional figures. Germany.

70th Infantry Division, 'Trail Blazers': a mountain landscape with an axe in the foreground. Saarbrücken, Moselle River.

71st Infantry Division: the divisional number on a circular background. Harz Mountains, Southern Germany.

75th Infantry Division: Ardennes, Bulge, Westphalia.

Plate 69. Shoulder Sleeve Insignia

Infantry and Airborne Divisions

76th Infantry Division: Luxembourg, Germany.

77th Infantry Division, 'Statue of Liberty': the division of New York State. Guam, Leyte, Okinawa.

78th Infantry Division, 'Lightning': Aachen, Roer River and Ruhr.

79th Infantry Division, 'Lorraine': the Cross of Lorraine commemorates World War 1 service in France. Normandy, Vosges Mountains.

80th Infantry Division, 'Blue Ridge': the hills in the badge stand for Pennsylvania, West Virginia and Virginia. Normandy, Moselle River, Relief of Bastogne.

81st Infantry Division, 'Wild Cat': Angaur, Peleliu, Ulithi.

82nd Airborne Division, 'All American': the 'airborne' tab was added to the pre-existing divisional patch. Sicily, Normandy, Nijmegen, Ardennes.

83rd Infantry Division, 'Ohio': the monogram in the centre of the patch reads 'Ohio'. Italy, Düsseldorf, Magdeburg.

84th Infantry Division, 'Railsplitters': the axe originates from the patch worn during World War 1. Ardennes, Hanover.

85th Infantry Division, 'Custer': the letters read 'Custer Division'. Rome, Po Valley.

86th Infantry Division, 'Black Hawk': Dachau, Ingolstadt, South Germany.

87th Infantry Division, 'Acorn': Ardennes, Germany, Czech Border.

88th Infantry Division, 'Blue Devil': a vertical and a horizontal '8' superimposed one upon the other. Rome, Volterra, Northern Italy, Trieste.

89th Infantry Division, 'Middle West': a 'W' which inverted becomes an 'M'. Bingen, Eisenach, Central Germany.

90th Infantry Division, 'Tough Ombres': the monogram 'TO', also stands for Texas and Oklahoma. The title means 'Tough Men'. Normandy, Metz, Czechoslovakia.

91st Infantry Division, 'Wild West': a fir tree. Gothic Line, Bologna, Gorizia.

92nd Infantry Division, 'Buffalo': a traditionally Negro division, so-called because the Indians used to call the Negro soldiers 'Buffaloes'.

93rd Infantry Division: the French helmet symbolises the Division's service in France during World War 1. Bougainville.

94th Infantry Division: Brittany, Siegfried Line, Moselle River, Saar.

95th Infantry Division: an Arabic '9' and a Roman 'V' interlaced. Metz, Moselle River, Siegfried Line, Saar.

96th Infantry Division: Leyte, Okinawa.

97th Infantry Division: a trident. Central Germany, Neumarkt.

98th Infantry Division: the shield and colours of New Amsterdam, with the head of an Iroquois Indian in its centre. It did not serve overseas.

99th Infantry Division: the patch is taken from the arms of Pitt. Ardennes, Remagen Bridgehead.

100th Infantry Division: Bitche, Remagen Bridgehead, Saar.

101st Airborne Division, 'Screaming Eagle': the eagle is Old Abe, the mascot of a regiment of the Iron Brigade during the Civil War. The black shield commemorates the Iron Brigade itself. Normandy, Bastogne.

102nd Infantry Division, 'Ozark': named after the Ozark Mountains. Siegfried Line, Ruhr, München-Gladbach.

103rd Infantry Division: Stuttgart, Austria.

104th Infantry Division, 'Timber Wolf': Rhine Crossing, Cologne, Ruhr.

106th Infantry Division: a lion's head. St. Vith, Battle of the Bulge.

Americal Division (23rd Infantry Division): the stars of the Southern Cross. Guadalcanal, Bougainville, Cebu Island.

Cavalry Divisions

Of the twelve cavalry divisions whose shoulder patches are illustrated in Plates 69 and 70, only the 1st saw active service in the Philippines. The basic colour of these patches was yellow, the colour of the cavalry; those of the 1st and 2nd Division were exceptionally large (14 × 10 cm).

Plate 70. Shoulder Sleeve Insignia

Army Ground Forces

The Army Ground Forces were generally composed of all U.S.-based units deployed in training, supplying and other supporting roles.

Eventually, with the expansion of the U.S. lines of communication all over the world, some of this personnel went overseas as well.

Technically, the A.G.F. was a separate service and its members wore a round patch evenly divided into blue, white and red.

The A.G.F. Replacement and School Command trained infantry, cavalry and artillery personnel; anti-aircraft personnel were trained by Anti-Aircraft Command. The Army Service Forces provided services and supplies for all army units and also trained its own personnel.

The triangular shoulder patch of the Armored Center portrays the colours of the infantry, cavalry and artillery. Army Corps wore the same patch but with black Roman numerals. Divisions used Arabic numerals.

The Ports of Embarkation shoulder patch was worn by personnel who organised the embarkation of units for overseas duty.

The Army Specialised Training Program trained young men in colleges; those under eighteen were trained by the A.S.T.P. Reserve.

Theaters

The shoulder patch of the U.S. Army Forces Pacific Ocean Area depicts the twelve stars of the Southern Cross constellation. The Southern Cross by itself is in the patch of the U.S. Army Forces South Atlantic, above the silhouette of Ascension Island.

The shoulder patch of the European Theater of Operations symbolised U.S. striking power. Within the E.T.O. Advance Base patch a small A.S.F. badge was also displayed.

A Moorish dome was appropriately the shape of the patch of the North African Theater of Operations. Similarly, the Chinese sun, together with the American star, were in the patch of the China–Burma–Indian Theater.

The white star in a red sky above a wavy blue sea was the patch of the U.S. Forces in the Middle East.

Plate 71. Shoulder Sleeve Insignia

Headquarters

The shoulder patch of the Supreme Headquarters Allied Expeditionary Forces was worn by General Eisenhower's staff during the north-west

European campaign. As with the patches of Allied Forces H.Q. and H.Q. Southeast Asia Command, it was worn by both American and British personnel. The patch of General H.Q. South West Pacific was used only by Americans.

Base and Defense Commands

The difference between Base Commands and Defense Commands can be deduced from their title: Defense Commands were employed in the actual defence of U.S. territory, while Base Commands were deployed for the same purpose outside the U.S. territory. London Base Command was an exception as it had nothing to do with U.S. defence. Its patch portrayed Big Ben in red, white and blue, the colours of both the Stars and Stripes and of the Union Jack.

Most of these shoulder patches are self-explanatory: that of Iceland Base Command shows an iceberg, that of Greenland Base Command the sea and the ice in a succession of blue and white wavy lines. The Atlantic Base Commands came under Eastern Defense Command and had a whale in the patch. The patch of Labrador, North-East and Central Canada Command depicted an igloo superimposed on an aurora borealis.

The Eastern and Southern Defense Commands administered most of the United States. The black part of the patch of Anti-Aircraft Artillery Command, Western Defense Command, symbolised the zone it administered, which was west of the Rocky Mountains.

There were also three other Anti-Aircraft Artillery Commands: the Eastern, Central and Southern Defense.

The Caribbean Defense Command's galleon patch appropriately demonstrated the area in which it operated.

The Military District of Washington was part of Army Service Forces and performed supply and administrative duties.

Frontier Defense Sectors

Personnel of Frontier Defense Sectors wore shoulder patches with red grenades as they were manning the batteries of the Coast Artillery. The five Defense Sectors, named after the territory they defended, were: Pacific Coastal, Chesapeake Bay, New England, New York–Philadelphia and Southern Coastal Frontier.

Plate 72. Shoulder Sleeve Insignia

Service Commands

The Service Commands were part of Army Service Forces and, numbered from one to nine, they administered all the territory of the United States.

1st Service Command: administered New England.
2nd Service Command: New York and New Jersey.
3rd Service Command: the Middle Atlantic States.
4th Service Command: the Southern States.
5th Service Command: Kentucky, Ohio, Indiana and West Virginia.
6th Service Command: Michigan, Illinois and Wisconsin.
7th Service Command: the North Central States.
8th Service Command: the South Central States.
9th Service Command: administered the Far West.

The composition and design of their patches suggested the Command's number. They were all coloured blue and white.

The North-West Service Command administered the Alcan Highway and Alaskan supply route. The Persian Gulf Service Command was in charge of the Lend-Lease supplies to the U.S.S.R.

Departments

Originally the territory of Alaska was administered by the Alaskan Defense Command whose badge depicted a seal with the aurora borealis in the background. Later, Alaska became a Department and a new badge was issued: a polar bear's head with a yellow star above it.

The Antilles Department supervised the area of the Western Caribbean, originally called the Puerto Rican Department. Its shoulder patch suggests the Morro Castle in red on a yellow background, the colours of the Spanish flag. The same colours are in the patch of the Panama Canal Department and its design symbolises the Canal itself.

The shoulder patch of the Philippine Department depicted a mythical sea lion and that of the Hawaiian Department the initial 'H' on an octagonal background.

Miscellaneous U.S. Units

Combat Team 442 was a unit raised among Japanese–Americans: it fought in Italy with the 5th Army. The 1st Special Service Force was a commando-trained unit formed from U.S. and Canadian personnel.

The shoulder patch of the Merrill's Marauders was a commemorative insignia as, in actual fact, this was a mixed force and no badges were worn except those of rank.

The Rangers were the counterparts of the British commandos and, deployed in battalions, they took part in operations in Italy and France. They generally wore shoulder flashes with the word 'Ranger' and the battalion number (from 1st to 7th), but it appears that a number of different shoulder flashes were also worn.

During World War 2, special shoulder patches were issued to Chinese and French troops training with U.S. units. Members of the U.S. Military Mission to Moscow had a patch with 'America', spelled in cyrillic lettering, above the American eagle. A patch was also authorised and worn at the H.Q. of the 1st Allied Airborne Army, during the invasion of Europe.

Personnel attached to the Veterans' Administration wore a round shoulder patch with the American eagle on a dark blue background.

Plate 73. Shoulder Sleeve Insignia

Miscellaneous U.S. Units

Shoulder patches worn by American, Hawaiian and Philippine units are illustrated in this plate.

The Panama 'Hellgate' Division shoulder patch was worn prior to that of the Panama Canal Department. There is also a shoulder title reading 'Panama' in yellow on red. An artillery grenade is depicted in the patch of the Hawaiian Separate Coast Artillery Brigade, and the taro leaf in that of the Hawaiian Division.

A bowie knife is shown in the patch of the Amphibious Training Force 9 which was at one time called Kiska Defense Force.

A special shoulder patch, with a Greek helmet and sword in its centre, is worn by personnel attached to the West Point Military Academy. The same motif also appears on the collar badges of the Academy staff, and on the cap badge of the cadets.

Airborne Troops

Some six different identification patches were worn on the forage cap by airbone troops. Light blue identified infantry units, while red identified artillery units in the three types of patch Glider Borne Paratroops, Glider Borne Troops and Paratroops.

The Identity Background Ovals were worn as a background to the metal wings; they also identified the branch of service of the wearer. The wings were often embroidered on the patch itself.

Sleeve Badges

U.S. servicemen also wore yellow stripes on the forearms above the cuff. They were 33 mm wide, and straight, one for each six months of service overseas. When worn on the left sleeve in the shape of 'V' chevrons, each represented six months of service overseas in the period 1917–23. When worn on the right sleeve they represented wounds.

If service stripes were worn as well (Plate 65) these yellow stripes were worn above them.

The meritorious patches were 49 mm square and were authorised for wear by personnel of units awarded a meritorious unit citation.

Germany

Germany is a relatively new European power, created only after the Franco-Prussian war of 1870. For centuries previously it was divided into a number of independent states, of which Prussia was the predominant power.

There were reasons that made the Prussians an aggressive militarist people: the vast plains of northern Europe did not provide stable geographical borders and wars were the only means of national survival.

In 1871, the King of Prussia became Emperor of Germany, with Bismarck as his Chancellor. The uniforms of the new German Army were standardised on the Prussian pattern, different badges and trimmings showing regimental and regional distinction.

The black, white and red cockade, adopted in 1897 as the emblem of the German Empire, subsequently saw the German soldier through two world wars.

The field grey service uniform was adopted in 1907 and during the years of World War I it was progressively simplified. Trench warfare soon called for the introduction of a solid steel helmet instead of the decorative *pickelhaube* of Prussian tradition.

After 1918, Germany was allowed to keep only a small army employed for internal security, and this was the base on which Hitler built his army which later overran most of Europe.

The Nazi emblems were given to the German armed forces in 1934. A year afterwards a new type of helmet was adopted, similar to, but slightly smaller than, the previous design, with the Nazi eagle depicted on the left and the national colours on the right.

All the German Army, except the armoured units, wore field grey uniforms, and although several differently appointed uniforms were worn for different duties, there were basically three officers' uniforms and only two uniforms for the other ranks.

All ranks wore the 'dress' uniform, the tunic having no pockets at the front, but false tail pockets at the back. The collar, cuffs, shoulder straps and the cap bands were lined with dark green material and, together with the tail pockets and the tunic's front overlap, were edged in coloured piping. Two coloured patches were stitched on each cuff.

The field service uniform was also worn by all ranks, its tunic having four patch pockets at the front and no tail pockets. The collar and shoulder straps were dark green with coloured piping; plain field grey cuffs for officers and no cuffs at all for the other ranks.

The tunic of the officers' 'undress' uniform could be described as one for field service with white metal, instead of grey buttons, and additional piping on the cuffs and along the front overlap.

A peaked cap was the common headdress of the German officer. It had twin silver cords for officers and gold cords for generals. A similar, but less elaborate cap, without chinstrap, was worn with the field service uniform. This was later replaced by a field cap, similar to that already worn by the other ranks.

The other ranks wore peaked caps with a leather chinstrap with 'dress' uniform; otherwise they wore a field cap. These were widely replaced during the war by the so-called 'mountain cap', originally issued only to mountain troops. It had soft peak and sides that could be folded down to cover the ears in cold weather.

Khaki uniforms were issued for use in hot climates, and white tunics were also worn for special occasions. Armoured troops wore a distinctive black uniform consisting of a short double-breasted jacket and long trousers which were tucked into the boots. Initially, armoured troops wore a padded black beret that was later replaced by a black field cap. Some special units wore a field grey uniform of the same design.

During the latter years of World War 2, although many 'utility' garments were introduced, the German uniform deteriorated both in quality and in appearance: the tunic's collar lost the dark green lining and the piping. New collar patches were issued, with small coloured stripes in the centre of the double bars and, in 1945, even these were discarded altogether.

The 'arm and service' colours the Germans call *Waffenfarbe*, were initially widely shown on the uniform in the form of piping on the head-dress and tunic; as a background to the collar and cuff patches, and also as a background to officers' shoulder straps. The colours were:

white	Infantry
yellow	Cavalry, Cyclists and Reconnaissance units
lemon yellow	Signals
red	Artillery—Ordnance
dark red	Smoke Troops (chemical)
black	Engineers
cornflower blue	Medical Corps
light blue	Motor Transport
light green	Jägers and Mountain Troops
pink	Armoured Troops and Anti-Tank units
crimson	General Staff and Veterinary Corps
violet	Chaplains
orange	M.P. and Engineer officers
grey-blue	Specialist officers

Administrative officials wore dark green *Waffenfarbe* and were divided into different branches, dependent upon the duty they performed. Each branch was represented by a different coloured piping on the dark green shoulder straps, collar and cuff patches.

The colours were:

red	Commissariat
crimson	H.Q. Officials
light blue	Legal Service
light green	Pharmacists
white	Paymasters
black	Technical Services
yellow	Cavalry Depot
orange	Recruiting Service
light brown	Training Specialists

Plate 74. Officers' Cap Badges, Collar and Cuff Patches

All ranks of the German Army wore two badges on the headdress: the Nazi eagle and the black, white and red cockade of Germany.

All officers, including generals, wore a white metal eagle on the crown of the peaked cap, and below, on the dark green band, was a metal cockade surrounded by a silver embroidered oak wreath (1).

Silver piping and chinstrap cords were worn by officers and gold piping and chinstrap cords by generals (2). During World War 2 embroidered eagles were also issued. They were larger than the metal type, embroidered in gold for generals and in silver for all other officers. Illustration No. 3 depicts the latter type of cap badge; a similar version, woven or embroidered, was also worn on the right breast over the pocket.

On field service caps only a smaller eagle and the cockade were worn, both woven or embroidered in silver.

Generals' collar patches (4) and cuff patches (8) of traditional design, were in gold on scarlet. On 3 April, 1941 new collar patches with three instead of two double ornamentations were adapted by the Field-Marshals. The buttons and the eagle breast badge were also gold. Their trouser stripes, the lapels of the greatcoat collar and the background cloth of the shoulder straps were scarlet.

All officers wore the traditional 'double bars' on the tunic collar and also on the cuffs of the 'dress' uniform, the cuff patches always being on a coloured background (10). There were two types of officers' collar patches: those embroidered in silver on a coloured background (5) and those embroidered on a dark green background, with a stripe of *Waffenfarbe* in the centre of each bar (7).

Staff officers' patches were embroidered in silver on crimson and their 'bars' were made with thicker wire, in order to distinguish them from other officers. Staff officers on permanent duty at Supreme Headquarters (OKW, OHK) wore patches embroidered in gold (5 and 9).

Officers' Rank Badges

German Army officers displayed their rank on the shoulder straps: three cords (two gold and one silver) interlaced for the generals' ranks; two silver double cords interlaced for senior officers. Junior officers had the same cords but they were straight, instead of being interlaced. Generals had gold buttons and silver 'pips' and all other officers had silver buttons and gold 'pips'. However, in 1941 the Field-Marshals' shoulder straps were changed to gold cords only, with the usual silver crossed batons pinned on to them.

The cords were made of bright gold and silver thread, or of frosted yellow or grey thread for field uniforms in order to give a matt appearance.

The shoulder straps of bandmaster officers were entirely different: senior bandmasters had interlaced cords similar to those of senior officers, but formed by two silver cords and a central red one. The double cords for junior ranks were comprised of one silver and one red cord and were set on a different *Waffenfarbe* background.

The officers of the Reserve wore normal shoulder straps with additional grey piping.

Plate 75. Non-Commissioned Officers and Other Ranks

Non-commissioned officers and other ranks wore the same badges as the officers on the peaked cap, but with a cockade and oak wreath made in white metal. On the field caps they wore the eagle and the cockade only (1); they were normally woven, the latter being woven on a diamond shaped background. A larger, grey, woven eagle was stitched over the right pocket of the tunic.

The patches on the collar and cuffs of the 'dress' uniform were double-bars of silver braid on coloured backgrounds (2 and 5). Those of the field uniform were generally woven in matt silver or grey yarn, with or without *Waffenfarbe* stripes on dark green or field grey background (3).

Armoured units wore special black collar patches with a 'skull and crossbones' badge, and pink piping (4).

The non-commissioned officers, except ensigns and specialist warrant officers, wore a stripe of silver braid around the edge of the collar (2) and on the cuffs of the 'dress' tunic, but only on the collar of the field tunic.

Regimental sergeant-majors were entitled to wear two stripes of silver braid on all tunic sleeves.

On fatigue tunics sergeants wore their rank badges in the form of a stripe surmounted by chevrons; regimental sergeant-majors wore two stripes.

The silver braid stripe around the edges of the shoulder straps stated all N.C.O.s' ranks; the white metal 'pips' were added for warrant officers' ranks, although officially they were still known as sergeants.

Ensigns and specialist warrant officers (of the Artillery, Medical and Veterinary Corps, Pharmacists and Paymasters) were entitled to wear officers' headdress.

Warrant officers specialising in Defence and Fortification Works wore interlaced black and white cords on the shoulder straps, with the cogwheel badge and 'pips' in white metal.

Warrant officers who were farrier instructors wore yellow interlaced cords on a crimson background with horseshoes and 'pips' in white metal.

The corporals and senior privates wore their rank badges on the left upper sleeve.

In peacetime, and during the first years of the war, the private's shoulder straps were intended to show the arm or service of the wearer in the form of coloured pipings and coloured figures and letters embroidered in the centre of the shoulder strap. The shoulder straps were then made in dark green cloth and, for instance, a red piping and red regimental number showed that the shoulder strap belonged to the artillery. Pink *Waffenfarbe* on black shoulder straps was worn by armoured units etc. Members of the *Grossdeutschland* Division had the letters 'GD', interlaced, embroidered on the shoulder straps in white, the colour of the infantry.

Plate 76. Arm Badges

Standard bearers wore a special badge on the right upper sleeve. It depicted two crossed regimental colours, with a black eagle clutching the swastika with a sprig of oak below it.

In August, 1944, snipers were granted a badge with 3 classes, 1st, 2nd and 3rd, which was to be worn on the right forearm. This was an embroidered badge: the 1st class had an oval gold cord frame, the 2nd class had silver cord and the 3rd class had no frame at all.

The Jäger (Rifle) Regiments' badge was three oak leaves with an acorn near the stem. A white metal version was worn on the headdress and an embroidered or woven one on the right upper sleeve, the latter enclosed in an oval frame.

The badge of the German mountain troops depicted an edelweiss; a white metal version was worn on the headdress and a woven oval version on the right upper sleeve. A similar badge in enamel, showing only the flower, with the the title *Heeresbergführer* below, was worn on the left breast pocket by the army's mountain guides.

Among the specialist's badges, those of helmsman and signaller were worn on the left upper sleeve, above the chevrons. Gunlayers and smoke troops operators (in other countries this section of the army was usually referred to as the Chemical Service) wore their badge on the left forearm. All the other badges worn by specialist non-commissioned officers and cadets, were sewn on the right forearm.

The badges for Army Specialists were embroidered on dark green cloth, while those for SS Specialists were on black.

The gothic letters, translated *literally*, are as follows:

F	*Feuerwerker*—fireworker	
S	*Schirrmeister*—harness master (motor maintenance)	
B	*Brieftaubenmeister*—pigeon-post master	
Fp	*Festungspioner*—fortifications pioneer	
Ts	*Truppensattlermeister*—troop saddler master	
V	*Verwaltung*—administration	
W	*Wallfeldwebel*—wall (fortifications) sergeant	

Cuff Titles

The German Army issued cuff titles, which are also called armbands, to commemorate outstanding campaigns or battles. They were intended to be worn around the left sleeve cuff of all uniforms, including greatcoats.

Members of the *Afrika Korps* were granted two cuff titles, the first, which was worn on the right sleeve, was adopted on 18 July, 1941, the second, which had the same status as a campaign award, on 15 January, 1943. It was embroidered in silver thread on sandy khaki cloth.

The cuff title *Kreta*, embroidered in yellow thread on white cloth, commemorated the German invasion of Crete and was approved on 16 October, 1942.

Another cuff title was instituted on 24 October, 1944, for the defence of Metz. It was embroidered in silver wire on black cloth, silver and black being the colours of the city of Metz. It appears that this title was not issued before the end of the war.

The last cuff title was approved on 12 March, 1945, as an award to the troops surrounded by the Russians in the region of Courland in Latvia. Specimens of this title were made in Courland before the capitulation. Contrary to the others that are 35 mm wide, this cuff title is 40 mm wide. It is grey with black lettering. The emblem on the left is that of Grand Master of the Order of the Teutonic Knights, that on the right the arms of Mitau, the capital town of Courland.

Plate 77. Shoulder Straps' Badges

A number of badges were worn on the shoulder straps by all ranks in order to show, together with the *Waffenfarbe*, the service branch of the wearer or, in some cases, to specify particular units or specialities. Badges worn by generals were in silver, those of officers in gilt, of the N.C.O.s in white metal, and of the other ranks in *Waffenfarbe*. At times, officers and other ranks of the same unit wore different badges: for instance, the officers of the Ordnance wore crossed cannons on the shoulder straps while qualified Ordnance N.C.O.s wore a crossed rifles badge on the forearm.

As many shoulder strap badges depicted simply the initial letter or letters of the title of the service they represented, a literal translation is given below together with the corresponding *Waffenfarbe* colour.

W (Gothic and Latin)	*Wache*—Guard. The Gothic 'W' was worn by the Guards Regiment in Berlin; the Latin 'W' by the Guards Battalion in Vienna—Wien. White.
P	*Panzerjäger*—Anti-Tank. Pink.
A	*Aufklärung*—Reconnaissance. Yellow. However, the same 'A' is worn by personnel of the army medical school together with cornflower blue *Waffenfarbe*.
K	*Kraftradfahrer*—Motor-cyclist. Pink.
R	*Reiter*—Mounted horse or bicycle. Yellow for cyclists, red for Horse Artillery.
M	*Maschinengewehr*—Machine-gun. White.
S	*Schule*—School.
MS	*Schule für Heeresmotorisierung*—Army Mot. Sch.
B	*Beobachtung*—Observation.
FS	*Feuerwerker-Schule*—Artillery School.
WS	*Heereswaffenmeister Schule*—Ordnance School.
KS	*Kriegs Schule*—War School. There were war schools in Potsdam, Dresden, Hanover and Munich. The towns' initials 'P', 'D', 'H' and 'M' were worn below to specify the school. White.
SS	*Heeressport Schule*—Army Sports School.
US	*Unteroffizier Schule*—N.C.O.s' School with 'P' for Potsdam, 'F' for Frankenstein and 'S' for Sigmaringen. White.
UV	*Unteroffizier Vorschule*—N.C.O.s' Preparatory School.
L	*Lehrtruppe*—Trainer units. Different *Waffenfarbe* depending on the unit.
BL (interlaced)	Observation trainer units. Red.
PL (interlaced)	Anti-Tank trainer units. Pink.

Fp	*Festungspioner*—Fortifications pioneer. Black.
V	Tank research units. Pink.
Gz	*Grenze*—Frontier. White.
D	Divisional headquarters staff. White for infantry divisions, pink for armoured divisions, etc.
G	Army Group headquarters staff. As above.
VH	*Versuchestelle*—experimental station—at Hillersleben. Red.
VK	Experimental station at Kummersdorf. Red.

Plate 78. Close Combat, Assault, Tank Battle and other badges

The Close Combat Clasp was worn on the left breast above the ribbons. It was instituted on 25 November, 1942, in three classes: gilt, silver and bronze, for, respectively 50, 30 and 15 days of unsupported close combat, or 40, 20 and 10 days in the case of wounded.

The white metal General Assault Badge, instituted on 1 June, 1940, was awarded for three assault actions on three different days. Originally only assault engineers were eligible for it. Later, on 22 June, 1940, two more types of the same badge were introduced, with the number of assaults added on a tablet at the base of the badge. The 25 and 50 Assaults Badge is altogether different from the 75 and 100 Assaults Badge. The eagle and crossed bayonet and grenade of the former are in black, and the wreath in silver, gilt replacing the silver in the latter. They were worn on the left breast pocket, by personnel not eligible for the Infantry Assault Badge or Tank Battle Badge.

These two awards, Infantry Assault and Tank Battle, were both instituted on 20 December, 1939, and worn on the left breast pocket. The former was originally in silver, but later, a bronze type was introduced for motorised infantry troops.

The Tank Battle Badge was awarded in silver to tank crews, in bronze to support troops. As in the case of the general Assault Badge, and on the same date, two other classes were instituted, the 25 and 50 Battles and the 75 and 100 Tank Battles, for tank crews; the former black and silver, the latter in gilt and silver. For other armoured vehicle's crews and personnel of Panzer-Grenadier divisions the first was in bronze, the second in bronze with a gilt wreath.

The Army Parachutists Badge was worn on the left breast pocket by all qualified parachutists of the Army from 15 June, 1937.

The Army Balloon Observer's Badge was instituted on 8 July, 1944, and had three classes, gilt, silver and bronze, and, as with the Army Anti-Aircraft Badge, it was an award. The Army A.A. Badge was granted on 18 June, 1941, and had only one class; it was made in grey metal.

Plate 79. Miscellaneous Badges

The marksmanship badges were worn on a lanyard made of twisted matt silver cords, worn from the right shoulder to the second button of the tunic.

The badge was awarded in three classes, each class divided into four awards, making up twelve separate awards. The classes were shown by different badges pinned on the lanyard at the shoulder. The awards of each class were shown by small acorns or grenades attached to the other end of the lanyard, none for the first award of each class, one for the second, and so on.

The Army eagle on a silver shield was the badge of the 3rd class; the eagle, with two crossed bayonets on a shield enclosed in an oak wreath, was the badge of the other classes, the 2nd made in silver, the 1st in gilt.

Tank marksmen wore badges similar to the Tank Battle Badge on the lanyard. That of the 3rd class marksman is illustrated; those of the other two classes, in silver or in gilt, are surrounded by an oak wreath.

The badges awarded 'for the single-handed destruction' of a tank or of an aircraft, were worn on the right upper sleeve, and were awarded in two classes. The 1st class depicts a gilt tank or aircraft on a gilt band edged with black, the 2nd a black tank or aircraft on a silver cord edged with black. Four consecutive silver badges could be worn on the sleeve, but with the achievement of the fifth, the gilt badge was awarded. The badge for Tank Destruction was instituted on 9 March, 1942, the other on 12 January, 1945. It is not known if any have ever been issued.

The Anti-Partisan War Badge was issued by the SS on 30 January, 1944, but it was given to any member of the armed forces engaged against guerrilla warfare. It was awarded in three classes: gilt, silver and bronze.

The Driver's Service Badge was awarded to drivers engaged in active military operations and could be worn in gilt, silver or bronze. It was instituted on 23 October, 1942, and was worn on the left forearm.

When on duty, the German military policeman wore a metal gorget on his chest, supported around the neck by means of a chain.

Mountain troops and Jägers wore their appropriate metal badges on the left side of the field cap and mountain troops wore an 'edelweiss', the flower only, on the peaked cap, between the eagle and the cockade. Chaplains wore the cross on the peaked cap in the same manner between the eagle and the cockade and some units were entitled to wear small white metal badges between the two normal cap badges to commemorate old regiments of great fame to which they belonged.

The illustrations on the bottom row represent the death's head traditional cap badge and was worn by the regimental staff of the 1st, 2nd, 4th, 5th, and 11th Squadrons of the 5th Cavalry Regiment.

The Dragoon eagle traditional cap badge was worn by the regimental staff of the 2nd and 4th Squadrons of Cavalry Regiment No. 6 and the 3rd Motor Cycle Battalion; and the death's head traditional badge was worn by the regimental staff of the 1st and 2nd Battalion H.Q. and the 1st, 4th, 13th and 14th companies of Infantry Regiment 17. It was also worn by the 2nd *Abteilung* and 4th Squadron of Cavalry Regiment 13.

Plate 80. Arm Shields

Arm shields were granted to commemorate battles and campaigns, and were worn on the left upper sleeve, one over the other or, in the case of three, one above and two below.

The first to be awarded was the Narvik Shield, on 19 August, 1940. It was in grey metal for the army and air force and in brass for the navy.

The Cholm Shield was instituted on 1 July, 1942, to commemorate the defence of the fortress of Cholm, on the Russian front, between January and May, 1942. The shield was in white metal.

The bronze Crimea Shield was issued on 25 July, 1942, to commemorate the German 1941–42 winter campaign in the Crimea.

Another shield that refers to the Russian front is the Demjansk Shield. It commemorates another surrounded German garrison, that of Demjansk, and the shield itself was issued in white metal.

The Kuban Shield, instituted on 20 September, 1943 was made in bronze and commemorates the defence of the Kuban bridgehead on the Russian Front.

The Warsaw Shield was issued to commemorate the suppression of the Warsaw rising. Permission for its issue was granted on 10 December, 1944, but it was never actually distributed to the troops.

The Lorient Shield commemorates the defence of Lorient, France. It was instituted in December, 1944, and subsequently made there with different metals available at the time.

The last shield to be issued was the Lapland Shield. The version of it illustrated is without the swastika as the shield could be a post-war reproduction made for use after the war by veterans.

Wounded Badges

These Wounded Badges were worn on the left breast pocket of the tunic, or just below the pocket, and were issued in three classes: gilt, silver and black. The first was instituted on 22 May, 1939 for Germans wounded in the Spanish Civil War. Its design was based on the World War 1 badge, with a swastika added in the centre. Only black and silver 'Spanish' badges were awarded.

The second badge was issued in September, 1939 as the World War 2 badge for wounded.

The third type illustrated relates to the 20 July, 1944 plot to assassinate Hitler. It carries the date and Hitler's signature.

The *Schutzstaffel* (Pl. 81–88)

The *Schutzstaffel* (Protection Squad) traced its origins back to the National-Socialist para-military forces raised in Germany during the early twenties.

The *Stosstrupp Adolf Hitler* (Shock Troop Adolf Hitler) was Hitler's first bodyguard and later similar small detachments of trusted Nazis were formed in several cities. The SS was raised on a national basis in 1925 as an élite political organisation, so much so that in 1929, when Himmler took command, the SS numbered less than 300 men. Heinrich Himmler set himself the task of reorganising and expanding this force and formed the *Stabswache* (Staff Guard), which became the first standing armed SS unit, and the *Totenkopfverbände* (Death's head unit) as a political police and for concentration camp duties.

The *Waffen* (Armed) SS should always be distinguished from the *Allgemeine* (General) SS which were employed on territorial duties.

In March, 1935 the *Stabswache* was transferred from Munich to Berlin and in September of the same year it was renamed *Leibstandarte Adolf Hitler* (Adolf Hitler's bodyguard regiment). Subsequently another three SS regiments were formed: *Germania*, stationed in Hamburg, *Deutschland*, stationed in Munich, and *Der Führer*, in Vienna. They were all part of the *Verfügungstruppe* (Reserve troops), with the exception of the *Leibstandarte Adolf Hitler*, which was independent. An SS artillery regiment was also added to the three infantry regiments of the *Verfügungstruppe* which, after the Polish campaign, became the *Verfügungs-Division*.

In the meantime, several so-called *Totenkopf* regiments were formed, and in October, 1939, the *Totenkopf* Division was formed.

About the same time another division was raised from policemen and was known as the SS-*Polizei-Division*.

SS members were drafted from the Hitler Youth by the following methods: a member of the Hitler Youth applied to join the SS at the age of 18 and, on the Reich's Party Day, 9 November, he became an SS-*Anwärter* (Candidate) and was given an SS identity card. Subsequently, he had to serve in the labour service and in the armed forces. When he had completed his conscription service he was then free to join the SS but, during the war, conscripts were not released from the armed forces, which left the SS with a recruiting problem.

However, after the Western offensive, Germany occupied countries whose 'Aryan' populations proved invaluable to SS expansion.

Danish and Norwegian volunteers formed the *Nordland* Regiment, and Dutchmen and Flemish Belgians formed the *Westland* Regiment. These, together with the *Germania* and the 5th SS Artillery Regiment, formed the *Wiking* Division in late 1940.

The *Verfügungsdivision*, together with a *Totenkopf* Regiment replacing the *Germania*, was renamed *Das Reich* Division.

The *Leibstandarte Adolf Hitler* became a brigade, and later a division, and another brigade, *Kampfgruppe Nord*, formed on the Finnish front from *Totenkopf* regiments, became a division in 1942.

In time the shortage of manpower compelled the authorities to recruit from 'non-Aryans' as well. The recruiting pattern was generally that of raising a legion of volunteers, which was later expanded to brigade strength, subsequently becoming a division.

A complete list of SS divisions as they were in the latter years of the war is as follows:

    1st SS-Panzer-Division *Leibstandarte Adolf Hitler*
    2nd SS-Panzer-Division *Das Reich*
    3rd SS-Panzer-Division *Totenkopf*
    4th SS-Polizei-Panzer-Grenadier-Division
    5th SS-Panzer-Division *Wiking*
    6th SS-Gebirgs-Division *Nord*
    7th SS-Freiwilligen-Gebirgs-Division *Prinz Eugen*
    8th SS-Kavallerie-Division *Florian Geyer*
    9th SS-Panzer-Division *Hohenstaufen*
    10th SS-Panzer-Division *Frundsberg*
    11th SS-Freiwilligen-Panzer-Grenadier-Division *Nordland*
    12th SS-Panzer-Division *Hitlerjugend*
    13th Waffen-Gebirgs-Division der SS *Handschar* (kroatische Nr 1)
    14th Waffen-Grenadier-Division der SS (galizische Nr 1)
    15th Waffen-Grenadier-Division der SS (lettische Nr 1)
    16th SS-Panzer-Grenadier-Division *Reichsführer SS*
    17th SS-Panzer-Grenadier-Division *Götz von Berlichingen*
    18th SS-Freiwilligen-Panzer-Grenadier-Division *Horst Wessel*
    19th Waffen-Grenadier-Division der SS (lettische Nr 2)
    20th Waffen-Grenadier-Division der SS (estnische Nr 1)
    21st Waffen-Gebirgs-Division der SS *Skanderbeg* (albanische Nr 1)
    22nd SS-Freiwilligen-Kavallerie-Division *Maria Theresia*
    23rd Waffen-Gebirgs-Division der SS *Kama* (kroatische Nr 2)
    23rd SS-Freiwilligen-Panzer-Grenadier-Division *Nederland*
    24th Waffen-Gebirgs-Division der SS *Karstjäger*
    25th Waffen-Grenadier-Division der SS *Hunyadi* (ungarische Nr 1)
    26th Waffen-Grenadier-Division der SS *Gömbös* (ungarische Nr 2)

27th SS-Freiwilligen-Grenadier-Division *Langemarck*
28th SS-Freiwilligen-Panzer-Grenadier-Division *Wallonie*
29th Waffen-Grenadier-Division der SS (Russian)
29th Waffen-Grenadier-Division der SS *Italien*
30th Waffen-Grenadier-Division der SS *Weissruthenien*
31st SS-Freiwilligen-Grenadier-Division *Böhmen-Mähren*
32nd SS-Freiwilligen-Grenadier-Division *30 Januar*
33rd Waffen-Kavallerie-Division der SS (Hungarian)
33rd Waffen-Grenadier-Division der SS *Charlemagne*
34th SS-Grenadier-Division *Landstorm Nederland*
35th SS-Polizei-Grenadier-Division
36th Waffen-Grenadier-Division der SS *Dirlewanger*
37th SS-Freiwilligen-Kavallerie-Division *Lützow*
38th SS-Panzer-Grenadier-Division *Nibelungen*

The various branches of the *Waffen* SS were distinguished by different colours that were worn on the uniform as piping and backing material under the shoulder cords. These colours were as follows:

	SS *Waffenfarbe*:
Infantry	white
Cavalry and Reconnaissance units	yellow
Signals	lemon yellow
Artillery	red
Rocket Artillery	dark red
Engineers	black
Medical Corps	dark blue
Mountain Troops and SS Police regiments	light green
Armoured Troops and Anti-Tank units	pink
Transport and Motor-maintenance Troops	light pink
Veterinary Corps	crimson
Military Police	orange
Replacement Service (until 1942)	orange-red
Supply units, Administrative and Technical Services	light blue
Concentration Camp units	light brown
Reserve Officers	dark green
Geologists	shell pink
Special Service N.C.O.s	dark blue/green

Plate. 81 Cap Badges

The eagle and swastika worn by the SS was different from that worn by the Army. Initially, in the 1930s, it was smaller, with pointed wings, the eagle itself being much smaller in proportion to the wreath it clutches.

White metal badges were worn on the black peaked cap, one over the other as illustrated; the traditional German skull and crossbones were also adopted by the tank units, but later the SS introduced their own pattern.

Eventually, a new SS eagle was introduced, much larger than that worn previously, with open wings. The middle feather of each wing was longer than the others.

When the front of the field cap was too short for both badges, the eagle was worn on the left side, the skull and crossbones on the front. There were several versions and sizes of this particular badge; one was in embossed metal on a button; some others were embroidered or woven in silver.

Finally, a cap badge was introduced with a smaller eagle and skull and crossbones, all woven into one badge.

All ranks of the SS wore the eagle and swastika on the upper left sleeve. That of officers was embroidered in silver thread, that of other ranks grey yarn. Eagles, embroidered in yellow and green, were worn respectively on the tropical and camouflage uniforms.

All ranks of the SS Police Division wore police badges on the head-dress and on the collar, plus an eagle and swastika on the left sleeve and the SS divisional cuff title. They adopted normal SS badges only in the latter years of the war.

Collar Patches

The 1933 style collar patches were changed in 1934 and again in 1942, as illustrated in Plates 84 to 87. The collar patches were intended to show the unit and the rank of the wearer: the unit on the right patch and the rank on the left. However, all the high-ranking officers, from colonels upward, wore the oak leaves on both sides. Their collar patches were made of black velvet. Cloth was used for other officers and other ranks. Generals and officers wore a 1·5 mm edging, made of silver aluminium twisted cords around both collar patches, although some officers ranks initially wore an edging made from black and silver aluminium cords. At the beginning of the war the SS N.C.O.s adopted the army N.C.O.s' silver braid around the collar and discarded the twisted cords around the collar patches which were previously worn.

The SS runes were worn on the right collar patch by most units except for the *Totenkopf* regiments, which wore the skull and crossbones. The foreign detachments generally wore their own devices on the right collar patch (Plate 83). Before the War the *Deutschland*, *Germania* and *Der Führer* regiments wore the regimental numbers 1, 2 and 3 in the bottom right-hand corner of the patch, as well as the SS runes. The first *Totenkopf* regiments also wore regimental numbers on the collar patch, and often other badges were worn, i.e. the lightning flash, worn by signal units, the crossed pick and spade of the pioneers, or small letters, initials of SS schools, etc.

Plate 81 also shows the *Odal* rune worn on the collar patches of the 7th SS Mountain Division *Prinz Eugen*. The same rune was also worn as an arm badge by the divisional commander.

Plates 81 and 82. Cuff Titles

All ranks of most SS divisions also wore cuff titles of the division or regiment to which they belonged; they were made in silver or grey thread on a black background. A selection of these have been illustrated in Plates 81 and 82.

Plate 83. Collar patches

A number of SS divisions, mainly formed from foreign volunteers, wore special badges on the right collar patch.

Scandinavian volunteers were mainly drafted into the 5th *Wiking* and 11th *Nordland* divisions. The 6th *Nord* was ethnically a German formation called *Nord* because it was a mountain division employed on the Finnish front.

Dutch and Belgian Flemish volunteers were drafted into the 23rd *Nederland*, the 27th *Langemarck*, and in the 34th Divisions, the latter being formed by two Dutch and one French regiment. The 28th *Wallonie* and the 33rd *Charlemagne* were formed mainly from French speaking volunteers. The latter originally had been raised as a Hungarian SS cavalry division. Hungary and the Balkans gave birth to the 18th, 22nd, 25th and 26th divisions, the 21st *Skanderbeg* was an Albanian division, and the 7th, 13th *Handschar* and 23rd *Kama* were formed from Yugoslavs. All ranks of the 13th and 23rd divisions were issued with a fez instead of the usual field cap: the *Handschar* had a flat-topped fez; the *Kama* a soft one.

The 15th and 19th Latvian and the 20th Estonian Divisions were raised in the Baltic.

A number of SS units were formed from Russian volunteers but their badges have no historical confirmation. Some units wore German and others Russian uniforms, complete with rank and cap badges, and an additional SS arm badge was worn on the left sleeve. Some units of the Russian SS wore plain black collar patches.

The only SS badge worn by the Italian SS of the 29th division was the skull and crossbones. Their cap badge and arm badge depicted the emblem of the Italian Social Republic. The Italian SS wore Italian uniforms and initially, the volunteer *Sturmbrigade*, wore plain red collar patches which were changed to black in the summer of 1944. Officers wore the rank badges on both patches and, probably towards the end of the war, the SS runes could have been adopted.

An Indian volunteer legion was raised in 1942 among Indian prisoners of war and it is believed that a small SS unit was also raised from British prisoners of war.

Plates 84, 85, 86 and 87. Rank Badges

The commissioned and non-commissioned officers of the SS were called leaders (*Führer*—leader) and had rank titles entirely different from those of the Army. Both wore rank badges on the collar and on the shoulder straps except for the lowest rank which was represented by a pip on the left upper sleeve.

Shoulder straps with cords were adopted in 1933 and until 1938 they were worn on the right shoulder only. They were intended to distinguish the different classes of rank, i.e. generals, senior officers, junior officers and the other ranks. The *Reichsführer* SS *H. Himmler* wore the general's shoulder strap with a small badge depicting three oak leaves and two acorns.

The other ranks' shoulder straps, that initially had black and white twisted cords, were changed in October, 1934, to black and silver.

In the years 1933–34 the junior officers had worn black and silver edgings on their collar patches and all the other ranks wore white edgings. This was changed in October, 1934, to silver-aluminium edgings for the junior officers to bring them into line with those already worn by all other officers, and black and silver for all other ranks.

In 1938 the *Waffen* SS adopted army rank badges: the shoulder straps of SS generals had a grey background and those of the other officers had SS *Waffenfarbe* piping and black underlay.

In 1942 some rank badges were changed and one rank, that of *Oberstgruppenführer*, was added. The oak leaves on the collar patches were also changed to a new design.

Waffenfarbe was worn in the form of piping on the shoulder straps and the first four élite SS regiments wore a regimental device embroidered on the shoulder straps in white silk.

The *Leibstandarte Adolf Hitler* wore the letters 'LAH' interlaced; the *Deutschland* and *Germania* regiments respectively wore a Gothic 'D' and 'G'; and *Der Führer* wore the initials 'DF' interlaced.

Some other chevrons, apart from those for corporals, could also be worn as appointment stripes. The appointment of SS-*Stabsscharführer*, given to N.C.O.s, was a lace chevron stitched onto the lower right sleeve.

The *Alter-Kämpfer* chevron was worn on the right upper arm by 'old campaigners' who were party members before 1933. The same chevron, with a round 'pip', was worn by ex-policemen and ex-soldiers who were members of the SS.

SS men who were ex-members of the *Stahlhelm* organisation wore a distinguishing black chevron on the left forearm.

Plate 88. Rank Badges for Camouflage Uniforms

There were several types of camouflage overalls for use in different seasons or on different terrain. The Army adopted a new type of rank insignia for uniforms without shoulder straps and in September, 1943, these badges were adopted also by the SS.

These rank badges were worn on the upper left sleeve only, and consisted of a combination of bars and oak leaves on a black rectangular or square background. The bars and oak leaves were yellow for generals and green for all the other ranks. Corporals wore the usual triangular chevrons also on camouflage clothing.

The same insignia, except No. 5, were also worn by Army personnel.

Index

This is not a complete Index but is intended only as a
cross reference between illustration and description

Army Badges and Insignia
Since 1945

Great Britain, Poland, U.S.A., Italy,
German Federal and Democratic
Republics, U.S.S.R., Belgium

To
my wife

Army Badges and Insignia Since 1945

Great Britain, Poland, U.S.A., Italy,
German Federal and Democratic
Republics, U.S.S.R., Belgium

Guido Rosignoli

BLANDFORD PRESS

POOLE·NEW YORK·SYDNEY

Contents

Introduction

The research necessary for the publication of my first book, *Army Badges and Insignia of World War 2*, left me with a great deal of additional information regarding the badges of the same armies used after 1945. I soon discovered that thousands of entirely new badges had been adopted in these last twenty-eight years and so became fascinated by this new field.

Although the publishers have agreed to add a few more pages of illustrations to the present book, I regret that space limitations, once again, have compelled me to deal solely with the regular armies, although some territorial badges have been included in particular cases when, by so doing, I could simplify the subject.

The reader will certainly realise that if I had attempted to illustrate all the British badges, including those of the territorials, little room would have been left for other armies, thus marring the original concept of this publication. I hope that in future I will be able to compile a separate book dealing only with the badges of territorial units, in the case of Britain worn since 1908, which will enable me to illustrate and describe all the changes and reorganisations that have taken place since then.

The translation of the N.C.O.s' ranks again presented an extremely difficult task, particularly with regard to the German ranks, and, as Germany is divided with two separate Armies, I had no choice but to refer to their original German-language titles.

I would like to thank the many readers who have written to me, and to the publishers, for showing their appreciation of my previous book.

G. Rosignoli,
Farnham, Surrey, 1973

Acknowledgments

I would like to thank:

The Belgian Embassy and Major Davreux for their help with the Belgian chapter.

The Embassy of the Federal Republic of Germany.

Mr K. Barbarski for his untiring help and his translations.

Sergeant-Major David W. Bruce, for giving his invaluable assistance in the wide field of the American shoulder sleeve insignia.

Mr A. Mollo who gave me access to all his files and constantly advised me.

Geom. L. Granata, who helped me with the Italian chapter.

I especially appreciate the kind help of Mr F. Ollenschläger who has given me the benefit of his knowledge through all the chapters of this book.

I also appreciate the help given to me by Mr B. W. T. Cockcroft, Mr A. L. Kipling, Mr H. L. King, Captain J. C. Cochrane, the Royal Irish Rangers, Mr J. E. Hankin, Major Frank Croxford, Major H. P. Patterson, Curator of the Royal Green Jackets Museum and Lt.-Col. H. N. Cole, O.B.E., T.D.

Lastly, my most sincere thanks to my wife who patiently transformed my manuscript into the text of this book.

OFFICERS' RANK BADGES

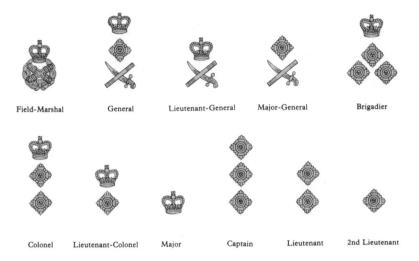

Field-Marshal General Lieutenant-General Major-General Brigadier

Colonel Lieutenant-Colonel Major Captain Lieutenant 2nd Lieutenant

WARRANT OFFICERS' AND N.C.O.s' RANK BADGES

S.S.M. (1st Class) Conductor W.O. (1st Class) R.Q.M.S. W.O. (2nd Class)

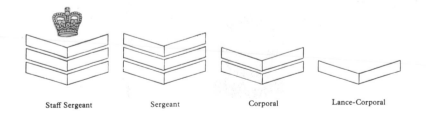

Staff Sergeant Sergeant Corporal Lance-Corporal

PLATE 1

CAP BADGES
Household Cavalry and Armoured Cavalry Regiments

Royals

H.C.

L.G.

R.H.G.

B. & R.

Q.D.G.

R.S.D.G.

4/7 D.G.

5 Innis D.G.

Q.O.H.

Q.R.I.H.

9/12 L.

R.H.

13/18 H.

14/20 H.

15/19 H.

16/5 L.

17/21 L.

PLATE 2

CAP BADGES
Arms and Services

R.T.R.

R.A.

R.A.C.

R.E.

R. Sigs.

R.H.A.

R.A.O.C.

R.M.P.

R.A.M.C.

R.C.T.

M.P.S.C.

R.A.V.C.

R.E.M.E.

G.P.R.

A.A.C.

R.A.D.C.

R.A.E.C.

PLATE 3

CAP BADGES
Arms and Services

R.A.P.C.

R.P.C.

I.C.

A.P.T.C.

G.S.C.

P.R.

Junior Leaders
Trng Regt

A.C.C.

S.A.S.

M.D.C

Army Dept
Fire Service

Army Legal
Services

W.R.A.C.

Q.A.R.A.N.C.

Royal Hospital
Chelsea

PLATE 4

CAP BADGES
Miscellanea

Control Commission
Germany

Army Dept
Constabulary

Army Dept Police
Cyprus

R.M.A.
Sandhurst

Mons Officer
Cadet School

R.M.S.M.

Small Arms
School Corps

Foot Guards

Grenadiers

Coldstream

Scots

Irish

Welsh

PLATE 5

CAP BADGES
The Brigade of Gurkhas

2nd

6th

7th

10th

Engineers

Signals

Staff Band

Transp. Regt

G.M.P.

Infantry Regiments

R. Lincolns

R. Leicesters

R. Hamps.

Dorset

Green Howards

Wilts

R.B.

Manch.

K.O.Y.L.I.

PLATE 6

CAP BADGES
Brigades

Lowland

Home Counties

Lancastrian

Fusilier

Forester

East Anglian

Wessex

Lignt Infantry

Yorkshire

Mercian

Welsh

North Irish

Highland

Green Jackets

PLATE 7

CAP BADGES
Infantry Regiments

Queen's

R. Anglian

Yorkshire

K.O.R.B.

Devon & Dorset

R.I.R.

Worc. & Sherwood
Foresters

Green Howards

Duke of Ed.'s

Staffs

R.H.F.

King's

Queen's Lancs

Glosters & Hamps.

Q.O. Hldrs

R.G.J.

PLATE 8

CAP BADGES

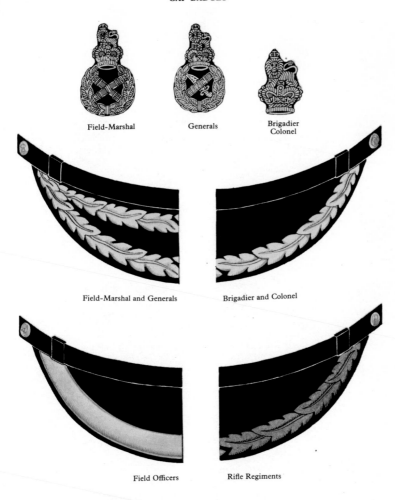

Field-Marshal

Generals

Brigadier
Colonel

Field-Marshal and Generals

Brigadier and Colonel

Field Officers

Rifle Regiments

R.A.Ch.D. Christian

Army Dept Fleet

R.A.Ch.D. Jewish

PLATE 9

FORMATION SIGNS

Home Commands

Scottish

H.Q.   Troops

Northern

Western

Eastern

South-Eastern

H.Q. Southern

Infantry

R.A.C.

R.A.

R.E.

R.A.O.C.

R.A.S.C.

R. Sigs

R.M.P.

R.A.M.C.

R.E.M.E.

R.A.P.C.

R.P.C.

I.C.

R.A.D.C.

A.C.C.

A.P.T.C.

R.A.E.C.

W.R.A.C.

Miscellaneous

R.A.D.C.

Northern and Eastern (1947)

Orkney and
Shetland Defences

A.A. Command

Garrisons and other formations

East and West
Ridings Area

Edinburgh Garr.

Catterick Garr.

Force 135
Channel Islands
Lib. Force

Shoeburyness Garr.

Br. Troops in Northern Ireland

PLATE 10

FORMATION SIGNS

Districts

Northern Ireland (2)

North Wales

South-Western

West Scotland

Lancs and Border

West Lancashire

South Wales

Salisbury Plain

London

North Highland

South Highland

North Riding

North Midland

South Midland

Hants and Dorset

Sussex

East Scotland

West Riding

Central Midland

East Anglian

East Kent

Northumbrian

East Riding and Lincs

Norfolk and Cambridge

North Kent and Surrey (2)

Northern Ireland

Northumbrian

East Anglian

South-Western

Aldershot

PLATE 11

FORMATION SIGNS
Army Corps

1st Corps

R.A.

R.E.

R. Sigs

R.A.S.C.

2nd Corps

Divisions

1st Division

R.A.

R. Sigs

R.A.S.C.

4th

40th

42nd

44th

44th

48th

54th

56th Armd

17th Gurkha

17th British

1st Commonwealth

Training Brigade Groups

Home Counties

Lancastrian

Midland

East Anglian

Wessex

Yorks & Northumberla

Mercian

Welsh

North Irish

Greenjackets

PLATE 12

FORMATION SIGNS

Brigades

1st Guards

2nd Guards

2nd

3rd

5th

6th

8th

H.Q. 12th

12th

17th

18th

19th

22nd Beach

23rd

25th Armd

25th

27th

29th

30th Armd

31st

39th

39th

49th

50th

51st

72nd

107th

155th

160th

161st

162nd

264th Beach

302nd

48th, 63rd and 99th Gurkha

PLATE 13

FORMATION SIGNS

British Forces Overseas

H.Q. Middle East
Land Forces

G.H.Q. Middle East
Land Forces

H.Q. Br. Troops
in Egypt

G.H.Q. Far East
Land Forces

Br. Troops
in Siam

Br. Troops
in Palestine

Malaya
Command

Persia and Iraq
Command

H.Q. Land Forces
Hong Kong

H.Q. Director of
Borneo Operations

Br. Troops
in Norway

Netherlands
District

Cyprus
District

BETFOR

Tripolitania
District

Cyrenaica
District

Singapore
District

Faroe Island
Force

North Palestine
District

Canal South
Distr. M.E.L.F.

H.Q. Br. Troops
in Aden

Land Forces
Adriatic

H.Q. B.C.O.F.
Japan-Korea

Allied Commn
Austria

Control Commn
Germany

Br. Troops
in France

Hamburg
District

Hanover
District

Br. Troops
in Berlin

H.Q. B.A.O.R.

Rhine Army
Troops

Rhine Army
Trng Centre

Sch. of Art
B.A.O.R.

Eng. Trng
Establ. B.A.O.R.

R.A.C. Trng
Centre B.A.O.R.

PLATE 14

FORMATION SIGNS

Army Groups, R.A.

| 1st | 2nd | 3rd | | 5th | 6th | 7th |

| 41st | 42nd | 84th | 85th | 86th | 87th | 88th |

| 89th | 90th | 91st | 92nd | 93rd | 94th | 95th |

| 96th | 97th | 98th | 99th | 100th | |

8th Trng Bde

1st Coast Art
Trng School

Coast Brigades, R.A.

| 101st | 102nd |

Guided
Weapons Regt

Maritime
A.A.Art.

oast Art. Trng
ntre, S.W. Distr.

Coast Art. School

105th

Coast Artillery

A.A. and Coast
Defence (C.M.F.)

A.A. Brigades, R.A.

| 30th | 31st | 33rd | 34th |

PLATE 15

FORMATION SIGNS
Engineer Groups

21st

22nd

23rd

24th

24th

25th

26th

27th

29th

Port Task Forces, R.E.

R.E. Base Group
Singapore

1st

2nd

3rd

R.E. Trng Bde

Transportation
Trng Centre R.E.

Bomb Disposal

Airfield Constr.
Groups, R.E.

Chem. Warfare

R.E. Depot

Miscellanea

R.A.C. Trng Bde

The War Office

Mil. Staff
Ministry of Supply

W.O. Controlled
units

Sigs Trng Regt

Sch. of Infantry

A.A.C.

Beach Groups

Special Trng
Centre

Air Despatch
Group

Air Formation Sigs

Army Dept Fleet

Air Liaison Sigs

PLATE 16

CAP BADGES

1st pattern   2nd pattern

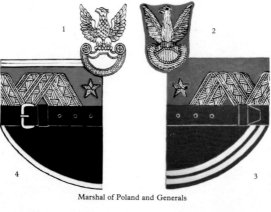

Marshal of Poland and Generals

Senior Officers

Junior Officers

Other Ranks

PLATE 17

OFFICERS' RANK BADGES

Marshal of Poland   General of Army   General   General of Division   General of Brigade

Colonel   Lieutenant-Colonel   Major

Captain   Lieutenant   2nd Lieutenant   W.O.

PLATE 18

WARRANT OFFICERS' AND N.C.O.s' RANK BADGES (1st pattern)

Staff Sergeant

Sergeant

Lance-Sergeant

Corporal

Lance-Corporal

(2nd pattern)

Senior Staff W.O.

Staff W.O.

Senior W.O.

W.O.

Junior W.O.

Senior Staff Sergeant

Staff Sergeant

Senior Sergeant

Sergeant

PLATE 19

RANK BADGES

Platoon Sergeant   Senior Corporal   Corporal   Lance-Corporal

COLLAR PATCHES (1949-52)

General – Infantry   Officer – Artillery

Engineers   Signals   Legal Service   Quartermaster Service

Administrative Service   Medical Service   Veterinaries   Mot. Transport Service

PLATE 20

COLLAR PATCHES FOR MARSHAL OF POLAND AND GENERALS (1952–60)

Armd/Mech. units

Warsaw Inf. Div.

Marshal of Poland

Generals – Inf.

Artillery

Eng./Mot. Transp.

Signals

Q.M. Admin.

Medical Service

Veterinaries

Legal Service

COLLAR PATCHES FOR OFFICERS AND OTHER RANKS (1952–60)

Chemical

Armd/Mech. units

Army

Officers' Schools

Armour

COLLAR BADGES

Infantry

Artillery

Armd/Mechanised

Signals

Ordnance

Pontoon units

Engineers

Chemical

Legal

Mot. Transport

Administrative

Q.M.

Construction Bns

Band

Mil. Railways

Medical

Veterinaries

PLATE 21

COLLAR BADGES (1961–73)

Infantry

Artillery

Marshal

Generals

Ordnance

Chemical

Engineers

Armour

Mech. units

Radiotechnical

Signals

Mot. Transport

Construction

Geographers

Mil. Transport

Administrative

Medical

Q.M.

Army Security

Legal

Veterinaries

Chaplains

Officers Schools

Mountain Troops

Army Tech. Ac.

Army Med. Ac.

N.C.O.s' Schools

SHOULDER-STRAP BADGES

Army Courses
in higher schools

W.O.s' School

Army Med. Ac.

Staff College

Army Tech. Ac.

Reg. N.C.O.s' School

PLATE 22

BREAST-POCKET BADGES FOR EXEMPLARY SERVICE

Exemplary Service

Rifleman

Light M.-Gunner

Reconnaissance

Driver

Marksman

Mortarman

Heavy M.-Gunner

Med. Orderly

Tankman

Sapper

Pontooner

Artilleryman

Cook

Baker

Miner

Exemplary Driver (3 classes)

ARM BADGES

Marines

Coastal Defence

N.C.O.s' School

PLATE 23

BREAST BADGES

1st Warsaw Inf. Div.

Grunwald badge

Frontier Defence

1st Warsaw
Cav. Div.

Inf. Trng Centre

Officers' Schools (12)

Inf. Officers'
School

Reg. N.C.O.s' School

Art. Off. School No. 1

Driver-Mech.

2nd Mot. Transp.
Trng Regt

13th
International Bde

Armd Corps

Parachutist

Youth Club

Inventiveness
Improvement

Exemplary Soldiers

Brotherhood of Arms

Driver-Mech. (Armour)

Officers' Schools and Academies

PLATE 24

ARM BADGES

6th POMORSKA Airborne Division

Specialists

Armour

Artillery

A.A. Defence

Ordnance

Mil. Transport

Topographer

Diver

Motor Transport

Quartermaster

Educational

Engineers

Chemical

Signals

Radiotechnical

PLATE 25

CAP BADGES

Warrant Officers

Enlisted Men

Generals – Field Officers   Officers – Warrant Officers

Special Forces

SPECIAL FORCES INSIGNIA

J. F. Kennedy
S.W.C.

1st   3rd   5th   6th

7th   8th   10th   11th   19th   46th

S.W.C.   Europe   Reserve   Trng   5th Combas   Arctic Rangers   Avn

PLATE 26

OFFICERS' RANK BADGES

General of the Army

General

Lieutenant General

Major General

Brigadier

Colonel

Lieutenant Colonel

Major

Captain

1st Lieutenant

2nd Lieutenant

WARRANT OFFICERS' RANK BADGES

CWO4 CWO3 CWO2 WO1 CWO4 CWO3 CWO2 WO1

SHOULDER ORNAMENTATION FOR ARMY BLUE UNIFORM

Lieutenant General

Major

Captain

Colonel

CWO3

PLATE 27

LINE N.C.O.s' RANK BADGES (1948)

First Sergeant

Master Sergeant

Sergeant 1st Class

Sergeant

Corporal

Private 1st Class

(1955)

First Sergeant

Master Sergeant

Sergeant 1st Class

Sergeant

Corporal

Private 1st Class

(1957-73)

Command Sgt Major

Sergeant Major

First Sergeant

Master Sergeant

Sergeant 1st Class

Staff Sergeant

Sergeant

Corporal

Private 1st Class

Private E-2

PLATE 28

SPECIALISTS' RANK BADGES (1956)

Master Specialist   Sp. 1st Class   Sp. 2nd Class   Sp. 3rd Class

(1958)

Sp. 9   Sp. 8   Sp. 7   Sp. 6   Sp. 5   Sp. 4

SHOULDER SLEEVE TABS

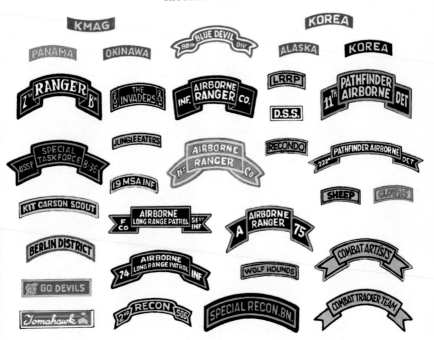

PLATE 29

OFFICERS' COLLAR BADGES

Officer's U.S.

Infantry

Armd Force

Artillery

Coast Art.

Engineers

Military Police

Chemical Corps

Finance

Ordnance

Quartermaster

Signal Corps

Nat. Guard Bur.

Band

Inspector G.S.

Transp. Corps

Judge Advocate

Civil Affairs
U.S.A.R.

Staff Specialist
U.S.A.R.

Intell. Security Branch

Chaplains

W.A.C.

Warrant Officer

Medical
Corps

Med.
Administration

Contract
Surgeon

Dental
Corps

Army Nurse
Corps

Pharmacy
Corps

Med. Specialist
Corps

Vet.
Corps

Adjutant General's
Corps

Hospital
Dietitian

Physical Therapy
Aid

Med.
Service Corps

Gen. Staff

Aides: The President

Vice President

Secretary
of Defense

Secretary
of the Army

Under-Secretary
of the Army

Chief of
Staff

to General
of the Army

General

Lieutenant
General

Major
General

Brigadier
General

PLATE 30

BREAST BADGES

Dept of Defense

White House
Service

Joint Chiefs
of Staff

General Staff

Honor Guard

Combat Infantryman

Expert Infantryman

C.I. 3rd Award

C.I. 2nd Award

Combat Field Artillery

Combat Armd Cavalry

Rigger

Parachutist

Senior Para

Master Para

Para Ranger

Glider

Nuclear Reactor
Operator, 1st Cl.

Senior Army
Aviator

Master Army
Aviator

Explosive Ordnance
Disposal

Exp. Ord. Disp.
Supervisor

Flight Surgeon

Expert Field
Medical

Combat Medical

C.M. 2nd Award

C.M. 3rd Award

C.M. 4th Award

PLATE 31

SHOULDER SLEEVE AND POCKET INSIGNIA

Recruiting and Training

F.A. School

Inf. School

Armed Forces
Information School

Army Avn
School

Air Def. School

V.N. Basic Trng
Center

U.S.A.R.S.

Special Warfare
Center

J.W.T.C.

Centers and Schools

F.A.

Missile and
Munitions

Signals

Q.M.

Transp.

M.P.

Ordnance

Helicopter School

Medical

Engr

Intelligence

Chemical

Combat Leadership
Trainee

Recondo Schools

Combat Surv.
Electr. School

Civil Affairs
School

G/75 Inf.

Judge Advocate
General's School

A.C.T.A.
2nd Div.

Command-G.S. College

Hawaii

U.S. Military Academy

5th Div.

54th Engr Professional
School

PLATE 32

Berlin Bde

Berlin District

Eur. Civil Affairs

Constabulary in Europe

U.S. Army Europe

Eur. Hqs E.T.O.

Tactical Cmd Austria

U.S. Forces Austria

Trieste U.S. Troops

U.S. Forces Far East

U.S.–Allied Control Commn–Hungary

Med. Cmd Europe

Guam Base

Ryukus Cmd

Japan Log. Cmd

West Pacific Far East Cmd

Military Government Korea

Japanese War Crimes Trial

Nurenberg District

U.S. TASCOM Europe

Communications Zone Korea

MAAG Laos

MAAG Taiwan

U.S. Army Missions

Civil Assistance Commn Korea

U.N. Partisan Force Korea

Engr Cmd Europe

Mil. Equipment Delivery Team Cambodia

Mil. Asst. Cmd V.N.

U.S. Army V.N.

Engr Cmd V.N.

1st Field Force

2nd Field Force

PLATE 33

SHOULDER SLEEVE AND POCKET INSIGNIA
Miscellaneous U.S. Units

China Hqs

Ledo Road

Marshall Task Force

158th Regt Comb. **Bushmasters**

480th F.A.

Katchin

Rangers
Jingpaw

O.S.S.–Special Force

99th Inf. Bn.

36th Engr Bn

2nd Cml M. Bn

83rd Cml M. Bn

Office of Strategic Services

49th A.A. Bde

98th F.A. Bn

1629th Engr Bn

93rd Cml M. Bn.

96th Cml M. Bn

Trng Engr

Engr Intell. Dept

Combat Development

Guided Missile Agency

Q.M.

SCARWAF

Security Agency

Army Avn Team

Defense Atomic Support Agency

Manhattan Project

Arctic Test Center

Sp. Forces Avn

1st Avn Bn Flight Sect.

Alaska Supply Group

Arctic Rangers

100th Cml M. Bn

Special Forces

Pathfinders

Alaska Cmd

PLATE 34

SHOULDER SLEEVE INSIGNIA

Ghost Units

1st Army Group

14th Army

31st Army Corps

33rd Army Corps

11th Div.

14th Div.

17th Div.

22nd Div.

46th Div.

48th Div.

50th Div.

55th Div.

59th Div.

108th Div.

119th Div.

130th Div.

141st Div.

157th Div.

National Guard Divisions

46th

47th

48th

49th

51st

Miscellanea

1st Army

2nd Army

19th Army Corps

5th Div.

40th Div.

89th Div.

11th Air Assault Div.
(Test)

PLATE 35

SHOULDER SLEEVE INSIGNIA

Regimental Combat Teams

4th

5th

25th

29th

33rd

38th

75th

103rd

107th

111th

150th

157th

158th

163rd

166th

176th

178th

182nd

187th Abn

196th

278th

295th

296th

298th

299th

351st

442nd

474th

508th Abn

99th Bn C.T.

187th Abn

65th

442nd (1st)

PLATE 36

SHOULDER SLEEVE INSIGNIA
Brigades

1st Inf.

2nd Inf.

11th Inf.

29th Inf.

32nd Inf.

33rd Inf.

36th Inf.

39th Inf.

40th Inf.

40th Armd

41st Inf.

45th Inf.

49th Inf.

49th Armd

53rd Inf.

67th Inf.

69th Inf.

71st Abn

72nd Inf.

81st Inf.

86th Armd

92nd Inf.

157th Inf.

171st Inf.

172nd Inf.

173rd Abn

187th Inf.

191st Inf.

193rd Inf.

194th Armd

196th Inf.

197th Inf.

198th Inf.

199th Inf.

205th Inf.

256th Inf.

30th Art.

256th Inf.

30th Art.

31st, 35th, 45th 47th, 49th, 52nd ARADCOM

32nd Air Defense

38th Art.

40th AA

107th Art.

PLATE 37

SHOULDER SLEEVE INSIGNIA

Brigades

| 7th Engr | 16th Engr | 18th Engr | 20th Engr | 130th Engr | 411th Engr | 412th Engr |

| 416th Engr | 420th Engr | 57th Ordnance | 1st Signal | 7th Signal |

| 1st Spt | 2nd Spt | 3rd Spt | 12th Spt | 13th Spt |

| 15th Spt | 35th Spt | 103rd Spt | 167th Spt | 301st Spt | 311th Spt | 377th Spt |

| 15th M.P. | 18th M.P. | 43rd M.P. | 220th M.P. | 221st M.P. | 258th M.P. | 290th M.P. |

| 7th Med. | 18th Med. | 44th Med. | 1st Avn | 107th Tpn | 125th Tpn | 143rd Tpn |

PLATE 38

SHOULDER SLEEVE INSIGNIA
Logistical Commands

1st

2nd

3rd

4th

5th

7th

8th

9th

300th

304th

305th

306th

307th

310th

312th

313th

315th

316th

319th

321st

322nd

323rd

324th

Transportation Commands

2nd

3rd

4th

5th

7th

11th

32nd

124th

184th

425th

PLATE 39

SHOULDER SLEEVE AND POCKET INSIGNIA

Commands

14th A.A.   Air Defense   Army Material   Special Amm. Support   Army Missile   300th M.P.–P.W.   Criminal Investigation

1st, 261st Signal

7th, 8th, 22nd, 23rd FASCOMs

Cavalry–Armoured and Airmobile

150th A.C.R.

F.A. Bde 1st Div.

29th Art. Regt

6th C.R.

17th Cav. Recon.

3rd A.C.R.

2nd A.C.R.

4th C. Group

14th A.C.R.

15th C. Group

6th C. Group

A/1st/9th

11th A.C.R.

101st A.C.R.

A/4th/12th A.C.R.

Heli. Medical Evacuation

C.M.P.P.

107th A.C.R.

163rd A.C.R.

PLATE 40

SHOULDER SLEEVE AND POCKET INSIGNIA

Armored Force

Hqs

3rd Armd Corps

1st Armd Div.

325th Armd Bn

The Armored Center

G.H.Q.

1st Armd Div.

3rd Armd Div.
Reconnaissance

30th Armd Div. N.G.

112th Armd Cav.

7th Cav. Regt

Demonstration
Regt

7th Army Tank
Training Center

17th Armd Group

510th Armd
Reconnaissance Bn

Tank Co. 39th Inf.

522nd Armd Engr Bn

1st Bn, 151st Armor

Special Airborne
Training Unit

70th Armd Regt

T.C.Q.C. Grafenwohr

628th Tank Destr.
Bn

PLATE 41

SHOULDER SLEEVE AND POCKET INSIGNIA

Para. Glider, Abn Infantry, Glider Infantry and Para. Infantry Regts

187th P.G.I.   187th A.I.R.   Mortar Btry 187th   188th A.I.R.

188th A.I.R.   1st Bat. Gp 325th   325th G.I.R.   Recon. Pl. 327th   501st P.I.R.

501st P.I.R.   502nd P.I.R.   503rd P.I.R.

503rd P.I.R.   504th P.I.R.   505th P.I.R.

H.G. 505th   506th P.I.R.   507th P.I.R.   508th P.I.R.   509th P.I.R.

509th P.I.R.   Recon. Pl. 509th   509th P.I.R.   511th A.I.R.

PLATE 42

Airborne and Parachute Infantry Regts and Miscellaneous Para. Units

511th A.I.R.

511th P.I.R.

513th P.I.R.

515th P.I.R.

517th P.I.R.

541st P.I.R.

542nd P.I.R.

550th P.I.R.

551st P.I.R.

555th P.I.R.

127th Abn Engr

Abn Eng (W.W.2)

460th Para F. A. Bn

674th P.F.A. Bn

370th Abn Engr

596th Abn Engr

462nd P.F.A. Bn

Aerial Supply

Abn School
Ft Benning

AIRBORNE

Aerial Supply

50th Abn Sig. Bn

Allied Forces Abn
Trng Center (W.W.2)

SEVENTH ARMY
PARACHUTE TEAM

U.S. ARMY
PARACHUTE TEAM
GOLDEN KNIGHTS

Parachute Teams

PLATE 43

U.S.A.

SHOULDER SLEEVE AND POCKET INSIGNIA
Airborne Divisions (O.R.)

1st/225th Inf. Regt

80th

84th

100th

108th

Ghost Airborne Divisions

6th

9th

18th

21st

135th

Airborne Brigades and Other Units

2nd

173rd

24th Inf.

187th A.I.R.
503rd A.I.R.

509th A.I.R.

2nd Field Force

82nd and 101st Airborne Divisions

Command and Control
82nd

82nd

101st

101st Abn Div. at
Ft Campbell

Intell. Det.
82nd

Sig. Bn
82nd

Divisional Recondos

7th Ranger Bn

Spt Cmd
101st

101st Abn Div
Reunion

PLATE 44

CAP INSIGNIA

General of Army Corps
A.C. General with Special Appointments

Other Generals

Cap bands and chinstraps

All officers

W.O.s and N.C.O.s

Generals

Senior Officers

Junior Officers

Warrant Officers

Rank badges worn on the field cap

Generals

Senior Officers

Junior Officers

Warrant Officers

Mountain Troops

Officers' feather holders

Rank badge (Major)

O.R.s' feather holders

PLATE 45

OFFICERS' AND WARRANT OFFICERS' RANK BADGES

A. C. General with Special Appointments   General of Army Corps   General of Division   General of Brigade

Colonel   Lieutenant-Colonel   Major   Captain   Lieutenant   2nd Lieutenant

Aiutante di battaglia   W.O. Major   Chief W.O.   W.O.

PLATE 46

OFFICERS' RANK BADGES (BLACK UNIFORM)

1st pattern

Generals

Senior Officers

Junior Officers

2nd pattern

Generals

Senior Officers

Junior Officers

SERGEANTS AND CORPORALS

Sergeant-Major

Sergeant

Corporal-Major

Corporal

CADETS

Officer

N.C.O.

Squad Commander

PLATE 47

CAP BADGES

Infantry

Inf. Folgore Div.

Bersaglieri

Lagunari

Grenadiers

Parachutists

Tanks

Lancers

Dragoons

Cavalry

Heavy Artillery

Medium Artillery

Field Artillery

Missile Artillery

Horse Artillery

Armoured Artillery

A.A. Artillery

Heavy A.A. Artillery

Art. Folgore Div

Terr. Air Defence

Engineers

Signals

PLATE 48

CAP BADGES

Railway Eng.

Miners

Bridging Eng.

Pionieri d'Arresto

Chaplains

Doctors

Pharmacists

Veterinaries

Motor Transport

Clerks

Administrative Service

Medical Service

Supply Service

N.B.C.

Commissaries

Technical Services

Legal Service

Fencing Instructors

Armd Troops
Training School

Military Academy

Military Schools

Military Postal Service

PLATE 49

MOUNTAIN TROOPS' CAP BADGES

Artillery

Engineers

Motor Transport

Administrative

Alpini

Supply

Signals

Medical

Commissaries

Doctors

Pharmacists

Veterinaries

Chaplains

O.R.s

ENAMEL BADGES

PLATE 50

COLLAR PATCHES

Grenadiers

Infantry

Mortars

Frontier Guards

Unassigned Infantry

Bersaglieri

Alpini

Tanks

Cavalry Depot

1st Nizza Cav. Regt

2nd Piemonte

3rd Gorizia

3rd Savoia

4th Genova

5th Novara

6th Aosta

7th Milano

8th Montebello

12th Saluzzo

14th Alessandria

15th Lodi

19th Guide

N.B.C.

Artillery

Engineers

Medical

Veterinaries

Commissaries

Supply

Administrative

Signals

Clerks

Fencing Instructors

Armd Infantry

Motor Transport

PLATE 51

COLLAR PATCHES

Mountain Troops   Armoured Troops

Parachutists

Parachutists   Folgore Inf. Division

Technical Services

Artillery   Engineers   Chemical   Geographical

Signals   Motor Transport

PLATE 52

Parachutists

Military Parachute Centre

Arm badges (1940–64)

Veterans
Folgore Div.

Air Supply

Breast badges (1964)

Para. Guastatore

Rigger

1st Tactical Group

Para. Artillery

Para. Saboteur

Lagunari

Breast badge

Collar patch

Cuff patch

PLATE 53

SPECIALISTS' BADGES

Metal Badges

Tank badges

Army Aviation Pilot

Motor-car and Motorcycle Drivers

Anti-Tank

Plastic Badges

Tank and Armd Car Crews

Fitter

Embroidered Badges

Guastatore

Artificer

Inf. Assault

Instructor Alpine School

Pioneer

Engine Driver

SPECIALISTS' ARM SHIELDS AND POCKET BADGES

PLATE 54

ARM SHIELDS

Infantry Divisions and Brigades

Folgore

Cremona

Legnano

Friuli

Mantova

Gran. di Sardegna

Aosta

Avellino

Pinerolo

Trieste

Armoured Divisions and Brigades

Ariete

Centauro

Somaliland
Security Corps

Pozzuolo del Friuli

Mountain Brigades

Taurineense

Julia

Tridentina

Orobica

Cadore

Miscellanea

Parachute Bde

Missile Bde

Garrison in Trieste

Frontier Guard

PLATE 55

TRAINING SCHOOLS' ARM SHIELDS

Electronic Def. Centre

Recr. Trng Centre

Armd Units Trng Camp

Mil. Riding School

N.C.O.s' School

War School

Army Avn Trng Centre

Mil. Medical School

Infantry

Signals

Mountain Troops

Engineers

Motor Transport

Army Sport Centre

Parachute

Veterinary

Commissariat,
Admin. and Supply

Mil. Phys. Trng School

Armoured Troops

Art. Electronic
Technicians

Artillery

A.A. Artillery

PLATE 56

CAP BADGES

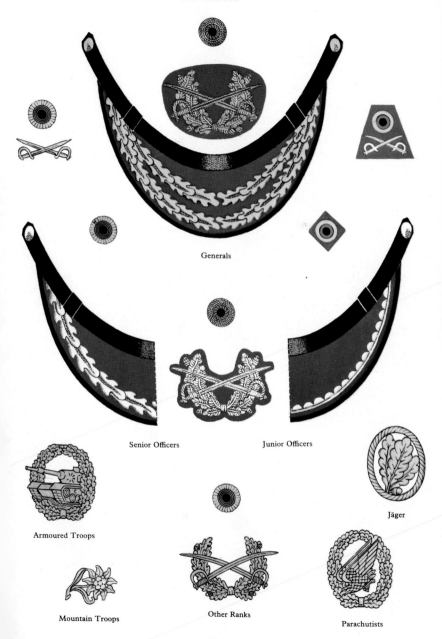

Generals

Senior Officers · Junior Officers

Armoured Troops

Mountain Troops

Other Ranks

Jäger

Parachutists

PLATE 57

OFFICERS' RANK BADGES (1955–62)

Lieutenant-General

Major-General

Brigadier-General

Colonel
(1955–56)

Colonel

Lieutenant-Colonel

Major

Captain
(1955–56)

Captain

1st Lieutenant

Lieutenant

PLATE 58

G.F.R.

N.C.O.s' RANK BADGES (1955–57)

Oberstabsfeldwebel

Stabsfeldwebel

Oberfeldwebel

Feldwebel

Stabsunteroffizier

Obergefreiter

Hauptgefreiter

Unteroffizier

Gefreiter

(1957–59)

Oberstabsfeldwebel

Stabsfeldwebel

Hauptfeldwebel

Oberfeldwebel

Feldwebel

PLATE 59

OFFICERS' RANK BADGES (1962)

General

Lieutenant-General

Major-General

Brigadier-General

Colonel

Lieutenant-Colonel

Major

Captain

1st Lieutenant

Lieutenant

PLATE 60

N.C.O.s' RANK BADGES (1962–1964 pattern)

Oberstabsfeldwebel   Stabsfeldwebel   Hauptfeldwebel

Oberfeldwebel   Feldwebel   Stabsunteroffizier   Unteroffizier

Hauptgefreiter   Obergefreiter   Gefreiter

Obergefreiter (1972)

PLATE 61

G.F.R.

Fähnrich

Oberfähnrich

Fähnrich

Fahnenjunker

Gefreiter OA

Officer Cadet star

Gefreiter UA

N.C.O. CADETS

FIELD UNIFORM RANK BADGES

PLATE 62

Infantry

Armour

Artillery

Signals

Anti-Tank

Anti-Aircraft

Engineers

Chemical

Ordnance

Medical

Quartermasters

M.P.

Band

Army Aviation

MISCELLANEOUS INSIGNIA

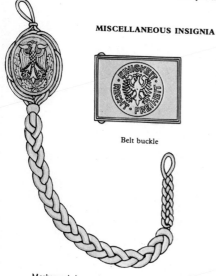

Belt buckle

Mountain Troops

Parachutists

Marksman's lanyard

Mountain Guide

Single-Handed Combat

PLATE 63

COLLAR PATCHES

Generals

G.S. Service

Infantry

Armour

Armd Reconnaissance

Artillery

Army A.A.

Engineers

Signals

Army Aviation

Band

M.P.

A.B.C. Defence

Technical Troops

Medical

Armd Infantry

Anti-Tank

Quartermasters

PLATE 64

PARACHUTISTS' WINGS

1

2

3

ARM BADGES

Medical

Pharmacists

Veterinaries

Dentists

Geographical

Storekeeper

Radio Operator

Book-keeper

Artificer

Repair Maintenance
Fitter

Radar
Fire Control

Helmsman

Diver

Fortification
Maintenance

Equipment
Inspector

Rigger

Air Protection

CUFF TITLES

Wachbataillon

Guard Battalion

Army Aviation

PLATE 65

FORMATION BADGES

Ministry of Defence

Military District
Command

H.Q. Corps and
Corps Troops

Depot

1st Armd Inf. Div.

2nd Armd Inf. Div.
(now Rifle Div.)

3rd Armd Div.

4th Armd Inf. Div.
(now Rifle Div.)

5th Armd Div.

6th Armd Inf. Div.

7th Armd Inf. Div.

1st Mountain Div.

1st Airborne Div.

10th Armd Inf. Div.
(now Armd Div.)

11th Armd Inf. Div.

12th Armd Div.

PLATE 66

CAP BADGES

Generals–Army

Officers–Border Troops

Other Ranks

BREAST BADGES

G.S. Academy
of the
Soviet Army

Military Academy
F. Engels

Mil. Medical Section
E.-M. Arndt University

Graduate
Officers

Military Academy
of the
Soviet Army

Exemplary Soldier

Proficiency
Army

Proficiency
Border Troops

Military Sports

Parachutist

PLATE 67

G.D.R.

OFFICERS' RANK BADGES

General of Army   Colonel-General   Lieutenant-General   Major-General

Colonel   Lieutenant-Colonel   Major

Captain   1st Lieutenant   Lieutenant   2nd Lieutenant

PLATE 68

N.C.O.s' RANK BADGES

Stabsfeldwebel

Oberfeldwebel

Feldwebel

Unterfeldwebel

Unteroffizier

Stabsgefreiter

Gefreiter

Bandsman

CADETS' RANK BADGES

SERVICE STRIPES

Officers' School

N.C.O.s' School

1st pattern

2nd pattern

PLATE 69

PATCHES/ARM-OF-SERVICE COLOURS

Generals' Collar and Cuff Patches

Army   Border Troops

Officers' Collar Patches

Infantry   Artillery   Armour   Services   Signals

Officers' and Other Ranks' Cuff Patches–O.R.s' Collar Patches

Engineers
Techn. Troops   Border Troops   Parachutists   Pioneers   Air Defence

PLATE 70

MISCELLANEOUS INSIGNIA

Proficiency Badges

All Arms

Armour

Qualification Badges

Tank Driver, 1st Class

Driver, 3rd Class

Signaller, 1st Class

Diver, 1st Class

Marksman's Lanyard

Infantry, Artillery and Armour

Belt Buckles

Officers

Other Ranks

PLATE 71

ARM BADGES

General Services

Chemical

Signals

Radio Location

Storekeeper

Motor-Driver
Tech. Service

Artificer

Radiotechnical

Medical

Legal

Information

Army Services

Armour

Artillery

Pioneer

Mil. Transportation

Armour
Tech. Service

Artillery
Ordnance

H.Q.
Messenger

Reconnaissance

Border Troops

Chief
Dog Handler

Diver

Pioneer

Ordnance

PLATE 72

SERVICE CHEVRONS (26.11.1945)

SHOULDER BOARDS (31.1.1947)

Generals and Officers on the Reserve List

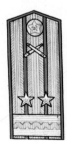

Generals and Officers on the Retired List

ARM BADGES

Parachutists (18.8.1947)   Railway Military Transport (13.2.1951)

PLATE 73

Railway Military Transport (13.2.1951)

SERVICE CHEVRONS (31.3.1952)

LAPELS OF PARADE AND ORDINARY UNIFORMS (9.4.1954)

Marshal of the Soviet Union   Supreme Marshals, Marshals and Generals

CUFFS OF PARADE UNIFORMS

PLATE 74

LAPELS AND CUFFS

Ordinary Uniforms (10.6.1954)   **Parade and Ordinary Uniforms (25.2.1955)**

Marshal
of the Soviet Union

Other Marshals
and Generals

Officers

VISORS AND CHINSTRAPS (10.6.1954)

All Marshals and Generals

Officers

BELTS (25.2.1955)

All Marshals and Generals

Officers

PLATE 75

PARADE PEAKED CAPS (1955)

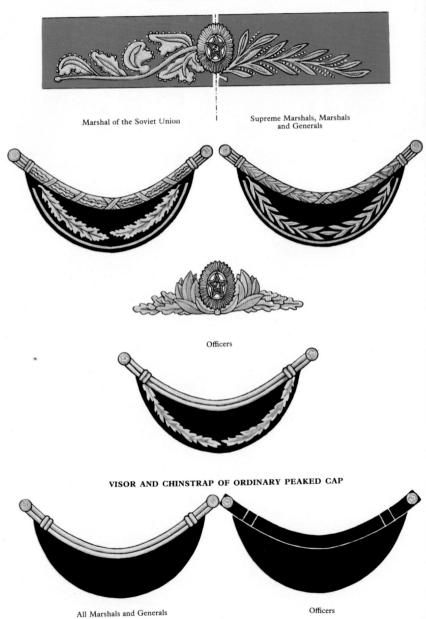

Marshal of the Soviet Union

Supreme Marshals, Marshals and Generals

Officers

VISOR AND CHINSTRAP OF ORDINARY PEAKED CAP

All Marshals and Generals

Officers

PLATE 76

ARM-OF-SERVICE BADGES (1955)

Mot. Rifle units

Parachutists

Artillery

Armour

Commissariat
Administrative

Engineers
Tech. Troops

Signals

Medical

Veterinary

Railway
Mil. Transport

Mot. Transport

Topographical

Tech. Troops

Legal

Pioneers

Band

COLLAR PATCHES FOR OVERCOAT (23.6.1955)

Marshal of the Soviet Union, Supreme Marshals, Marshals and Generals

Marshal of the Soviet Union

Medical–Veterinary

Legal

Mot. Rifle units

Artillery–Armour

Technical–Commissariat

Officers

Mot. Rifle units
Commissariat–Legal

Artillery–Armour
Technical Troops

Medical–Veterinary
Administrative

PLATE 77

Orchestra of the Regimental Garrison at Moscow (11.3.1955)

Officer and Soldier of the Honorary Guards (1.8.1955)

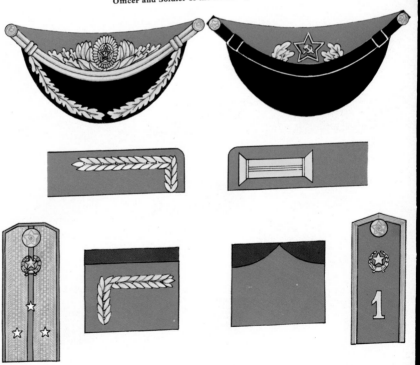

PLATE 78

Parade and Walking-Out Uniforms (22.9.1956)

Marshal of the Soviet Union   Supreme Marshals   Marshals

29.3.1958

General of Army   Colonel-General   Lieutenant-General   Major-General

Colonel   Lieutenant-Colonel   Major

PLATE 79

OFFICERS' RANK BADGES

Parade and Walking-Out Uniform (29.3.1958)

Captain

Senior Lieutenant

Lieutenant

Junior Lieutenant

Ordinary Uniform

Marshal
of the Soviet Union

Supreme Marshals

Marshals

Colonel-General

Lieutenant-Colonel

Senior Lieutenant

PLATE 80

OFFICERS' RANK BADGES

Field Uniform (29.3.1958)

All Marshals, Generals and Officers

N.C.O.s' RANK BADGES

Parade/Walking-Out and Ordinary/Field Uniforms (30.12.1955)

| Sergeant-Major | Senior Sergeant | Sergeant | Junior Sergeant | Corporal |

29.3.1958

Parade/Walking-Out   Ordinary   Field Uniform

PLATE 81

CAP BADGES AND LAPELS (29.3.1958)

Ordinary

Parade/Walking-Out

Field

Ordinary Uniforms   **Parade and Ordinary Uniforms**

Marshal
of the Soviet Union

Other Marshals
and Generals

Officers

SHOULDER BOARDS AND SERVICE CHEVRONS

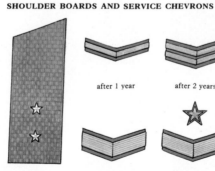

after 1 year   after 2 years   after 3 years

after 4 years   after 5–9 years   after 10 years and over

Sergeant-Major
(1963)

Warrant Officer
(1.1.1972)

BREAST BADGES

Inf. Specialist

Extended Service

Tank crew

Proficiency

PLATE 82

ARM BADGES

Traffic Controller

Mot. Rifle units

Airborne

Other Ranks
(Shoulder Strap)

Armour

Artillery

Signals

Engineers

Chemical

Railway Mil. Transport

Motor Transport

Pipeline Troops

Construction Troops

Medical/Veterinaries

Band

PLATE 83

GENERALS' AND SENIOR OFFICERS' RANK BADGES

Generals

Lieutenant-General

Major-General

Brigadier-General

Colonel-Brigadier

Senior Officers

Colonel

Lieutenant-Colonel

Major

PLATE 84

JUNIOR OFFICERS' AND WARRANT OFFICERS' RANK BADGES

Junior Officers

1st Captain

Captain

Lieutenant

2nd Lieutenant

W.O. 1st Class

Warrant Officers

W.O.

OTHER COLLAR PATCHES

Advocate Generals

Judge Advocates

Ingénieurs des
Fabrications Militaires
(Lieutenant-Colonel)

Clerks

Medical Service
(O.R.)

PLATE 85

SERGEANTS' AND CORPORALS' RANK BADGES

1st Sergeant-Major

1st Sergeant

Sergeant

Corporal

Private 1st Class

1st Sergeant-Major

1st Sergeant

Sergeant

Corporal

Private 1st Class

FRONT LINE WOUND STRIPES

SERVICE CHEVRONS

ARMLETS

Military Police

Regimental Police

PLATE 86

Royal Military School's Shoulder Cords and Badges

1st year 2nd year 3rd year 4th year 5th year

Cadet

Instructor

Polytechnic

Arm-of-Service Schools

Bde Schools and Graduates

N.C.O.s' School

Wings

Parachutist

S.A.S.

Para-Commando

Commandos Trng Centre

Parachute Instructor

P.T. Instructors

PLATE 87

FORMATION SIGNS

1st Army Corps

2nd

Home Defence
Forces

Commandos

Ground Forces Base

Airborne

1st Inf. Division   2nd Inf. Division   3rd Inf. Division   4th Inf. Division   5th Inf. Division   16th Armd Division

ARM-OF-SERVICE BADGES

Generals

General Staff

Commissaries

Advocate Generals

Judge Advocates

Medical, Veterinary
and Pharmacist Officers

Protestant, Catholic and Jewish Chaplains

Ingénieurs des
Fabrications Militaires

PLATE 88

ARM-OF-SERVICE BADGES

Carabiniers

Chasseurs-on-Foot

Grenadiers

Chasseurs of
the Ardennes

Training Centre

Parachutists

Infantry

Base Personnel

'Liberation' Bn

M.P.

Commandos

Guides

Chasseurs-on-Horse

Security

Engineers

Armd Troops School

Lancers

Royal Mil. School

Pioneers

R.A.S.C.

Artillery

Military Railways

R.A.O.C.

Band

Belgian Lion

R.E.M.E.

PLATE 89

ARM-OF-SERVICE BADGES

Trumpeters

Med. Vet. Pharm.
Service (O.R.s)

Legal Service
Clerks

Administrative Service

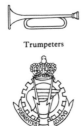

Logistical Corps

Tank Bns (Inf. Divs)

SHOULDER-STRAP NUMERALS

BERET BADGES

R.A.S.C.

Artillery

Logistical Corps

R.E.M.E.

Engineers

Administrative

Signals (1st)

R.A.O.C.

Signals (2nd)

M.P.

Medical

Army Aviation

PLATE 90

BERET BADGES
Chasseurs-on-Horse

| 1st | 2nd | 3rd | 4th |

Guides

| 1st | 2nd | 3rd | 4th |

Lancers

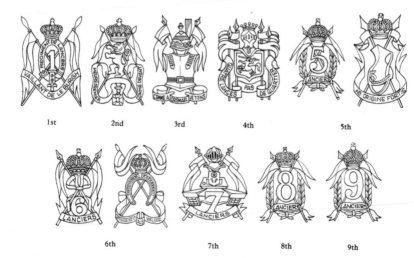

| 1st | 2nd | 3rd | 4th | 5th |

| 6th | 7th | 8th | 9th |

PLATE 91

BERET BADGES
Infantry

1st Infantry

2nd

3rd

4th

5th

6th

7th

8th

9th

11th

12th

13th

14th

Grenadiers

Chasseurs of the
Ardennes

1st Para.
Bn

2nd Commando
Bn

3rd Para.
Bn

Mortar Coy

Carabiniers

1st Chasseurs-on-
Foot

2nd

3rd

PLATE 92

BERET BADGES
Schools and Training

Royal Military School

Infantry School

Artillery School

Armoured School

Inf. Training
Staff

Engineers School

Armd Troops
Demonstration Det.

Armd Troops
Trng Centre

Cadets School

Armoured Units

1st Heavy Tank Bn

1st Heavy Tank Bn

4th Heavy Tank Bn

Carabiniers

1st Recce Sq.
(1–4)

Recce Sqs

16th Armd Div.

Missile Coy (Inf. Bde)

PLATE 93

Great Britain

Great Britain was once one of the most powerful nations in the world but, as it was a colonial power, the major share of the glory usually went to the Royal Navy.

Armies were raised in time of trouble and hurriedly disbanded as soon as peace was restored. Later, the Standing Army was divided into two separate branches, the first consisting of regular soldiers, the second of territorials (militia, volunteers, yeomanry, etc.). In peacetime both regulars and territorials were, and still are, volunteers.

In 1902 a khaki service dress was adopted and the traditional coloured uniforms were finally discarded during World War 1, and during the following decades most armies of the world adopted khaki uniforms as well.

At the end of World War 2 the British soldier wore a khaki battledress which consisted of a beret (or helmet), a blouse and trousers tucked into anklets. The belts and anklets were made of woven 'webbing' material. The berets were khaki except for those of the armoured and airborne forces and the Commandos, who wore black, maroon and green berets respectively, and the 11th Hussars, who had a beret with a scarlet band.

The officers also wore the same battledress with a peaked cap, or a service dress composed of a peaked cap, jacket with open collar and four patch pockets and trousers.

Troops serving in hot climates had appropriate uniforms made of light materials, of a sandy-yellow colour.

National Service returned after the war in 1947 and lasted until 1960. During this period the battledress was considerably improved: dark blue berets were issued to the infantry and the collar of the blouse was opened up to show the shirt and tie. Collar badges were therefore re-adopted by most regiments and some coloured shoulder titles replaced the white and red ones previously used. For instance, the Essex Regiment adopted new ones with the word 'ESSEX' in yellow on a violet background, the Green Howards with white lettering on a green background and the North Staffordshire Regiment with white and black titles.

During 1961 and 1962 battledress was replaced by the new No. 2 dress, consisting of single-breasted belted jacket of khaki barathea, with four patch pockets and matching trousers, to be worn by officers and other ranks. A combat dress of disruptive-pattern camouflage material was introduced for certain units at the same time.

Plate 1. Officers' Rank Badges

The officers' ranks have not changed since the War and the rank badges also have remained the same, with the exception of the crown which, after the coronation of Elizabeth II in 1953, was changed to the St Edward's pattern.

Field-Marshals and generals wear crossed batons and crossed baton and sword respectively; generals with stars and crowns added for each rank. The batons and swords are also shown in the cap badge. The officers of field rank wear the crown, with additional stars; the subalterns only the stars.

Since the 1950s the officers' rank badges have also been made in anodised metal, although the previous gilded and embroidered patterns are still in use.

The chaplains of the Royal Army Chaplains' Department rank as follows: Chaplain-General – Major-General; Deputy Chaplain-General – Brigadier; Chaplain 1st Class – Colonel; Chaplain 2nd Class – Lieutenant-Colonel; Chaplain 3rd Class – Major; Chaplain 4th Class – Captain.

Warrant Officers' and N.C.O.s' Rank Badges

The basic ranks are those of Warrant Officers of First and Second Class, Staff Sergeant, Sergeant, Corporal and Lance-Corporal, and a number of appointment ranks are held as well.

The title of Corporal replaces that of Sergeant in the Household Cavalry which, together with the Brigade of Guards, has no one-chevron rank.

Four chevrons pointing upwards below a crown are worn on both forearms by Squadron Quartermaster-Corporals and Staff Corporals of the Household Cavalry while Pipe-Majors of the Brigade of Guards, and Drum-Majors, Pipe-Majors, Bugle-Majors, etc., wear a small drum, bagpipe and bugle above the four chevrons. The Master Gunners and Sergeants of the Royal Artillery wear a small gun together with their rank badges; the Sergeants of the Royal Engineers have a small grenade and those of the Royal Corps of Signals wear the figure of Mercury above their chevrons. A lyre is the badge of the bandsmen.

The brass badges of the Staff Sergeant-Major, Regimental Quartermaster-Sergeant and warrant officers, and also the brass crowns, guns, drums, etc. worn with chevrons, are currently made in anodised metal. Some smaller chevrons for summer wear are also made in anodised brass. Those of the Staff Sergeant have a small crown attached to the top.

During the war the N.C.O.s' chevrons used to be composed of individual stripes whilst now they are machine-embroidered in white cotton in one, two or more stripes on khaki felt. White cotton chevrons are used on summer uniforms.

Cap Badges

All British servicemen wear the badge of the corps, department or regiment they belong to on the head-dress. The officers' and other ranks' cap badges are usually similar, although the officers have badges made of superior metals, i.e. gilt and silver plate, instead of anodised metal, and some officers' badges are also embellished with coloured enamels. The first badges made of anodised aluminium were introduced in the early 1950s and soon became the official standard O.R.s' cap badges, replacing the old brass and white metal badges previously in use.

The officers of some corps and regiments wear embroidered cap badges on the forage cap or beret and some of these badges differ from the standard pattern used on the peaked cap. All the officers of the Gurkha battalions and Gurkha Engineers wear a small variation of their usual cap badge mounted on a coloured cord boss on the peaked cap, forage cap and beret. I have illustrated only the cap badges worn by other ranks, if not stated otherwise.

The badges of the Royal Artillery, Royal Armoured Corps, Royal Engineers and the other corps and services, schools, etc., have been grouped together under the title of Arms and Services. The following is the order of precedence of the corps, etc., of the British Army:

The Life Guards and the Blues
 and Royals
Royal Horse Artillery
Royal Armoured Corps
 (Armoured Cavalry Regiments)
Royal Tank Regiment
Royal Regiment of Artillery
Corps of Royal Engineers
Royal Corps of Signals
Regiment of Foot Guards
Regiments of Infantry
Special Air Service Regiment
Army Air Corps
Royal Army Chaplains'
 Department
Royal Corps of Transport
Royal Army Medical Corps
Royal Army Ordnance Corps

Corps of Royal Electrical and
 Mechanical Engineers
Corps of Royal Military Police
Royal Army Pay Corps
Royal Army Veterinary Corps
Small Arms School Corps
Military Provost Staff Corps
Royal Army Educational Corps
Royal Army Dental Corps
Royal Pioneer Corps
Intelligence Corps
Army Physical Training Corps
Army Catering Corps
General Service Corps
Queen Alexandra's Royal Army
 Nursing Corps
Women's Royal Army Corps

Plate 2. Cap Badges
Household Cavalry and Armoured Cavalry Regiments

The Royal Dragoons (1st Dragoons), known as the Royals, was the first cavalry regiment to change cap badge after World War 2. The new badge commemorated the capture of the standard of the 105th French Regiment at Waterloo and was used previously by the Royals before 1898 and unofficially during World War 1. Finally, in 1948, the French Eagle replaced the Royal Crest and was worn until 1969, when the Royals were merged with the Royal Horse Guards to form a new regiment, the Blues and Royals.

In 1953 the Household Cavalry (Life Guards and Royal Horse Guards badges and Household Cavalry badge with Garter, used by both regiments) adopted the St Edward's Crown and the cypher of Elizabeth II on their badges.

The 1st King's Dragoon Guards and the Queen's Bays (2nd Dragoon Guards) were amalgamated in 1959 to form the Queen's Dragoon Guards. The new regiment wears the old cap badge of the King's Dragoon Guards and the collar badges of the Bays, now with the new crown.

A new cap badge was also adopted by the Royal Scots Dragoon Guards (Carabiniers and Greys), a new regiment formed by merging the 3rd Carabiniers (Prince of Wales's Dragoon Guards) and the Royal Scots Greys (2nd Dragoons). In November 1958, the Queen's Own Hussars was formed by the amalgamation of the 3rd King's Own Hussars and the 7th Queen's Own Hussars while a month earlier the 4th Queen's Own Hussars and the 8th King's Royal Irish Hussars were reformed as the Queen's Royal Irish Hussars. Later, in 1969, the 10th Royal Hussars (Prince of Wales's Own) and the 11th Hussars (Prince Albert's Own) were also amalgamated into one regiment: the Royal Hussars (Prince of Wales's Own).

The 9th Queen's Royal Lancers and the 12th Royal Lancers (Prince of Wales's) were amalgamated in September 1960 under the new name of 9th/12th Royal Lancers (Prince of Wales's).

The 4th/7th Royal Dragoon Guards and the 17th/21st Lancers are the only two regiments still wearing their old wartime badges, although now made in anodised metal. Some others changed to the St Edward's Crown and the Prussian Eagle of the 14th/20th King's Hussars at present is black, with gilded orb and sceptre.

Plate 3. Cap Badges
Arms and Services

Shortly after World War 2 a number of corps were granted the title 'Royal' in recognition of service rendered during the War: they were the Corps of Royal Military Police, The Royal Army Educational Corps, the Royal

Army Dental Corps and the Royal Pioneer Corps. The R.A.E.C. and the R.A.D.C. changed cap badges as well; the former adopted the symbolic torch of learning and the latter a dragon's head holding a sword with its teeth. New cap badges were also made for the M.P.s, with the title 'Royal' added in the scroll.

The cap badge of the Corps of Royal Engineers, then still with the 'GRVI' cypher and King's crown, was slightly changed after the war as new issues were made with a white metal wreath.

The scroll of the Royal Army Medical Corps's cap badge was changed to white metal, the motto *In Arduis Fidelis* replacing the Corps title.

After the War new cap badges were also issued to the Royal Corps of Signals, the Royal Army Ordnance Corps and the Royal Electrical and Mechanical Engineers.

During the reigns of George VI and Elizabeth II the cap badges of the Royal Army Service Corps's officers were made of silver (or chromed white metal), gilt and enamel, and those of other ranks were made of brass.

On 15 July 1965 the R.A.S.C. became the Royal Corps of Transport and, although the basic design of the badges was not altered, the new title was inscribed on the scroll and new anodised bi-metal badges were issued to the other ranks.

The Army Air Corps was formed in 1942 and its badges were worn by the Parachute Regiment and by the Glider Pilot Regiment. The year after a new badge was issued for the Parachute Regiment while the Glider Pilot Regiment continued to wear A.A.C. badges until 1950, when the A.A.C. was disbanded and a proper badge was adopted for the Glider Pilot Regiment. In due time, in 1957, the G.P.R. was also disbanded and its personnel taken over by the newly-raised Army Air Corps.

A new badge was adopted by the Army Air Corps in 1957, somewhat similar to the 1942 pattern, but without the lettering 'A.A.C.' Beret badges are worn on a dark blue square backing, and personnel of R.A.M.C., R.A.P.C., etc, attached to the A.A.C., wear their own cap badges on the blue backing.

After 1953, with the accession to the throne of Elizabeth II, all the crowns and cyphers were changed to those of the new monarch. The cap badge of the Military Provost Staff Corps is a good example as the crowned cypher is actually its badge. New badges were issued also to the Royal Horse Artillery, with the new crown and cypher, while only the crown was changed in the case of the Royal Artillery, Royal Armoured Corps, Royal Tank Regiment and Royal Army Veterinary Corps.

Plate 4. Cap Badges
Arms and Services

The crown was also changed on the badges of the Royal Army Pay Corps, Royal Pioneer Corps, Intelligence Corps, etc., illustrated in this plate. The General Service Corps has now only one badge and it also has a different role, while the former badge of the G.S.C. (Training Units) is now worn by the Junior Leaders Training Regiment.

A small white metal brazier was added to the all-brass cap badges of the Army Catering Corps after the War and, in 1973, a scroll with the words 'We Sustain' was added at the bottom.

The Mobile Defence Corps was created in 1955 as a link between the Armed Forces and the Civil Defence Forces; it was disbanded in 1959. The Special Air Service was raised in 1940 and ten years later became part of the Regular Army as a regiment.

The Women's Royal Army Corps and Queen Alexandra's Royal Army Nursing Corps were both formed on 1 February 1949 as part of the Regular Army. They are the successors of previous women's services which were raised during both World Wars.

The badge of the Army Legal Services was adopted in 1958; the officers previously appointed to the Army Legal Services Staff wore the Royal Crest, the badge of the Extra-Regimentally Employed List.

The wording on the badge of the Army Department Fire Service has been slightly changed as the letters 'W.D.' (War Department) have since disappeared and the title now reads 'Army Fire Service'.

The badge of the Royal Hospital, Chelsea, was adopted in 1945 and it is worn by the Hospital's staff.

Plate 5. Cap Badges
Miscellanea

The Control Commission, Germany, was a post-war organisation formed in the British Zone of occupied Germany. Its personnel also wore a special formation sign, illustrated on Plate 14.

The War Department Constabulary and the War Department Police (Cyprus) changed their titles in 1964: the former became the Army Department Constabulary and the latter the Army Department Police (Cyprus) and is now a depot.

The Royal Military School of Music is at Kneller Hall, Twickenham, Middlesex, and its badge was adopted in 1907. The Small Arms School Corps was formed in 1929 by the previous (1926) amalgamation of the Small Arms School and Machine Gun School. The Royal Military Academy and the Mons Officer Cadet School both train the future officers of the British Army.

Foot Guards

The cap badges of the five regiments of the Foot Guards have remained the same, with the exception of that worn by warrant officers, N.C.O.s and musicians of the Grenadier Guards, whose cypher has been changed to that of the reigning monarch. All guardsmen now wear badges made of anodised metal.

Plate 6. Cap Badges
The Brigade of Gurkhas

Gurkha soldiers have fought for the British Crown since the Pindaree War of 1817 and in 1825, at Bhurtpore, they gained their first battle honour. In 1947 there were ten Gurkha regiments and on 1 January 1948 four of these became part of the British Army while the others remained in the new Indian Army. The four regiments, together with the Gurkha Engineers, Signals, Transport Regiment, the 5th Gurkha Dog Company and the Gurkha Independent Parachute Company, were formed into the Brigade of Gurkhas which later became the bulk of the 17th Division, formed by the 48th, 63rd and 99th Gurkha Infantry Brigades (Plate 13) and other British units.

After peace was re-established in Borneo the Gurkhas were regrouped once again into the Brigade of Gurkhas, but now at reduced strength.

The 2nd King Edward VII's Own Gurkha Rifles (The Sirmoor Rifles) was raised in 1815 as the Sirmoor Battalion. The 6th Queen Elizabeth's Own Gurkha Rifles was raised in 1817, and designated the 6th Gurkha Rifles in 1903, and it assumed the present title on 1 January 1959. On the same date, the 7th Gurkha Rifles, originally raised in 1902, became the 7th Duke of Edinburgh's Own Gurkha Rifles. The 10th Princess Mary's Own Gurkha Rifles was raised in 1890 as the 1st Regiment of Burma Infantry; it became the 10th Gurkha Rifles in 1901 and Princess Mary's Regiment in 1949.

The officers wear a regimental badge similar to that of the other ranks on the slouch hat while on the peaked cap, forage cap and beret they wear a small replica of the same badge on a coloured cord boss; red for the 2nd and black for the other regiments and for the Engineers. The officers of the Sirmoor Rifles have a red and green diced cloth backing under the slouch hat badge, the other ranks wear black badges on red backing. The small badge worn on the cord boss by the officers of the 10th Gurkha Rifles has no scroll.

The Royal Crown and the cypher of the Duke of Edinburgh were added on the badges of the 6th and 7th Gurkha Rifles in 1959 when they became affiliated to the Queen and the Duke of Edinburgh.

The Gurkha Engineers, Signals, Transport Regiment and Military

Police were all formed after 1948 and the last was disbanded in 1965. The Transport Regiment was formed in 1958 as the Gurkha Army Service Corps: it was renamed the Gurkha Transport Regiment in 1965.

A cap badge similar to that of the Staff Band, but with 'Boys' between the handles of the kukris, is worn by the Boys' Company.

Infantry Regiments

In 1946 the title 'Royal' was granted to the Lincolnshire, Leicestershire, and Hampshire Regiments in recognition of their past service, and the new title was added onto their cap badges. In the case of the Royal Lincolnshire, the word 'Egypt', on a tablet below the Sphinx, was changed from Old English to modern lettering.

In 1951 the Dorsetshire Regiment was renamed the Dorset Regiment and its title changed on the scroll. The following year a new badge was granted to the Green Howards (Alexandra, Princess of Wales's Own Yorkshire Regiment). It should be mentioned that there are two versions of the previous cap badge of the Green Howards as, during World War 2, some were made with the king's crown instead of the traditional coronet.

In 1956 Prince Alfred's cypher in the centre of the Wiltshire Regiment's cap badge was changed to that of Philip, Duke of Edinburgh, who in 1954 became Colonel-in-Chief of the regiment.

Two years later the Rifle Brigade adopted a new cap badge, with a Guelphic crown and without battle honours on the surrounding wreath. Sometime after World War 2 the fleur-de-lis of the Manchester Regiment and the cap badge of the King's Own Yorkshire Light Infantry were changed to white metal.

Post-War Reorganisation of the British Army (Brigades)

Traditionally, each regiment of the British infantry was composed of two regular battalions and a number of territorial battalions. One regular battalion was normally at home and the other overseas so that a man's service could be spent partly in Britain and partly abroad, still in the same regiment. After World War 2 the Army was reorganised and the infantry regiments lost their second regular battalion.

In 1947 all the battalions were organised into the Training Brigade Groups (Plate 12), each battalion representing its regiment.

Following the recommendations contained in the 1957 White Paper all the regiments of the Infantry of the Line were grouped into fourteen brigades, as far as possible on the basis of regional affinity. Each brigade should have been composed of three or four battalions, each representing a regiment of the 1957 Regular Army. However, as there were too many battalions to fit into the fourteen brigades, a number of regimental amalgamations became necessary.

Between the years 1958 and 1961 the following amalgamations took place:

20 January 1959
The Royal Scots Fusiliers } The Royal Highland Fusiliers
The Highland Light Infantry } (Princess Margaret's Own Glasgow
  (City of Glasgow Regiment) } and Ayrshire Regiment)

14 October 1959
The Queen's Royal Regiment (West Surrey) } The Queen's Royal Surrey
The East Surrey Regiment } Regiment

1 March 1961
The Buffs (Royal East Kent Regiment) } The Queen's Own Buffs,
The Queen's Own Royal West Kent Regiment } The Royal Kent Regiment

1 October 1959
The King's Own Royal Regiment (Lancaster) } The King's Own Royal
The Border Regiment } Border Regiment

1 September 1958
The King's Regiment (Liverpool) } The King's Regiment (Manchester and
The Manchester Regiment } Liverpool)

1 July 1958
The East Lancashire Regiment } The Lancashire Regiment
The South Lancashire Regiment } (Prince of Wales's Volunteers)
  (The Prince of Wales's Volunteers) }

29 August 1959
The Royal Norfolk Regiment } 1st East Anglian Regiment (Royal Norfolk
The Suffolk Regiment } and Suffolk

1 June 1960
The Royal Lincolnshire Regiment } 2nd East Anglian Regiment (Duchess of
The Northamptonshire Regiment } Gloucester's Own Royal Lincolnshire
  } and Northamptonshire)

2 June 1958
The Bedfordshire and Hertfordshire Regiment } 3rd East Anglian Regiment
The Essex Regiment } (16th/44th)

17 May 1958
The Devonshire Regiment } The Devonshire and Dorset Regiment
The Dorset Regiment }

9 June 1959

The Royal Berkshire Regiment
   (Princess Charlotte of Wales's) } The Duke of Edinburgh's
The Wiltshire Regiment (Duke of Edinburgh's) Royal Regiment (Berk-
shire and Wiltshire)

6 October 1959

The Somerset Light Infantry (Prince Albert's) } The Somerset and Cornwall
The Duke of Cornwall's Light Infantry   Light Infantry

25 April 1958

The West Yorkshire Regiment
   (The Prince of Wales's Own) } The Prince of Wales's Own
The East Yorkshire Regiment   Regiment of Yorkshire
   (The Duke of York's Own)

31 January 1959

The South Staffordshire Regiment
The North Staffordshire Regiment } The Staffordshire Regiment (The
   (The Prince of Wales's)   Prince of Wales's)

7 February 1961

The Seaforth Highlanders (Ross-shire Buffs,
   The Duke of Albany's) } The Queen's Own Highlanders
The Queen's Own Cameron Highlanders   (Seaforth and Camerons)

Plate 7. Cap Badges
Brigades

The remaining infantry regiments, reduced to battalion strength, were grouped into fourteen brigades whose personnel wore brigade cap badges and regimental collar badges. The Midland Brigade was retitled Forester Brigade and was disbanded in 1963.

The following is the list of these brigades with their component regiments:

The Lowland Brigade
   The Royal Scots (The Royal Regiment)
   The Royal Highland Fusiliers (Princess Margaret's Own Glasgow and Ayrshire
      Regiment)
   The King's Own Scottish Borderers
   The Cameronians (Scottish Rifles)

The Home Counties Brigade
   The Queen's Royal Surrey Regiment
   The Queen's Own Buffs, The Royal Kent Regiment
   The Royal Sussex Regiment
   The Middlesex Regiment (Duke of Cambridge's Own)

The Lancastrian Brigade
The King's Own Royal Border Regiment
The King's Regiment (Manchester and Liverpool)
The Lancashire Regiment (Prince of Wales's Volunteers)
The Loyal Regiment (North Lancashire)

The Fusilier Brigade
The Royal Northumberland Fusiliers
The Royal Fusiliers (City of London Regiment)
The Lancashire Fusiliers
The Royal Warwickshire Fusiliers – formerly part of the Forester Brigade

The Midland Brigade – retitled Forester Brigade – disbanded in 1963
The Royal Warwickshire Regiment
The Royal Leicestershire Regiment
The Sherwood Foresters (Nottinghamshire and Derbyshire Regiment)

The East Anglian Brigade
1st East Anglian Regiment (Royal Norfolk and Suffolk)
2nd East Anglian Regiment (Duchess of Gloucester's Own Royal Lincolnshire
and Northamptonshire)
3rd East Anglian Regiment (16th/44th)
The Royal Leicestershire Regiment – formerly part of the Forester Brigade

The Wessex Brigade
The Devonshire and Dorset Regiment
The Gloucestershire Regiment
The Royal Hampshire Regiment
The Duke of Edinburgh's Royal Regiment (Berkshire and Wiltshire)

The Light Infantry Brigade
The Somerset and Cornwall Light Infantry
The King's Own Yorkshire Light Infantry
The King's Shropshire Light Infantry
The Durham Light Infantry

The Yorkshire Brigade
The Prince of Wales's Own Regiment of Yorkshire
The Green Howards (Alexandra, Princess of Wales's Own Yorkshire Regiment)
The Duke of Wellington's Regiment (West Riding)
The York and Lancaster Regiment

The Mercian Brigade
The Cheshire Regiment
The Worcestershire Regiment
The Staffordshire Regiment (The Prince of Wales's)
The Sherwood Foresters (Nottinghamshire and Derbyshire Regiment) –
formerly part of the Forester Brigade

113

The Welsh Brigade
The Royal Welch Fusiliers
The South Wales Borderers
The Welch Regiment

The North Irish Brigade
The Royal Inniskilling Fusiliers
The Royal Ulster Rifles
The Royal Irish Fusiliers

The Highland Brigade
The Black Watch (Royal Highland Regiment)
Queen's Own Highlanders (Seaforth and Camerons)
The Gordon Highlanders
The Argyll and Sutherland Highlanders (Princess Louise's)

The Green Jackets Brigade
1st Green Jackets (43rd/52nd)
2nd Green Jackets (The King's Royal Rifle Corps)
3rd Green Jackets (The Rifle Brigade)

Officers' and other ranks' versions of the brigade cap badges have been used during the decade of their existence. The former wore gilded and silver plated badges as a rule, the latter anodised badges, although some embroidered and enamelled variations have been made for the officers. There are also two sizes of the officer's cap badge of the East Anglian Brigade.

Some regiments used to wear coloured cloth backings under the cap badges, for instance the Lancashire Regiment wore a $1\frac{3}{4}$-in. square yellow backing, the King's Own Royal Border Regiment a $1\frac{3}{4}$-in. square scarlet backing, and the King's Regiment a $1\frac{3}{4} \times 2$-in. scarlet backing. All three were part of the Lancastrian Brigade.

Divisions

The brigades lasted until 1968 when, on 1 July, the infantry was reorganised into the divisional structure. Six divisions were created, each formed by a number of regiments; thus the brigade cap badges were gradually replaced by regimental cap badges.

The Brigade of Guards became the Guards Division, formed by the old five regiments: the Grenadier, Coldstream, Scots, Irish and Welsh Guards.

A list of the other divisions, with their component regiments, is given below:

The Queen's Division
    The Queen's Regiment
    The Royal Regiment of Fusiliers
    The Royal Anglian Regiment

The King's Division
    The King's Own Royal Border Regiment
    The King's Regiment (Manchester and Liverpool)
    The Prince of Wales's Own Regiment of Yorkshire
    The Green Howards (Alexandra, Princess of Wales's Own Yorkshire Regiment)
    The Royal Irish Rangers (27th (Inniskilling) 83rd and 87th)
    The Queen's Lancashire Regiment
    The Duke of Wellington's Regiment (West Riding)

The Prince of Wales's Division
    The Devonshire and Dorset Regiment
    The Cheshire Regiment
    The Royal Welch Fusiliers
    The Royal Regiment of Wales (24th/41st Foot)
    The Gloucestershire Regiment
    The Worcestershire and Sherwood Foresters Regiment (29th/45th Foot)
    The Royal Hampshire Regiment
    The Staffordshire Regiment (The Prince of Wales's)
    The Duke of Edinburgh's Royal Regiment (Berkshire and Wiltshire)

The Scottish Division
    The Royal Scots (The Royal Regiment)
    The Royal Highland Fusiliers (Princess Margaret's Own Glasgow and Ayrshire
        Regiment)
    The King's Own Scottish Borderers
    The Black Watch (Royal Highland Regiment)
    Queen's Own Highlanders (Seaforth and Camerons)
    The Gordon Highlanders
    The Argyll and Sutherland Highlanders (Princess Louise's)

The Light Division
    The Light Infantry
    The Royal Green Jackets

Plate 8. Cap Badges
Infantry Regiments

The Home Counties Brigade was reorganised as a 'large' regiment on 31 December 1966. The newly-born Queen's Regiment was formed by four battalions:

    1st Bn The Queen's Regiment (Queen's Surreys)
    2nd Bn The Queen's Regiment (Queen's Own Buffs)

3rd Bn The Queen's Regiment (Royal Sussex)
4th Bn The Queen's Regiment (Middlesex)

A new cap badge and new collar badge were adopted, incorporating the motifs of the four previous regimental badges.

On 23 April 1968 (St George's Day) the Fusiliers Brigade became the Royal Regiment of Fusiliers, composed of the former Brigade's four battalions.

The Brigade's cap badge and collar badges were retained by the Regiment, but the red and white hackle was adopted by all the battalions, instead of the different colours previously worn.

The third regiment of the Queen's Division is the Royal Anglian Regiment, which was formed on 1 September 1964 from the East Anglian Brigade. Its battalions are:

1st (Norfolk and Suffolk) Bn
2nd (Duchess of Gloucester's Own Lincolnshire and Northamps) Bn
3rd (16th/44th Foot) Bn
4th (Leicestershire) Bn, the Royal Anglian Regiment

The design of the cap badge remained similar to that of the Brigade; however the title in the scroll was changed to 'Royal Anglian'. Each battalion retained its individual collar badge.

The King's Division was formed on 1 July 1968 by the Lancastrian and Yorkshire Brigade and by the Royal Irish Rangers, formerly the North Irish Brigade.

The Lancastrian Brigade contributed three regiments only, as the Lancashire Regiment (Prince of Wales's Volunteers) and the Loyal Regiment (North Lancashire) were amalgamated in March 1970 to form the Queen's Lancashire Regiment. New cap badges were issued to all three regiments.

The York and Lancaster Regiment, of the Yorkshire Brigade, was disbanded in December 1968 and the remaining three regiments joined the King's Division. The Duke of Wellington's Regiment (West Riding) resumed its old pre-1958 cap badge, while the other two regiments adopted new ones.

On 1 July 1968 the North Irish Brigade was converted into one regiment, the Royal Irish Rangers, formed by three battalions. The 3rd Battalion was disbanded at Catterick in December 1968, and its operational role was taken over by the 1st Battalion, which moved up to Catterick from Worcester. The battalions are known simply as the 1st and 2nd Bns of the Royal Irish Rangers. The regimental cap badge is similar to that of the Brigade except for the title scroll which now reads 'Royal Irish Rangers'. A new collar badge has also been adopted.

The Wessex, Mercian and Welsh Brigades contributed to the formation of the Prince of Wales's Division.

The four battalions of the Wessex Brigade regained regimental status, although the Glosters and the Royal Hampshires were due to amalgamate in 1970. The latter readopted their old regimental cap badges while the other two regiments, the Devonshire and Dorset and the Duke of Edinburgh's, used their previous brigade's collar badges as head-dress badges.

The Worcestershire Regiment and the Sherwood Foresters were amalgamated at Bulford on 28 February 1970 and a 'combined' cap badge was adopted by the new regiment known as the Worcestershire & Sherwood Foresters. The other two units of the Mercian Brigade, the Cheshire and the Staffordshire Regiments, became independent regiments, the former with its old cap badge while the latter adopted its previous collar badge as cap badge.

The Welsh Brigade contributed with only two regiments as, in 1969, the South Wales Borderers and the Welch Regiment were merged to form the Royal Regiment of Wales (24th/41st Foot).

The Royal Welch Fusiliers resumed their own pre-1958 regimental cap badge.

The Scottish Division was formed on 1 July 1968 by the Lowland and Highland Brigades. Originally, it was planned to disband the fourth regiment of each brigade, but only the Cameronians (Scottish Rifles) were disbanded in May 1968; the Argyll and Sutherland Highlanders were reduced to a small 'tradition' detachment, the Balaklava Company. One year after, however, the Argylls were back, at battalion strength, as a regiment of the Scottish Division.

New cap badges were adopted by the Royal Highland Fusiliers (Princess Margaret's Own Glasgow and Ayrshire Regiment) and Queen's Own Highlanders (Seaforth and Camerons) while the other regiments were issued with pre-1958 badges, now made of anodised metal.

The Light Division was formed by two newly-constituted regiments: the Light Infantry and the Royal Green Jackets.

The Light Infantry Brigade became a regiment on 10 July 1968 (Light Infantry Day) and the Brigade's four regiments became the 1st, 2nd, 3rd and 4th Bns, The Light Infantry. The cap badge remained that of the Light Infantry Brigade and a smaller version of it was adopted as a regimental collar badge. As is usual for bugle badges, they are worn in pairs, mouthpieces towards the opening of the collar.

Already in 1958 the battalions of the Green Jackets Brigade had established a common drill, except for the mess kit and the regimental titles worn on the shoulder straps. Although remaining regiments in theory, the components of the Brigade assumed numerical Battalion denomination and finally, on 1 January 1966, the Brigade was redesig-

nated the Royal Green Jackets, a 'large' regiment composed of the
following battalions:

> 1st Bn the Royal Green Jackets (43rd & 52nd)
> 2nd Bn The Royal Green Jackets (The King's Royal Rifle Corps)
> 3rd Bn The Royal Green Jackets (The Rifle Brigade)

A new cap badge was adopted by the regiment and on 15 June 1968 a
new shoulder title, the same for all three battalions, was taken into use. It
consists of the letters 'RGJ' in Old English script, surmounted by a bugle.

The process of amalgamation and integration of these regiments has
been long and painful. Several of them, already reduced to company
strength, were subsequently reformed as battalions. The projected
amalgamation of the Gloucestershire and Royal Hampshire Regiments
should have taken place in 1970. A new cap badge was made for the new
regiment which, however, never materialised.

Plate 9. Other Cap Badges

Field-Marshals wear an embroidered cap badge consisting of two crossed
batons on a wreath, surmounted by the Royal Crest. Generals wear a
similar badge but with a sword and a baton, instead of crossed batons, in
its centre. Brigadiers and Substantive (full) Colonels wear only the
Royal Crest.

Field-Marshals and Generals (including Chaplains-General) are also
entitled to a double row of gold oak leaves on the visor of the peaked cap
and the Brigadiers and Substantive Colonels (including chaplains of
equivalent rank), to one row only, embroidered at the front of the visor.

Field officers (not Rifle and Light Infantry regiments) have a plain gold
$\frac{3}{4}$-in. stripe, while field officers of the Rifle regiments wear one row of
black oak leaves and those of the Light Infantry regiments a silver $\frac{3}{4}$-in.
stripe.

The officers below field rank wear peaked caps with plain visor, although
gold stripes are worn by all officers of some regiments and gold or brass
stripes by the other ranks of the Guards.

The chaplains, both Christian and Jewish, are all officers and wear cap
badges made of silver, gilt and enamel, or plain black ones.

A special badge is worn by personnel of the Army Department Fleet,
formerly known as the War Department Fleet. The formation sign worn
by these units is shown on Plate 16.

Formation Signs

A great number of wartime formation signs which were worn on the upper
sleeve were kept in use for years after World War 2 and many are still worn
nowadays. Due to the post-war reorganisation of the British Army many

new formation signs have been adopted as well. However, the great majority of World War 2 signs have by now (1973) disappeared and the old ones still in use are normally slightly different from the originals; thus they can easily be recognised as modern patterns.

As it is difficult to separate the signs of the Regular Army from those worn by the territorials without creating confusion, both types have been illustrated together. Many of these had already been adopted during the last war but were in use after the War as well.

Formation signs worn by units smaller than brigades have not been included.

Plate 10. Formation Signs
Home Commands

During World War 2 the United Kingdom was militarily divided into Home Commands which, in turn, were divided into Districts. The same organisation, although modified in its structure, was maintained for many years after the War.

The South-Eastern Command was disbanded in 1944 and its former territory absorbed by the Southern and Eastern Commands. The formation sign of the latter was changed in 1947 and also, during the same year, the small sign of the Northern Command was replaced by the shield-shaped badge.

The Northumbrian District, the North Midland District and the three Yorkshire Ridings were all part of the Northern Command.

The badge of the Southern Command is based on a simplified design of the Southern Cross constellation and each branch of service of the Command wore the same badge, but in its arm-of-service colours. Miscellaneous units of the Southern Command wore their own sign, horizontally divided into black and red; however, some embroidered signs have been made with dark blue, instead of black, felt at the top. The colours have also been misplaced on some other Southern Command formation signs as in the case of the last shield illustrated, worn by the R.A.D.C. Note the difference between this badge and the one above, which is the correct one.

Garrisons and Other Formations

The formation sign of the Orkney and Shetland Defences was a red fouled anchor embroidered on dark blue felt. The same anchor, but smaller and on a round background, was adopted after the War by the local T.A. units, nominally the Orkney and Zetland Battery, 540 Regt (The Lovat Scouts), R.A.

After the War the White Rose of Yorkshire on a black background became the emblem of the East and West Ridings Area (Northern Command) and the Tudor Rose was adopted by the newly-formed Catterick

District in 1947. The District previously had been part of the Northumbrian and also of the North Riding Districts and, in 1952, it became part of the Northumbrian District once again. In the 1960s Catterick Camp was the headquarters of the Yorkshire District and the Tudor Rose on green background was the formation sign of the District. Northumbrian District ceased to exist on 31 December 1972 and the new North East District with headquarters in York took over all the territories previously controlled by Northumbrian and Yorkshire Districts.

The formation sign of Force 135 (Channel Islands Liberation Force) represents the three lions of the arms of Jersey and Guernsey.

There are two patterns of the Anti-Aircraft Command's formation sign, both in embroidered and printed variations. The main difference is that in the first pattern the bow was round, and without the handle.

The British troops in Northern Ireland and the personnel of 6th Corps wore a similar sign, the former a red gate and the latter a green gate, both on black rectangular background.

Plate 11. Formation Signs
Districts

All the Scottish districts belonged to the Scottish Command; only two districts remained after the War, the Highland District, now wearing the formation sign of the former North Highland District, and the Lowland District, with the sign of the former West Scotland District.

The first formation sign of the Northern Ireland District showed a bird in a nest (the Latin for nest is *nid*). Subsequently, the badge was changed to the typical 'Irish' gate, in white on emerald green background.

The formation sign of the West Lancashire District consists of the emblems of Cheshire, Lancashire and Staffordshire. It ceased to exist in 1944 when its territory was absorbed by its neighbouring districts of Western Command: the Lancashire and Border District, renamed North Western District, and the North Wales District, which became the Midland West District.

The Central Midland District was renamed East Central District and remained part of the Eastern Command.

The County of Essex was initially administered by the 2nd Corps and, subsequently, by the Essex and Suffolk District (Eastern Command) whose formation sign depicted the Suffolk Castle and the Seaxes of Essex on a shield, in full colour. The colours were changed to black and yellow in 1944 when it became part of the East Anglian District and, finally, in 1946 the District adopted the viking's head as its emblem.

The disbandment of the South-Eastern Command in 1944 also caused many changes in the organisation of the Southern District: the Hampshire and Dorset District became the Aldershot and Hampshire District and

Dorset joined Wiltshire (previously Salisbury Plain District) to form the new Wiltshire and Dorset District. Most of the forces which invaded Europe in June 1944 embarked from the counties of Hampshire and Dorset; thus the District's badge symbolises Victory setting out for the invasion. The Aldershot District was formed in 1948.

During the war the North Kent and Surrey District (South-Eastern Command) used two formation signs both depicting the rampant White Horse of Kent. The first badge was round and showed only the horse's head.

A Canadian Corps administered the area that later became the Sussex District of South-Eastern Command. The East Kent District, also, was part of the same Command and later, as Home Counties District, it became part of the Eastern Command.

The reorganisation of several districts has taken place since the war and many badges have been abolished or modified. The St Oswald's Shield in the formation sign of the Northumbrian District, initially composed of six red and yellow stripes, was later changed to eight stripes and the francolin partridge of the South Western District (Southern Command) was replaced by the Golden Hind on a green background. The London District was part of the Southern Command.

The bell in the formation sign of the South Midland District (Southern Command) is the Great Tom of Christ Church, Oxford, and the archer in the badge of the North Midland District (Northern Command) is Robin Hood. In 1948 a new formation sign depicting the Irish Harp was adopted by the North Ireland District.

Plate 12. Formation Signs
Army Corps

The 1st Corps was reformed in Germany in the early 1950s and, once again, the white spearhead became its emblem. It should be noted that during the War each branch of service of the Corps wore the spearhead on a background divided in arm-of-service colours.

The first pattern of the 2nd Corps badge was a fish on a blue and white wavy background but later a much simpler badge was devised, similar to that of 1st Corps. It is a figure '2' on a red diamond.

Divisions

The white triangle of the 1st Infantry Division symbolically stands for the top of the spearhead of the 1st Corps badge, as the Division is the first division of 1st Corps. This formation sign used to be on a black or khaki background or on its own. Specimens can also be found with a narrow red edging, worn by infantry units, or with yellow edging for the divisional armoured units. The divisional artillery, signals, etc., wear the white triangle on a diamond-shaped background of arm-of-service colours.

The formation sign of the 4th Division initially was the fourth quadrant of a circle made of red felt. Later it was changed to a red circle with the fourth quadrant detached, on a white background. A third pattern has since been adopted in printed or woven variations, similar to the second but on a black background.

The 40th Division was formed in 1949 and took part in the Korean War. Its badge is represented by a cockerel on a black square or rectangular background and originates from a similar badge worn by the homonymous division during World War 1.

The 1st Commonwealth Division also fought in Korea and was raised out there from British and Commonwealth troops in 1951. There are in existence two slightly different variations of the same badge.

The 42nd (Lancashire) Division was raised in 1947 as one of the new territorial divisions, in place of the 42nd (East Lancashire) and 55th (West Lancashire). The new divisional sign incorporates the red diamond of the 42nd and the red rose of the 55th Divisions.

The wartime badge of the 44th (Home Counties) Division was a plain red oval which in 1947 was combined with the shield of the East Kent District, and later changed to a third pattern, with a yellow trident in its centre.

Both 48th (South Midlands) and 54th (East Anglian) Divisions adopted brand new formation signs when they were re-raised after the war as T.A. divisions. The Saxon Crown is the centrepiece of both badges.

In 1947 the 56th (London) Division became an armoured T.A. division and adopted a new emblem, the knight's helmet and the sword, more suited to its new role. In 1950, however, the wartime badge, Dick Whittington's Cat, was resumed, now with a sword superimposed on the cat.

Another black cat, but on a khaki background, was the badge of the 17th Indian Division from 1943. Later the background was changed to yellow and the Division became the 17th British Division in Malaya, which in 1965 became the Malaya District.

The badge of the 17th Gurkha Division was worn during the War by the 43rd Lorried Infantry Brigade.

Some other divisions have been reformed as well in the last twenty-eight years but wear their old wartime formation signs. Some brigades wear old divisional signs. Although the design of these badges has remained the same, the manufacture has often changed. There are now formation signs of the 6th Armoured Division with the mailed fist on a blue background and many modern badges are considerably smaller than their wartime counterparts.

Training Brigade Groups

The first post-war army reorganisation took place in 1947 with the creation of the Training Brigade Groups, intended to group the existing infantry regiments on the basis of their regional affinity.

Each group wore a new formation sign, embroidered on felt or printed, on the left sleeve of the battledress.

Plate 13. Formation Signs
Brigades

A number of these formation signs used to be worn during the War and others have been adopted since 1945.

The 1st and 4th Guards Brigades have readopted the old badge of the Guards Armoured Division with the addition of Roman figures 'I' and 'IV' below the eye. The 2nd Guards Brigade's badge was adopted in Malaya in 1947 whilst the 2nd Infantry Brigade initially wore the white triangle of the 1st Division, later changed to the badge illustrated.

The 3rd was an Infantry Brigade Group. After the War the 2nd Division was stationed in the Far East and its 5th Brigade was part of the British Commonwealth Occupational Forces in Japan. In 1946 the 53rd (Welsh) Division, then in Europe, was renamed the 2nd Division. Thus the 4th, 5th and 6th Brigades of the latter, still in the Far East, became independent and were renumbered the 24th, 25th and 26th Independent Infantry Brigades. The 5th Brigade had the same sign as the 2nd Division, but slightly smaller and, as 25th Independent Infantry Brigade, adopted a new formation sign which incorporated the divisional crossed keys and a 'Torii' gate to commemorate its service in Japan. Only one key, crossed with a bayonet, is shown in the latest badge of the 5th Infantry Brigade and the 6th has the same motif but with inverted colours. The 8th is also an Infantry Brigade and the 11th used to wear the woven formation sign of the former 78th Division. There are two versions of the 12th Infantry Brigade badge as the H.Q. personnel wore a fouled anchor on a blue diamond. The personnel of the 17th Infantry Brigade also wore two different badges; the triangular one symbolised the Nile Delta but later, in 1952, it was changed to a yellow arrow pointing upwards on a scarlet rectangle. The 18th Infantry Brigade was also composed of British and Gurkha units, thus a bayonet and a kukri are represented on its badge. The first pattern of the formation sign of the 19th Infantry Brigade had the top point of the triangle cut off; the second pattern is illustrated.

A penguin was the symbol of the 22nd Beach Brigade and the badge of the 264th (Scottish) Beach Brigade (T.A.) was composed of the St Andrew's Cross of the former 52nd (Lowland) Division and the sign of the Beach Groups (Plate 16). The 23rd, the 29th and the 72nd were the British

Brigade Groups stationed in India after the War. As well as the 25th Infantry Brigade there was a 25th Armoured Brigade which had a badge similar to that of the former 1st Armoured Division.

The badge of the 27th Independent Infantry Brigade was used until 1949, when the Brigade became part of the 40th Division; some have red and others yellow numerals.

The Cross of St Andrew is present in the formation sign of the 30th (Lowland) Independent Armoured Brigade (T.A.) and again in that of the 155th Independent Infantry Brigade.

Another three badges have been worn by T.A. units, namely the 107th (Ulster) Independent Brigade Group and the 161st and 162nd Independent Infantry Brigade Groups.

The 39th was also an Independent Infantry Brigade Group which has worn, in turn, two different badges. The 31st, 49th, 50th and 51st are Independent Infantry Brigades; the 160th and 302nd are Infantry Brigades.

The formation signs of the Brigades of Gurkhas are similar: they all show the crossed kukris on different coloured backgrounds.

Plate 14. Formation Signs
British Forces Overseas

A great number of formation signs have been worn by British forces stationed overseas but obvious space limitations compel me to show only part of these. Therefore I have purposely left out all the formation signs which, together with cap badges, I will be able to show, properly grouped into separate chapters, in another volume, i.e. Africa, India, West Indies, Gibraltar, Malta, etc.

Some of the badges illustrated have been worn during the War and others after the War. The designs of all the formation signs of the British Army of the Rhine (B.A.O.R.) derive from that of the 21st Army Group which became the B.A.O.R. in 1945. The blue cross on red or yellow shields was worn by line of communication troops in France and in the Netherlands respectively. The British troops in Berlin originally wore a red ring on a black circle and the title was added only in 1952.

In 1945 the 8th Army occupied Austria while its 13th Corps remained in the North-East of Italy where it became the British Element Trieste Force (BETFOR). In Austria the former 8th Army sign was usually worn and the personnel of the Allied Commission, Austria, wore the same badge with the letters 'ACA' added above the shield. Personnel of the H.Q. British Commonwealth Forces in Japan wore the formation sign which later was adopted by the British Commonwealth Forces in Korea.

The Cyrenaica and Tripolitania Districts were administrative organisations created during the war. The first pattern of the Cyrenaica District's badge was black on a white background and some slightly different variations exist of the Tripolitania District's badge as well. A Malayan kris on maroon background was the badge of the H.Q. Commonwealth Overseas Land Force.

The two small white triangles in the badge in the Canal South District (Middle East Land Forces) stand for a boat's sail and its reflection in Suez Canal waters. In the badge of the Canal North District the boat is at the top right of the formation sign. A blue fish was the emblem of the North Palestine District.

Plate 15. Formation Signs
Army Groups, Royal Artillery

Regular and Territorial Army formation signs of the A.G.R.A. have been illustrated side by side and the backgrounds of most show the colours of the Royal Artillery, red and blue.

The 2nd A.G.R.A. adopted the symbol of Taurus, the second sign of the zodiac, whilst the 86th A.G.R.A. (T.A.) wore the badge used by the 6th during the war, the sixth sign of the zodiac. The 3rd A.G.R.A. had two badges, a gun barrel and later the Roman 'III' on R.A. colours.

The 84th and 85th were Scottish territorial units and so was the 87th A.G.R.A. (Field), which used at one time to wear the badge of the 55th (West Lancashire) Division. The 88th, 89th, 90th and 91st were all Field Artillery units and most of the following were Anti-Aircraft Artillery units.

The formation sign of the 94th A.G.R.A. (A.A.) (T.A.) shows the Cheshire Garb and the Red Rose of Lancashire and that of the 96th, the Liver Buildings on the River Mersey. The Eros of Piccadilly Circus is the centrepiece of the formation sign of the 97th, a London A.A. unit.

An East Anglian windmill is depicted in the badge of the 98th and the Sussex Martlets is that of the 99th. The Hampshire Rose and the white and green bars of Wiltshire appear in the badge of the 100th A.G.R.A. (A.A.) (T.A.), together with the Royal Artillery colours.

Coast Brigades, Royal Artillery

Four Coast Brigades wore the three badges illustrated as the 102nd Brigade adopted the sign of the former 104th, a unit of Western Command. The 105th was a Scottish unit and all were part of the Territorial Army.

Anti-Aircraft Brigades, Royal Artillery

The 30th, 31st, 33rd and 34th Anti-Aircraft Brigades, R.A., wore their own formation signs; the 30th initially adopted a badge similar to that of the A.A. Command (Plate 10), later changed to the Roman 'XXX' on Royal Artillery colors.

A number of other Royal Artillery formation signs have been illustrated at the bottom of this plate: they mainly refer to training units. The Maritime Anti-Aircraft Artillery was formed in 1941 and consisted of A.A. gunners aboard ships which were not part of the Royal Navy. They wore a typical naval formation sign with the additional letters 'AA' which were later changed to 'R A' alongside the anchor.

Plate 16. Formation Signs
Engineer Groups

The Engineer Groups were all territorial units whose local connections were usually displayed on their formation signs. For instance, the first pattern of the sign of the 22nd Engineer Group (T.A.) was that of the Northumbrian District with the R.E. grenade embroidered on the St Oswald shield. The 24th Engineer Group (T.A.) had three different patterns of formation sign. The first one had a small replica of the badge of the 55th (West Lancashire) Division in its centre; in the second pattern the Staffordshire Knot was added below the rose and the final badge was a yellow shield with the Red Rose of Lancashire, the Cheshire Garb and the Staffordshire Knot. The 25th was a unit of Essex and the White Horse of Wiltshire was on the formation sign of the 26th. The 29th was a Scottish engineer group.

Port Task Forces, Royal Engineers

All three formation signs of the Port Task Forces have a blue background and depict marine symbols.

Some other formation signs illustrated in this plate belong to training units, depots and specialised branches of the Royal Engineers.

Miscellanea

The formation signs of the War Office and of the War Office Controlled Units were adopted in 1946; the Royal Crest of the latter now has the St Edward's Crown.

The Army, the Navy and the R.A.F. contributed in the formation of the Beach Groups, specialist units created for amphibious operations. They wore a special round badge with a red anchor within a red border, on a light blue background.

The War Department Fleet is known now as the Army Department Fleet and all its personnel wear a special formation sign and the cap badge illustrated on Plate 9. The service is composed of Royal Corps of Transport (former R.A.S.C.) personnel equipped with a variety of motor boats and amphibious crafts. The Air Despatch Group, R.A.S.C., was created in 1944 with the task of maintaining and supplying the ground forces by air. Its formation sign depicts a yellow Dakota aircraft on a rectangular blue background.

Formation signs of the Air Liaison Signals can also be found with the regimental numbers '2', '7' and '14' above the wings. The light blue, blue and green of the badge of the Air Formation Signals represent the sky, the sea and the land. The diving eagle is currently worn by all ranks of the Army Air Corps.

Poland

Poland became a unified nation in the tenth century and lost its independence in the eighteenth century and, more recently, in 1939 when it was invaded by the Germans and the Russians. After World War 2 Poland regained its national sovereignty on a territory which had moved considerably westwards.

The present Polish Army is descended from Polish units raised in the U.S.S.R. during World War 2. The first of these Polish formations was the 1st Tadeusz Kościuszko Infantry Division which was formed in 1943 and, as the new Polish Army advanced westwards, its ranks were swelled by Poles released from German concentration and prison camps. At the end of the War there were two Polish armies, the 1st and 2nd, whose ranks fought courageously at Lenino, Studzianki, and the Pommernstellung, to mention only a few names. Polish troops also took part in the capture of Berlin.

The first uniforms, adopted in 1943, were Russian ones on which Polish badges were worn accompanied by the characteristic square caps. However, as the months went by, their uniforms gradually assumed a more Polish appearance until, in 1945, except for minor details, they wore the same style uniforms as before the War.

The officers wore an ordinary and an evening uniform and all had square peaked caps, except for the officers of the Warsaw Infantry Division who wore rounded caps with a yellow band. The armoured troops used to wear khaki uniforms, as did the rest of the army, with orange cap bands and orange and black collar pennons, until 1947, when all ranks were issued with new steel-grey uniforms and rounded peaked caps. Their cap bands were initially steel-grey but, in 1949, black cap bands were introduced for all ranks. During these years the traditional square-topped peaked cap, known as the *czapka*, was gradually replaced by rounded caps until, during 1950–1, it was only permitted as head-dress for officers off duty.

The officers had winter and summer uniforms, technically divided into service and walking-out dress. The Sam Browne belt was usually worn without shoulder belt and the latter, together with pistol holder, was worn for field duties. The sword, decorations and medals were added for parade and ceremonial duties. The tunic with pointed collar and four patch pockets was the same as that used before the War. Tradition prescribed breeches for the cavalry, artillery and engineers and trousers for the rest of the army. The generals had two large blue stripes, divided by blue piping, on the sides of the trousers and silver-embroidered zigzag ornaments on the cap band, collar patches and shoulder straps and on the cuffs of the tunic and greatcoat.

The other ranks were issued with summer and winter uniforms. The steel-grey uniforms of the armoured troops were replaced by khaki uniforms in 1950 and the generals' trouser stripes were changed from blue to light carmine and later, in 1958, they were changed back to blue.

In 1952 an evening dress, consisting of khaki peaked cap and tunic and dark blue trousers, was adopted for the officers. A new khaki jacket was adopted for service dress; it had an open collar showing the shirt and tie, and four patch pockets of Polish pattern, with rectangular flaps. A white tunic with buttoned-up collar and four patch pockets was also adopted.

In 1952, the colours of the cap bands, collar patches and piping were also reviewed; the generals had light carmine, the armoured and mechanised troops, black, and the rest of the army, dark carmine. However, the Warsaw Division kept the yellow cap bands and collar patches, now worn with dark carmine trouser stripes and piping. The internal security forces retained their old colours, i.e. the Internal Security Corps (*Korpus Bezpieczeństwa Wewnetrznego* – K.B.W.) wore dark blue and the Frontier Defence units (*Wojska Ochrony Pogranicza* – W.O.P.) wore light green. Later, in 1957, the newly-formed Army Security Units (*Wojskowa Służba Wewnętrzna* – W.S.W.) were given white cap bands and patches, and part of their equipment (belts, pistol holsters, etc.) was white as well. In the same year a maroon beret was adopted for all ranks of the newly-formed Airborne Division and in 1964 a light blue beret was adopted for the Coastal Defence units.

Armoured troops wore black berets. A brigade of mountain troops formed part of the Internal Security Corps: its personnel wore the traditional stiff feathered felt hat, the wide cape and dark blue patches with traditional zigzag on the collar of the tunic. The same uniform is still worn nowadays by these mountain troops, although jackets with an open collar have replaced the tunics, and collar patches are not used any more.

In 1952, when the jackets with open collar were adopted, new smaller patches were issued to fit the new collar. Metal badges were worn on these patches until, in 1960, the patches were abolished altogether and the year after a new set of collar badges was taken into use. In 1957 the coloured cap bands were abolished, except for those of the Warsaw Division, Internal Security Corps, Frontier Defence and Army Security units.

Double-breasted greatcoats were introduced in 1960 and at about that time new field uniforms were issued to all ranks. They are still in use at present although they have been modernised since introduction. The field uniforms are made of the typical olive-khaki striped material used by the armies of the Warsaw Pact.

Plate 17. Cap Badges

All ranks of the Polish Army wear the traditional Polish Eagle on all types of head-dress. The original eagle, worn until 1945 by the Polish armies in the West, used to be crowned, whilst the Polish armies in the East have worn the eagle without crown since 1944.

White metal cap badges (1) were worn by officers on the peaked cap until 1957 when peaked caps with brown visor and chin strap, and khaki cap bands, were introduced. In the following years the officers started to wear silver-embroidered badges (2) made in the shape of the previous metal cap badge. Another embroidered cap badge, slightly different (3), was adopted in 1970 for the regular officers while reserve officers continued wearing the old embroidered pattern.

The other ranks wear white metal oxidised badges on the peaked cap and machine-embroidered badges (4) on the field caps. These badges are embroidered in white thread on khaki, black, maroon and light blue felt; the backing felt matches the colours of the different head-dresses. There are two patterns of O.R.s' cap badges; as with the officers' badge, one was worn before and the other after 1970.

Since the War, two patterns of peaked cap have been used regardless of the shape of the crown (square or rounded). The cap worn until 1957 had black leather visor and chin strap; a metal rim around the visor was originally worn by the officers and later by all ranks. The generals had a silver zigzag embroidered all around the cap band, below a narrow stripe of braid; the senior officers wore a double stripe of braid at the top of the cap band and the junior officers had a single stripe. The rank of the wearer was shown by silver stars embroidered at the front, below the cap badge. Small silver chevrons and stripes, embroidered in place of the stars, showed N.C.O. rank.

The peaked cap of the 2nd pattern is in use at present. The rank stars, chevrons and stripes are still at the front, below the cap badge, but now the senior officers have two silver stripes on the brown leather visor, the junior officers one stripe only. Besides the two stripes on the visor, the generals have a silver zigzag embroidered on the cap band.

Plate 18. Officers' Rank Badges

The army rank badges are worn on the head-dress and, of course, on the shoulder straps also. Generals (including Marshals of Poland) have a silver zigzag embroidered at the end of the shoulder straps, senior officers, two silver stripes, and junior officers, only the stars of rank.

Until 1954 the Polish Army had three generals' ranks, plus that of

Marshal of Poland. The General of Army wore four stars from 1954 to 1958, when finally this rank was abolished. In the early 1950s the three-star rank (General), which still exists, applied to the generals of the corps and services.

During and after the War the ranks were those used in 1939, except for the rank of Warrant Officer which became an officers' rank in 1943 in order to keep in line with the three lieutenants' ranks of the Red Army. When the warrant officers' ranks were readopted in 1963 the one-star officer disappeared; thus at present the 2nd Lieutenant wears two stars.

The rank badges worn on the field cap and on the beret are similar to those worn on the shoulder straps. The generals wear stars above a small zigzag and the officers, stars above double bars, or stars alone, on the left side of the head-dress.

The Marshal of Poland always wears the crossed batons instead of the stars.

Plate 19. Warrant Officers' and N.C.O.s' Rank Badges

The sergeants and corporals wore the pre-war silver lace with red edging until 1961, when a new all-silver lace was introduced. Both ranks still have their badges on the shoulder straps in the form of chevrons and stripes.

As the officers became more academically qualified, the reinstatement of the warrant officers' ranks became necessary. Thus the Warrant Officer and Senior Warrant Officer were created in 1963 and another three W.O.s' ranks were added in 1967. They all have a silver stripe worn all around the loose sides of the shoulder straps and stars from one to four; the junior W.O. wears a star above one chevron.

In 1967 another three sergeants' ranks were added to the existing ones and their rank titles were changed as well.

Plate 20. Rank Badges

The corporals also changed their stripes to the new all-silver lace in 1961 and later, in 1970, a new rank was added, that of Platoon Sergeant, with four stripes.

Collar Patches (1949–52)

New dress regulations, introduced in 1949, dealt with the army collar patches which, with the exception of the armoured troops, were still worn on the collar of the khaki tunic. Personnel of the armoured units by then wore jackets with open collar without any patches. The new collar patches continued to be made in the usual shape in order to fit the pointed collar of the tunic and all ranks wore them with the traditional zigzag as they did before the war. Only the generals' and officers' pattern of embroidery have been illustrated on the first two collar patches; the other patches should be considered simply as a colour guide. The sergeants had a 5-mm zigzag embroidered in silver and the other ranks' zigzag consisted of a 5-mm. stripe of silver lace. The patches were dark carmine with a narrow stripe of arm-of-service colour at the outer end.

The colours were as follows:

	Patch	*Piping*
Infantry	dark carmine	dark blue
Artillery	dark carmine	emerald-green
Engineers	dark carmine	black
Signals	dark carmine	royal blue
Legal Service	dark carmine	light carmine
Quartermaster Service	dark carmine	cornflower-blue
Administrative Service	dark carmine	brown
Medical Service	dark carmine	violet
Veterinaries	dark carmine	grey
Motor Transport Service	dark carmine	silver

The chaplains were all officers and did not wear collar patches. They had the officer's zigzag embroidered on the collar and a plain cross in the corner between the embroidery.

The two colours, dark carmine and the arm-of-service colour, were also worn on the collar of the greatcoat in the form of two 5-mm. stripes, the former at the bottom, the other above it.

These new patches were adopted by regulations published on 1 March 1949, which became compulsory only after 1 January 1951, and the old uniforms could still continue to be worn until the end of that year.

The colours of the collar patches of the internal security forces were not affected by these regulations and the Internal Security Corps continued wearing the dark blue collar patches. Frontier Defence units wore light green triangular pennons with a dark blue stripe, adopted on 1 May 1946.

No collar patches were worn on the field uniform.

Plate 21. Collar Patches for Marshal of Poland and Generals (1952–60)

Collar patches of an entirely new shape were introduced in 1952 for the newly-adopted jackets with open collar; the pointed patches were still worn on the tunic. All the generals, with the exception of those of armoured and mechanised units and of the Warsaw Division, had light carmine patches with piping in the arm-of-service colours. These colours were as follows:

	Patch	*Piping*
Infantry	light carmine	dark blue
1st Warsaw Inf. Div.	yellow	dark blue
Armoured/Mechanised Units	black	light carmine
Artillery/Ordnance	light carmine	Nile-green
Engineers/Mot. Transport	light carmine	black
Signals	light carmine	cornflower-blue
Quartermaster/Admin. Service	light carmine	sky-blue
Medical Service	light carmine	violet
Veterinaries	light carmine	grey
Legal Service	light carmine	scarlet

The Marshal of Poland wore light carmine patches without piping, with the silver eagle clutching the crossed batons embroidered in the centre. The generals had only the eagle embroidered on their patches.

Collar Patches for Officers and Other Ranks (1952–60)

All the officers and other ranks wore the same collar patches between 1952 and 1960: personnel of the armoured and mechanised units wore black patches with dark carmine piping and the rest of the army had dark carmine patches. The different branches of service were distinguished one from the other by metal badges which were pinned onto the patches. The cadets wore tunics with buttoned-up pointed collars: thus they had different-shaped patches, black for armour and dark carmine for the rest of the army. They wore coloured shoulder straps as well.

Collar Badges

These were the collar badges worn by officers and other ranks on the collar patches between 1952 and 1960 and later on their own, pinned on the lapels of the jacket. They were made of white metal (nickel-plated brass), except that of the Medical Service which was made of brass, in order to distinguish it from the white metal badge of the Veterinary Service.

Only the badges for Armoured/Mechanised units, the Administrative, Medical and Veterinary Services and the Construction Battalions, were worn in pairs.

Plate 22. Collar Badges (1961–73)

By 1960 the collar patches were abolished altogether and later new collar badges were adopted. The embroidered eagles of the Marshal of Poland and generals remained basically the same, whilst most of the other badges were changed, and some new ones were added as well.

The Armoured units and the Mechanised units each obtained their own badges and the same applies to the personnel of the Medical and Veterinary Services. The chaplains, who previously wore only the cross, now wear a cross surrounded by a wreath of laurel. Only the badges of the Infantry, the Artillery and the Legal Service remained more or less the same.

The edelweiss of the Mountain Troops is worn as a feather holder, on the hat, and on the collar of the cape.

Shoulder-Strap Badges

All cadets of the Officers' School wear the letters 'SO' on the shoulder straps: the badge of the 1st was introduced in 1952 and subsequently modified in 1961. The badge for cadets at the N.C.O.s' School (*Szkoła Podoficerska*) was also adopted in 1961 but later a new badge was adopted for the N.C.O.s and cadets of the Regular Army, and also another badge for the Warrant Officers' School.

The Polish title of the Army Technical Academy is *Wojskowa Akademia Techniczna*; hence the letters 'WAT' on the badge. The letters 'WAM' on the badge of the Army Medical Academy refer to the Polish title *Wojskowa Akademia Medyczna*. The letters 'SW' stand for *Studium Wojskowe*.

The three remaining badges, illustrated at the bottom of the plate, were adopted some years later and are currently in use.

Plate 23. Breast Pocket Badges for Exemplary Service

The Exemplary Service badges were granted to meritorious other ranks and were worn on the right breast pocket of the jacket. They are made of white metal and coloured enamel, and the ears of wheat on the sides are painted gold.

These badges were introduced in 1951, one for each branch of service, and the first on the left, with the spread eagle in its centre, was introduced in 1953 for personnel who could not qualify for any of the others. The Infantry badges have a red background, Artillery badges have a green background, Armour and Engineers a black background and all branches of the Quartermaster Service have badges with a light blue background.

In 1958 the Driver's badge was awarded in three classes and later an Exemplary Service badge was also instituted for Miners.

Arm Badges

The Polish Marines are part of the Army and therefore they wear army uniforms but have a white metal fouled anchor on the lower left sleeve. The personnel of the Coastal Defence units wear a light blue beret and an arm badge of the same colour depicting an anchor surrounded by a wreath.

The badge of the Regular N.C.O.s' School is embroidered and it is worn on the left arm.

Plate 24. Breast Badges

The badge of the 1st Warsaw Infantry Division is made of white metal and coloured enamels and was adopted soon after the war to commemorate the victorious march from Lenino to Berlin. In its centre there is a portrait of Tadeusz Kościuszko, after whom the Division is named.

The first Grunwald badges were made in bronze, but later others were made in white metal. A smaller replica of this badge is the centrepiece of the Brotherhood of Arms badge, adopted in 1963. The personnel of the Frontier Defence Units and of the 1st Warsaw Cavalry Division wore their own special breast badges made in metal and coloured enamel. The Frontier Defence badge has been adopted recently, while the other is a wartime badge. The meaning of the letters 'WOP' has already been given in the previous pages, whilst the lettering on the badge of the cavalry division stands for *Warszawska Dywizja Kawalerii.*

A number of different badges of schools and training establishments have been worn since 1945. For instance, there are twelve variations of the Officers' School badge, with different lettering at the top as listed below:

OSP	*Oficerska Szkoła Piechoty*
	Officers' School of Infantry
OSA	*Oficerska Szkoła Artylerii*
	Officers' School of Artillery
OSAPlot	*Oficerska Szkoła Artylerii Przeciwlotniczej*
	Officers' School of A.A. Artillery
OSI	*Oficerska Szkoła Inżynierii*
	Officers' School of Engineers
OSL	*Oficerska Szkoła Łączności*
	Officers' School of Signals
OSK	*Oficerska Szkoła Kwatermistrzowska*
	Officers' School of Quartermasters
OSU	*Oficerska Szkoła Uzbrojenia*
	Officers' School of Ordnance
OSPW	*Oficerska Szkoła Polityczno-Wychowawcza*
	Political-Educational Officers' School
OSWS	*Oficerska Szkoła Wojsk Samochodowych*
	Officers' School of Motor Transport
OSBP	*Oficerska Szkoła Broni Pancernej*
	Officers' School of the Armoured Corps

The two remaining badges, with 'OSL' and 'OSMW' lettered at the top, are those of the Air Force and Naval Officers' Schools. One single school trained both the cadets of the Armoured Corps and of the Motor Transport (*Oficerska Szkoła Broni Pancernej i Wojsk Samohodowych*) but the two courses had different badges.

These badges were all adopted between 1947 and 1950 and in 1953 they were superseded by the diamond-shaped badges shown at the bottom of the plate. The badges of the academies had a white enamel background, those of the schools a red background, and most were named after Polish national heroes and military leaders. The lettering on each badge stands for the branch of service title, as follows:

ASG	*Akademia Sztabu Generalnego*
	General Staff Academy (Gen. K. Świerczewski's)
WAP	*Wojskowa Akademia Polityczna*
	Army Political Academy (F. Dzierżyński's)
WAT	*Wojskowa Akademia Techniczna*
	Army Technical Academy (J. Dąbrowski's)
WAM	*Wojskowa Akademia Medyczna*
	Army Medical Academy
FWM	*Fakultet Wojskowo – Medyczny*
	Army Medical Faculty
OSWZ	*Oficerska Szkoła Wojsk Zmechanizowanych*
	Mechanised Units Officers' School (T. Kósciuszko's)
OSWPanc	*Oficerska Szkoła Wojsk Pancernych*
	Armoured Units Officers' School (S. Czarnecki's)
OSA	*Oficerska Szkoła Wojsk Rakietowych i Artylerii*
	Rockets and Artillery Officers' School (Gen. J. Bem's)
OSWOPL	*Oficerska Szkoła Wojsk Obrony Przeciwlotniczej*
	A.A. Defence Officers' School (M. Kalinowski's)
OSI	*Oficerska Szkoła Wojsk Inżynieryjnych*
	Engineer Officers' School (J. Jasiński's)
OSUZBR	*Oficerska Szkoła Uzbrojenia*
	Ordnance Officers' School (Lt W. Baginski's and 2nd Lt A. Wieczorkiewicz's)
OSL	*Oficerska Szkoła Łaczności*
	Signals Officers' School (B. Kowalski's)
OSWOPch	*Oficerska Szkoła Wojsk Chemicznych*
	Army Chemical Officers' School (S. Ziaj's)
OSS	*Oficerska Szkoła Samochodowa*
	Motor Transport Officers' School (Gen. A. Waszkiewicz's)
OSR	*Oficerska Szkoła Radiotechniczna*
	Radio-Technical Officers' School (Capt. S. Bartosik's)
OSWOP	*Oficerska Szkoła Wojsk Ochrony Pogranicza*
	Frontier Defence Units Officers' School
OSKBW	*Oficerska Szkoła Korpusu Bezpieczeństwa Wewnętrznego*
	Army Security Officers' School (M. Nowotka's)
OSP	*Oficerska Szkoła Piechoty*
	Infantry Officers' School

A white enamel badge with the lettering 'W S M W' was also introduced for the Naval Academy and another two badges, both made of brass and red enamel, for the Air Force, one with the letters 'TSWL' and the other with the letters 'OSL'.

On 30 October 1958 new Exemplary Service badges were adopted to replace those illustrated in the preceding plate. They are granted to the other ranks and are worn on the right breast pocket. There are two grades of the same badge, silver and bronze. Later, the silver (white metal) badge was awarded in three classes, shown by numerals on the badge itself.

The wing-shaped badge of a Driver-Mechanic of Tanks and Self-Propelled Guns is also worn on the right breast pocket and it is awarded in four classes. The badge of the top class has an 'M' in the shield, the others have numerals from 1 to 3. It was instituted in 1960.

The keen soldier, in certain cases, can also be awarded the Inventiveness –Improvement badge, in silver after three successful projects, and in gold for five or more projects.

The qualified parachutists wear their badge with the number of jumps in the wreath. The parachute instructors wear the same badge but with a gold wreath. The badge of the 13th International Brigade is worn by ex-members of that Brigade, which was raised in Spain during the Civil War.

Plate 25. Arm Badges
6th POMORSKA Airborne Division
A number of badges have been worn by the personnel of the Division although the round badge last on the right is the divisional badge.

Specialists
These embroidered badges are worn on the left upper sleeve. The numbers, from 1 to 3, show the specialist class of the wearer.

U.S.A.

The United States is a relatively young nation, formed in 1783 by the union of thirteen North-American states, formerly British colonies. A long period of territorial expansion and internal reassessment followed until at the turn of the last century the U.S.A. began to be involved in European affairs. By the end of World War 2 it had become one of the most powerful nations in the world and American troops were stationed on all the world's continents.

The soldier wore different uniforms for different duties and those worn during the latter period of the war were kept in use until the 1950s. He has an elegant appearance, wearing well-tailored uniforms made with good material and embellished by colourful badges. A peaked cap or forage cap, blouse and trousers, all made of khaki material, were usually worn in temperate climates whilst the summer uniform, which is still in use, consisted of a head-dress, shirt and trousers made of a lighter, sandy yellow material. The same shirt was worn with both uniforms, with the same tie, which was usually darker.

On 1 July 1957 the Army Green uniform replaced the old khaki one: it is composed of a head-dress, jacket with open collar and four patch pockets, and trousers made of a greyish-green material.

Currently officers and warrant officers are also required to own the Army Blue uniform for wear on appropriate occasions; it is similar in style to the A.G. uniform, consisting of a peaked cap, jacket and trousers. The jacket and trousers of the generals' uniform are both made of the same blue cloth while the officers and warrant officers wear lighter blue trousers. Special short shoulder straps with insignia of rank on branch colours are worn on the blue uniform (Plate 27), together with cuff stripes, ornamented cap bands and stripes on the trousers, respectively double gold lace stripes for generals and a single stripe, $1\frac{1}{2}$ in. in width, for the others.

The Army White is an optional uniform, identical in style with the A.G. uniform but made of white material.

The Army Blue or White Mess uniforms are also authorised for optional wear by officers and warrant officers. The former is all made of blue cloth (with lighter blue trousers for officers and W.O.s), while the latter is composed of a white peaked cap, jacket and waistcoat, together with black trousers. The peaked caps used with the mess uniforms are the same as worn with the Army Blue and Army White uniforms.

The short jackets have shoulder cords and the rank insignia are on the cuffs, gold oak leaves and stars for the generals, and gold stripes and loops for the officers, with the insignia of branch in between. 2nd Lieutenants and W.O.s do not wear shoulder cords. The blue jackets have lapels with branch colour facings, and the metal-enamel insignia centred upon them, on both sides. A cummerbund is worn instead of a waistcoat. The blue trousers have gold lace stripes, as prescribed for the Army Blue uniform.

The Army Evening Dress is another optional uniform which consists of the peaked cap, jacket and trousers of the Army Blue Mess uniform worn with full dress shirt with wing collar, white bow tie and white waistcoat. A similar dress uniform but with a tail coat was worn officially until 1969 and will be optional until 1 July 1975.

Branches and corps of the Army have official colours which appear as piping on uniform components, in facings, and in the blue and white dress uniforms. They are:

Adjutant General's Corps	dark blue piped with scarlet
Armor	yellow
Army Medical Department	maroon piped with white
Artillery	scarlet
Chaplains	black
Chemical Corps	cobalt-blue piped with golden yellow
Civil Affairs U.S.A.R.	purple piped with white
Corps of Engineers	scarlet piped with white
Military Police Corps	green piped with yellow
Finance Corps	silver grey piped with golden-yellow
Infantry	light blue
Inspector General	dark blue piped with light blue
Military Intelligence	oriental blue piped with silver-grey
Judge Advocate General's Corps	dark blue piped with white
National Guard Bureau	dark blue
Ordnance Corps	crimson piped with yellow
Permanent Professors of United States Military Academy	scarlet piped with silver-grey
Quartermaster Corps	buff
Signal Corps	orange piped with white
Staff Specialist, U.S.A.R.	green
Transportation Corps	brick-red piped with golden-yellow
Women's Army Corps	old gold and moss-tone green
Warrant Officers	brown
Unassigned to Branch	teal-blue piped with white

Plate 26. Cap Badges

The peaked cap and the forage cap are the principal head-dresses worn by all personnel of the U.S. Army, although soft caps, fur caps and helmets are used as well for particular duties or in particular climates. Berets are worn by personnel of the Special Forces.

The eagle from the coat of arms of the United States of America is worn by officers and enlisted men on the peaked cap; on its own by the former and on a brass disc by the latter. The warrant officers have a different badge, depicting a different eagle, clutching two arrows, surrounded by a wreath of laurel.

Generals and field grade officers have gold-embroidered oak leaves on the visor of the ordinary service caps, while all the others have plain black leather visors. The peaked cap of the Army Blue uniform shows the wearer's rank on the cap band as well. Generals have gold-embroidered oak leaves on the blue cap band as well as on the visor, while all officers have gold stripes on the cap band. Field grade officers only have gold oak leaves on the visor; other officers have a plain leather visor. Warrant officers wear a plain visor with only one stripe on the cap band.

The officers' and warrant officers' chin strap is covered with gold wire lace, whilst that of the enlisted men is made of black leather, matching the visor.

The American Eagle is now also worn by all personnel of the Women's Army Corps: the officers wear a cap badge a little smaller than that of the male officers and the W.A.C. enlisted women wear the same badge, but surrounded by a metal ring.

Officers' and warrant officers' rank badges are worn on the left side of the forage cap, known as a garrison cap, and the piping around the top edge of the curtain shows rank distinction as well.

Generals wear gold piping, all other officers wear gold and black piping, warrant officers silver and black piping and enlisted men, piping of their branch of service colour.

Special Forces Insignia

The Special Forces originate from the Special Warfare Center at Fort Bragg, N.C. In June 1960 the U.S. Army activated the 1st Special Forces which assumed the heritage and honours of the wartime 1st Special Forces and of the Ranger battalions. It also became the parent unit for the 1st, 7th and 10th Special Forces Groups (Airborne) stationed respectively at Okinawa, North Carolina and Bad Tölz (Germany).

The 10th Special Forces Group (Airborne) was raised in June 1952 and in September 1953 the 77th was raised from personnel drafted from the 10th, then to be transferred to Germany. In June 1960 the 77th S.F.G.A. was renumbered the 7th and from the spring of 1961 until October 1962 the Group was deployed in Laos under the operational control of the Military Assistance Advisory Group. Several other groups have been raised and many different beret flashes have been adopted since then.

All ranks of the Special Forces wear the green beret and on the beret, their unit's flash, which is a coloured shield, generally woven, on which the officers have the rank badge and the other ranks have the distinctive insignia of the Special Forces, illustrated at top left. The distinctive insignia on the right is that of the Special Warfare Center.

The first flashes adopted were yellow, red, green and blue and some were later modified: for instance, a black border to commemorate J. F. Kennedy's death was added to the yellow flash of the 1st, and the German national colours were added to the flash of the 10th S.F.G.A. – Europe, stationed in Germany. The colours of the South Vietnamese flag are on the flash of the 5th S.F.G.A. from which the 5th Combat Assistance developed, with a flash of its own. The U.S. Advisors in Cambodia, a training group, wore a flash similar in design to the latter: it is dark blue with golden yellow border, with three white stars on red background at the top left and a white silhouette on the right.

The 3rd S.F.G.A. was formed by personnel of the 1st, 5th and 7th, and the yellow, black and red colours of its parent units are part of its flash. The Special Forces Aviation and the Special Warfare Center, named after President Kennedy, have their own flashes, and also wear particular shoulder patches (Plates 32 and 34) differing from the arrowhead patch of the Special Forces (Plate 34).

Plate 27. Officers' Rank Badges

In the U.S. Army silver rank badges have seniority over gold ones; for instance in the case of the badges of Lieutenant Colonel and Major and those of lieutenants. They were all adopted during the last century except for the generals' stars which were adopted some time earlier. Initially, the U.S. Army had only two generals' ranks: Brigadiers and Major Generals. The rank of Lieutenant General was instituted in 1799 and from that year to 1802 the rank of General of the Armies of the United States existed as well and was later conferred on John J. Pershing in 1919. The rank of General of the Army was instituted in 1866 and once again in 1944.

The officers' rank badges are usually worn on the shoulder straps of the jacket and overcoat or on the right side of the shirt collar when the jacket is not worn. They are also worn on the left side of the garrison cap and on the head-dress of the field and work uniforms.

These badges are made of metal or are embroidered in metal wire; machine-embroidered or woven rank badges are usually worn on field and work uniforms.

Warrant Officers' Rank Badges

Brass and enamel bars with rounded ends became the rank badges of the

Warrant Officer and of the Chief Warrant Officer in 1942 but, some years after the Korean War, in 1956, two new ranks were instituted. Thus there are now one warrant officer rank (W1) and three chief warrant officer ranks (W2, 3 and 4). The rank badges were changed to rectangular bars with three enamel blocks for CWO4 and CWO2 and only two enamel blocks for CWO3 and WO1; the bars of the two top ranks were made of white metal whilst those of the two lower ranks were made of brass.

As these badges caused a great deal of visual confusion, new badges have been adopted since 1 December 1972. The new badges are all made of white metal with black enamel blocks, one for each warrant rank. There are also subdued versions for field and work uniforms.

Shoulder Ornamentation for Army Blue Uniform

On the Army Blue uniform the rank badges are embroidered on special rectangular straps, previously used on blue uniforms during the last century. The straps are surrounded by a gold nylon or rayon border, ⅛-in. in width with a single line of gold Jaceron on either side. The strap background is of blue-black velvet for generals and, for officers, of cloth in the branch-of-service colours. If the branch of service has two colours the first named colour constitutes the background and the second replaces the inner line of Jaceron. The warrant officers have a brown background.

The generals and the colonels wear one set of stars or, respectively, one eagle for each strap, whilst the other officers and warrant officers wear one badge on each side of the shoulder strap.

Plate 28. Line N.C.O.s' Rank Badges (1948)

The American N.C.O.s wore the wartime chevrons (80 mm. in width) until 1948, when both the ranks and the rank badges were changed. The technician (T) ranks were all abolished and the three-chevron ranks of (Buck) Sergeant were abolished as well. The new badges adopted in 1948 were considerably smaller (48 mm. in width) and were woven, the same as the shoulder sleeve insignia. Combatant personnel wore blue chevrons on a yellow background and non-combatant personnel wore yellow chevrons on dark blue.

The American N.C.O.s' ranks are related to their pay grade which until 1948 went from E-1 (M/Sgt and 1st Sgt) to E-7 (Soldier). In 1948 the succession of pay grade was inverted, i.e. the M/Sgt and the 1st Sgt became the seventh enlisted man pay grade.

1955

In 1955 larger chevrons (80 mm. in width) were once again introduced for the line N.C.O.s' ranks together with four new specialists' ranks. The chevrons of the former were machine-embroidered in khaki silk on a dark blue gabardine material; those of the specialists were considerably smaller (50 mm. in width) with the American Eagle embroidered in the centre

1957–73

When the new Army Green uniforms were adopted in 1957, new yellow chevrons were adopted as well for both the line N.C.O.s and the specialists (Plate 29) and several new ranks were introduced in the following years.

The following were the ranks in use until 1958:

Pay Grade	Line N.C.O.s	Technicians
E-7	First Sergeant	Master Specialist
	Master Sergeant	
E-6	Sergeant 1st Class	Specialist 1st Class
E-5	Sergeant	Specialist 2nd Class
E-4	Corporal	Specialist 3rd Class
E-3	Private 1st Class	none
E-2	Private	none
E-1	Recruit – under four months' service	none

In 1958, the three-chevron rank of Sergeant (E-5) was re-introduced and the former rank of Sergeant, with four chevrons, became that of Staff Sergeant (E-6). As a result the pay grade was pushed forward one grade all along the line and a new rank, that of Sergeant Major (E-9), was created, with six chevrons and a star.

On 1 September 1965, a wreath was added around the star on the rank badge of the Sergeant Major and his previous badge, with six chevrons and the star, was taken on by the new rank of Chief Master Sergeant, which was re-titled Staff Sergeant Major in 1968 and Sergeant Major on 1 July 1969. The chevrons with the star and wreath became the badge of the Command Sergeant Major in 1968. Both these two N.C.O.s' ranks belong to the E-9 pay grade.

Another E-9 rank is that of Sergeant Major of the Army, created in July 1966. This rank is covered by a single man serving at the Pentagon who wears on the sleeves the chevrons of the Command Sergeant Major, plus special brass and enamel collar badges.

A new rank badge consisting of one chevron with another round one below was adopted in 1965 for the new Lance Corporal rank (E-3) and the Private 1st Class took the E-2 pay grade. Later, in 1968, the Lance Corporal became a Private 1st Class (E-3) and the one-chevron rank was renamed Private E-2.

The Platoon Sergeant wears the same chevrons as the Sergeant 1st Class and both ranks belong to the E-7 pay grade.

Plate 29. Specialists' Rank Badges (1956 and 1958)

New specialists' ranks were adopted in 1955 represented by badges embroidered in yellow on greyish-green gabardine material. The lowest specialist's class corresponded to the line N.C.O.'s rank of Corporal and to the E-4 pay grade.

The specialist's rank and rank badges were changed in 1958. New larger rank badges were adopted and the specialists were named after their corresponding pay grade number. Until 1968, however, all the specialists were technically subordinated to the line N.C.O. of the rank of Corporal, while since June of that year they have been subordinated to the line N.C.O. of identical pay grade and above the N.C.O. of the lower pay grade.

The ranks of Specialists 8 and 9 have never been worn.

Shoulder Sleeve Tabs

Traditionally the U.S. Army did not use shoulder tabs as a means of unit recognition. The Ranger battalions, however, wore the familar numbered scroll tabs during World War 2. Another 'RANGER' tab, with its title in white on a red straight tab, was worn at that time by personnel of the 5th Army. A curved 'RANGER' tab, yellow on black, appeared some years later during the Korean War. It also had the title 'AIRBORNE' below.

Tabs of U.S. Army locations were, and still are, in use. The tab 'KOREA' can also be found with white lettering on blue background. 'KMAG' stands for Korea Military Advisory Group and was worn below the patch of the Military Government of Korea (Plate 33).

The 'INVADERS' tab was worn by the band of SHAEF during the latter stage of the war and some personnel of the 88th Division wore the unofficial scroll tab 'BLUE DEVIL' above the divisional patch. The Division was then stationed in the region of Venezia Giulia, in the North-East of Italy. In 1947 the Free Territory of Trieste was formed, and the 88th Division composed the nucleus of TRUST (Plate 33), the U.S. Army contingent stationed in Trieste. The close relation between the 88th Division and TRUST can be seen in the similarity of both the patches and tabs worn by the two units.

In later years, the raising of Special Forces and Long Range Patrols started an urge for individuality among the units of the U.S. Army, and particularly in the Vietnam theatre of operations dozens of tabs were adopted although most were unofficial.

Divisional and regimental Airborne-Ranger and Pathfinder-Airborne detachments and Long Range patrols were raised and adopted their own self-explanatory tabs which were worn above the shoulder patch. For instance, the scroll tab with 'AIRBORNE-RANGER/INF.CO.' embroidered in white with red edging was worn above the patch of the Americal Division. The letters 'LRRP' stand for Long Range Reconnaissance Patrol and 'RECONDO' for Reconnaissance Commando.

When all the Airborne-Ranger Companies were organised as part of the 75th Infantry Regiment (see Marshall Task Force, Plate 34) the tabs of the companies in Vietnam were standardised, with the company's letter ('A', 'B', 'C', etc.) on the left and '75', the regimental number, on the right. 'AIRBORNE-RANGER' was in the scroll's centre.

The 'AIRBORNE-RANGER' tabs with the company letter were worn on field uniforms while on the ordinary service uniforms an 'AIR-BORNE' tab (white on blue or yellow on black) was added above the patch of wearer's unit, as in the following list:

Abn Ranger Company	Unit
A	197th Inf. Bde
B	7th Corps
C	1st Field Force
D	2nd Field Force
E	9th Inf. Division
F	25th Inf. Division
G	Americal Division
H	1st Cav. Division (Airmobile)
I	1st Inf. Division
K	4th Inf. Division
L	101st Abn Division
M	199th Inf. Bde
N	173rd Abn Bde
O	3/82nd Abn Division
P	5th Inf. Division (Mech.)

Some variations exist, for instance, in the case of L Company, 'CO' and 'INF' are added on the scroll ends, which in this case are square.

The red and black scroll tab 'USSF/SPECIAL TASK FORCE/B-36' was worn on the right shoulder by the Team B-36, 5th Special Forces in Vietnam.

The Tomahawk patch is worn by the 5th Bn, 23rd Infantry Regiment and the motto 'Go Devils' belongs to the 1st Bn, 60th Infantry Regiment of the 172nd Infantry Brigade.

Only a selection of shoulder-sleeve tabs has been illustrated, and many others can be found by the collector, embroidered in various colours or in the subdued black on olive-green variation.

Plate 30. Officers' Collar Badges

The U.S. Army officers wear four badges on the collar and lapels of the jacket: two U.S. national insignia, one for each side, at the top, and the service branch badges at the bottom. On the collar of the summer shirt the rank badge is worn on the right and the branch badge on the left.

The infantry badge illustrated belongs to an officer of the 349th Infantry Regiment, of the 88th Division, and it was worn soon after World War 2.

During the last twenty-eight years several collar badges have been modified in conformity with the Army's reorganisation, and some others have been abolished as the branch of service they represented no longer exists.

The Armored Force adopted a new badge, the design of which links the cavalry with its armoured role, although the cavalry and the tank units still keep their separate identity. Personnel of cavalry units have now readopted the crossed sabres. The use of numerals above the crossed sabres is permitted but not squadron numbers or letters.

In the late 1950s, when missiles became standard equipment of the Artillery, a 'composite missile' was added to the traditional crossed cannons.

The letters attached to the Medical Corps badges were made of brass or maroon enamel, but soon after another pattern, with black letters, was introduced, which is worn currently.

The Aide-de-Camp badges were introduced in 1902, initially for Aides to Brigadier, Major and Lieutenant General; in 1918 the badge for General's Aide was adopted, with four stars in the chief.

These early devices were entirely different from the later types: they were slightly larger, as it was only in 1921 that their height was standardised at $1\frac{1}{4}$ in. and until 1924 the stars were made of gold. The shield of early badges was convex and its top edge was usually straight. Some shields had pointed upper corners, others were with the eagle's wings overlapping onto the corners of the shield. As the latter type appeared in the U.S. Marine Corps regulations, it is technically a U.S.M.C. badge, although often used by Army personnel as well.

Both types were also made in bronze and smaller Aides' badges were worn on the shirt collar. Other types were embroidered respectively on dark brown or khaki, olive-drab, olive-green and white material. Subdued badges are made of black silk on olive-green.

The badge for Aide to the General of the Army was adopted in 1944, and in 1951 a round badge was introduced for Aides to the President. Two years later, in May 1953, this badge was replaced by another which conforms to the usual pattern. In May 1969 a similar badge, but with inverted colours of enamel, was approved for the Aide to the Vice President.

In 1951, badges for the Aides to the Secretary of Defense and Secretary of the Army were also introduced and in February 1963 those for Aides to the Under-Secretary of the Army and to the Chief of Staff.

The coat of arms of the latter is superimposed on a white star. The arm and service badges worn by enlisted men are similar to those of the officers, but entirely made of brass and superimposed on a brass disc.

Plate 31. Breast Badges

The Department of Defense Identification badge, known at present as the Office of the Secretary of Defense Identification badge, is worn on the left pocket by individuals who have served not less than one year, after 13 January 1961, in the Office of the Secretary of Defense.

The Presidential Service badge was instituted on 1 June 1961 and it is awarded to individuals who have served for not less than one year at the White House. It is worn on the right breast pocket.

The Joint Chiefs of Staff Identification badge is worn on the left pocket by individuals who have served not less than one year in the organisation.

The Army General Staff Identification badge is the oldest badge of this type as it was authorised on 23 October 1933 for officers who, since 1920, had served for not less than one year on the General Staff. It is worn on the right pocket.

The Guard, Tomb of the Unknown Soldier, Identification badge is worn on the right breast pocket by members of the Honor Guard in Washington, D.C.

The Expert Infantryman and the Combat Infantryman badges are made of silver and blue enamel and are worn above the ribbons; the former is awarded to infantrymen who have satisfactorily completed a number of proficiency tests, the other is awarded for meritorious combat performance. The Combat Artillery and Armored Cavalry badges are unofficial.

There are three classes of parachutists' badges: the Master Parachutist badge is awarded for sixty-five jumps, including twenty-five with combat equipment, four at night and five mass tactical jumps: the wearer must be a qualified 'jumpmaster' or have served as jumpmaster on at least one combat jump or thirty-three non-combat jumps.

The badge of Senior Parachutist is awarded after thirty jumps, including fifteen with combat equipment, two at night and two mass tactical jumps. The wearer must be a qualified jumpmaster or have taken part in one or more combat jumps or fifteen non-combat jumps as a jumpmaster.

The Master and Senior Parachutists must have served on jump status for respectively thirty-six and twenty-four months.

All the other army-qualified parachutists wear the winged parachute illustrated, worn above the unit's identification oval. Ranger-qualified parachutists wear the same badge with the Ranger tab.

The Glider badge is no longer awarded, but it is still worn by those who have qualified for it.

There are three types of Army Aviation badges in existence, each divided into three classes: the plain wings, the wings surmounted by a star, and the badge with the star surrounded by a wreath. The badges are worn respectively by the Master and Senior Army Aviator and by the Army Aviator; by the Senior Flight Surgeon, Flight Surgeon and Aviation Medical Officer; and by the Master, Senior and Aircraft Crewman.

There are four badges for nuclear reactor operators, awarded to graduates of the Nuclear Power Plant Operators Course, and after periods of such duty. The Reactor Commander badge and the Shift Supervisor badge are identical but the former is worn by officers. There are also the Operator First and Second Class badges and the Operator Basic badge.

The Explosive Ordnance Disposal Specialist and the Supervisor wear similar badges, that of the latter with a star.

Medical personnel wear the Expert Field Medical badge after completion of proficiency tests whilst the Combat Medical badges are worn by personnel who have satisfactorily performed their duty on active ground combat.

Plate 32. Shoulder Sleeve and Pocket Insignia

Coloured patches are worn by army personnel on the upper sleeves of the jacket and overcoat and on the shirt when it is worn as an outer garment. The same patches, but of the subdued type (black and olive-green), are worn on field work and other utility uniforms. They come in two versions, woven or machine-embroidered in black on an olive-green cloth.

All personnel wear the patch of the unit in which they currently serve on the left upper sleeve. Individuals who have earned merit in combat operations during World War 2 (7 December 1941 – 2 September 1946), the Korean War (27 June 1950 – 27 July 1954), in Korea after 1 April 1968, in Vietnam after 1 July 1958 and in the Dominican Republic after 29 April 1965, are entitled to wear the patch of the unit they belonged to at that time on the right upper sleeve.

A great number of coloured and subdued patches are also worn on one of the breast pockets of field and utility uniforms.

Most patches are currently woven, or partly woven on felt, although others have been hand-embroidered in the Far East, particularly in Vietnam.

Several units retain the badge they wore during World War 2 but even the woven badges made nowadays are considerably different from the old ones. Before the adoption of the Army Green uniforms many patches used to have a khaki background or a narrow khaki border; these backgrounds are now Army Green and many patches are now made with a thick woven coloured border.

Recruiting and Training

The U.S. Army Recruiting Service initially had a shield-shaped patch, later changed to an oval one, with the Liberty Bell surrounded by the stars of the first thirteen states of the Union.

The Armed Forces Information School existed in the late 1940s and early 1950s at the Carlisle Barracks, Pa, and the three stars in the patch symbolised the Army, Navy and U.S.A.F., which it served. The Army Aviation School is located at Fort Rucker, Ala. The Helicopter School, whose pocket patch is illustrated below, is part of the Army Aviation School.

The Psychological Warfare Division was established in 1950 at the Army General School at Fort Riley, Kansas. Two years later it was transferred to Fort Bragg, N.C., and it became the Psychological Warfare Center, renamed the Special Warfare Center in December 1956. This establishment is dedicated to President J. F. Kennedy.

The Jungle Warfare Training Center was created in 1951 at Fort Sherman, Panama Canal Zone, and in May 1960 it became an independent command under the U.S. Army, Caribbean.

Centers and Schools

The first patch of the Field Artillery School depicted a cannon only but when, later, it became the Artillery and Missile School the black missile was added to the patch. In July 1970 a third patch was adopted, without the missile but of a different design from the first one. Similar diamond-shaped patches were adopted for the Training Commands of the various branches of service, and later they were all renamed Center and School (i.e. Missile and Munitions Center and School, etc.).

Four patches of Recondo (Reconnaissance Commando) Schools have been illustrated among others at the bottom of the plate. They are only a selection as many others are in existence and all are usually in the shape of an arrowhead. Company G, 75th Infantry Regiment, was the Recondo unit of the American (23rd) Division, and Company P was raised by the 5th Division. The other two are patches of independent Recondo units raised respectively in Hawaii and by the U.S. Military Academy.

The Imjin Scout insignia is worn as a pocket patch by personnel and graduates of the Advance Combat Training Academy of 2nd Division, stationed near the Demilitarised Zone in Korea. It is also worn below a 'SNIPER' tab and on armbands worn on the left sleeve by personnel of the DMZ Police. Patches exist with and without the letters 'DMZ' at the bottom, below the map of Korea.

The 54th Engineers Professional School, previously a battalion, has now been renamed 130th Engineers Brigade Professional School.

The full title of the first patch on the fifth row is Combat Surveillance Electronic School.

Plate 33. Shoulder Sleeve and Pocket Insignia
U.S. Forces Overseas

The shoulder patch of the U.S. Army, Europe, is similar to the patch of the former Supreme Headquarters Allied Expeditionary Force, except that its background is now blue, instead of black. The same patch with the word 'BERLIN' as part of the patch, at the top, was adopted by the U.S. troops stationed in Berlin. The U.S. troops stationed in Trieste from 1947 to 1953 wore a modified patch of the 88th Division, to which they used to belong, with the halberd of the town of Trieste in its centre and an additional self-explanatory scroll. Some patches of the Tactical Command, Austria, can also be found with two scrolls, one at the top, similar in shape to that of the 'TRUST' with the inscription 'AUSTRIA' and another at the bottom which reads 'LINZ'.

The U.S. Forces in Austria used to wear a patch made in the Austrian colours, with a sword and a twig of laurel in its centre. The patch of the U.S. Forces, Far East, depicts Mount Fujiyama and later, with an additional scroll, it became the badge of the 29th R.C.T. (Plate 36). A Torii gate is depicted on the shoulder patch of the Ryukyus Command, with its headquarters at Okinawa. The U.S. personnel in Guam have in turn worn two different badges. Both have been illustrated.

The fleurs-de-lis are present on the badge of the U.S. TASCOM, Europe, because this organisation was originally formed on 25 April 1953 in France; the central arrow represents the flow of supplies. On 6 August 1964 it was renamed U.S. Army Communications Zone, Europe, and on 26 September 1969 it became the U.S. Theater Army Support Command, Europe. Similar logistical organisations were also set up in Japan and Korea and wore their own patches. They were later organised as part of a network of logistical commands, whose patches are illustrated on Plate 39.

A number of new patches have been adopted in recent years by units in Vietnam, and by the various Military Assistance Advisory Groups and similar organisations raised in the Far East.

The bell-shaped patch of the former Military Government of Korea has a tab fitted at the bottom (Plate 29). The letters 'KMAG' of this tab stand for Korea Military Advisory Group.

Plate 34. Shoulder Sleeve and Pocket Insignia Miscellaneous U.S. Units

The China Headquarters, Ledo Road, the Marshall Task Force and the Jingpaw and Katchin Rangers were all formations which fought the Japanese during World War 2 and most of their shoulder sleeve insignia were worn by veterans after the war, on the right sleeve.

The patch of the Marshall Task Force is very similar except for the tab, to that of the Merrill's Marauders, although it also had another patch with 'MARS TASK FORCE' written in blue, all on one line, on a curved green tab. The same shield, without any tab, became the distinctive insignia of the 75th Infantry Regiment, raised on 5 December 1968 as the parent unit of all the Long Range Reconnaissance Patrol units.

The 75th is descended from the 475th Infantry Regiment which, together with the 24th Cavalry Regiment, 612th and 613th Field Artillery Battalions and a Chinese infantry regiment, formed the 5332nd Brigade (Provisional) then, in 1944, stationed in India. This American formation was first known as Galahad Force, organised on 10 September 1943 and renamed 5307th Composite Unit (Provisional) on 1 January 1944. It was stationed at Camp Deogarth, India, and later, under the command of Brigadier Frank D. Merrill, it was deployed in the recovery of Northern Burma in operations which led to the construction of the Ledo Road, linking the Indian Railway station of Ledo with the Burma Road to China.

The 5332nd Brigade was later sent to China where it was used as a training unit for Chinese troops; the 475th Regiment was disbanded on 1 July 1945. It was reactivated as the 75th Infantry Regiment at Okinawa on 20 November 1954, disbanded on 21 March 1956 and re-raised once again in 1968.

At that time there were twelve L.R.R.P. units in Vietnam which all became companies of the new regiment (Plate 29).

The wings of the Office of Strategic Service Special Force were worn on the right sleeve, halfway between the shoulder and the elbow, by about a hundred Americans attached to the British S.O.E.

There are several variations of the Bushmasters' patches, particularly of the infantry one, as it was originally worn by units stationed in the Panama Canal Zone, later becoming a Regimental Combat Team and subsequently Brigade (Plate 36).

A number of Chemical Mortar Battalions wore shoulder patches during World War 2 and that of the 100th, for instance was hand-embroidered in Italy where the battalion was stationed in 1944. The Training Engineers units have rectangular patches in arm-of-service colours, with the engineers' castle in its centre, and often with the battalion number embroidered above. The Quartermaster Corps badge is depicted on the Quartermasters' patch, on a blue circular background. The winged sword can be seen in the shoulder patch of the Special Category Army With Air Force (SCARWAF), an organisation formed in 1952.

The U.S. Army Alaska Supply Group was previously known as 69th General Support Group, and before that as the U.S. Army Support, Alaska. The Arctic Rangers is also an Alaskan-based unit: its personnel wear the green beret with a Special Forces flash (Plate 26).

Finally, the arrowhead shoulder patch of the Special Forces was worn alternately with two different airborne tabs. The Army Aviation personnel of the S.F.G.A. wear a different self-explanatory patch.

Plate 35. Shoulder Sleeve Insignia
Ghost Units, National Guard Divisions and Miscellanea

A number of shoulder patches, never actually worn on uniform, are commonly known as patches of 'ghost units'. Most are insignia of Infantry and Airborne (Plate 44) divisions whose patches were designed and put into production during World War 2, but the units themselves were never formed.

Some National Guard divisions were activated in the early 1950s and subsequently disbanded, after the Korean War.

Many shoulder insignia have been modified since the end of World War 2: Army Green has replaced khaki in order to match the colour of the uniforms adopted in 1957. In the case of the 89th Infantry Division, whose background was solely khaki, a new coloured patch was adopted altogether. The 40th Infantry Division, known as the 'Ball of Fire', adopted a new patch while serving in Korea.

The original patch of 1st Army was a black 'A' on a khaki background but personnel of the Army's different branches of service had their branch colours added to the patch. A different patch was issued after the War with the 'A' on a white and red background, without additional colours.

The 19th Army Corps used to have a blue and white insignia during the War which subsequently was slightly modified to the pattern illustrated. Special units of some divisions had scrolls, letters or numerals added to their original patches, as in the case of the Honor Guard and Long Range Reconnaissance Patrol of the 5th Infantry Division. A number of modified patches have also been adopted, especially by the 7th, 24th and 25th Infantry Divisions, during spells of active service in the Far East.

The 11th Air Assault (Test) Division was formed on 1 February 1963 and on 3 July 1965 it became the 1st Cavalry Division (Airmobile). As its title suggests, it was an experimental formation whose units tested the new tactic of airborne-helicopter warfare.

Plate 36. Shoulder Sleeve Insignia
Regimental Combat Teams

The Combat Team 442 was a unit raised among Japanese–Americans which fought as an independent formation during World War 2. It is the first regimental team to have its own insignia and, as a matter of fact, its personnel wore two different shoulder patches in turn. The second pattern was also used after the War when the 442nd became a Regimental Combat Team. The 25th R.C.T. also existed during World War 2.

The Regimental Combat Team consisted of an infantry regiment, a field artillery battalion and a company of engineers and services, thus forming a self-supporting fighting unit. Three R.C.T.s formed the Triangular Division of the early 1950s. During the mid 1960s they were gradually replaced by the newly-formed brigades.

There are also two variations of the patch of the 5th R.C.T., one with two crossed rifles and the other with a yellow thunderbolt on the pentagon. A tab was worn as well, with the lettering '5 R.C.T.' in white on a red background bordered white. The latest patch of the 75th R.C.T. was slightly different from that illustrated: the shield was light blue, without the white inner border.

The 103rd R.C.T. was a unit from Maine and the 107th a unit from New York. The shoulder patch of the 111th contains a silhouette of Benjamin Franklin. The black diamond of the 150th symbolises the coal mines of West Virginia and the Mount Rushmore figures are on the patch of the 196th R.C.T.

Personnel of the 187th Airborne R.C.T. have worn about twelve variants, all slightly different, of the same badge, plus two of the three pocket patches illustrated at the bottom of this plate.

The 298th and 299th were Hawaiian units, and the patch of the former shows the face of King Kamehameha I and a Hawaiian spear. The spear and a kahili are depicted on the patch of the other.

The shoulder patch of the 351st R.C.T. is made in the shape of an axe head. The 74th Infantry Regiment was raised during the War and later became the 474th R.C.T. Its badge depicts a blue Viking ship surmounted by a small Ranger scroll, all on a red arrowhead; in some of these badges, however, the positioning of the blue and red have been inverted.

The black and white patch on the bottom row is the pocket patch of the 65th R.C.T., a unit raised in Puerto Rico.

Plate 37. Shoulder Sleeve Insignia
Brigades

All the shoulder sleeve insignia illustrated in this plate belong to Infantry and Artillery brigades, most of which were raised in the 1960s. All information concerning these patches is given below in an abbreviated form.

1st and 2nd Infantry Brigades	Originally part of 1st Inf. Div. Both were transformed to Abn Bdes in the summer of 1943. The 1st was disbanded the following January, the 2nd (Plate 44), in 1945. Both became independent Inf. Bdes in 1958 and in 1962 were returned to 1st Inf. Div.
11th Infantry Brigade	Insignia officially approved on 26 July 1966.
29th Infantry Brigade	Hawaiian N.G. (National Guard). Insignia approved on 9 September 1964 and 16 May 1968.
32nd Infantry Brigade	Insignia of former 32nd Div. Wisconsin N.G. approved for the Inf. Bde on 17 May 1968.
33rd Infantry Brigade	As above, Illinois N.G. 1 July 1968.
36th Infantry Brigade	Texas N.G. Brigade. 10 May 1967.
39th Infantry Brigade	Arkansas N.G. 24 September 1968.
40th Infantry Brigade	Insignia of former 40th Inf. Div. California N.G. readopted on 1 May 1968.
40th Armored Brigade	California N.G. 30 January 1969.
41st Infantry Brigade	12 June 1969.
45th Infantry Brigade	Insignia of former 45th Inf. Div. Oklahoma N.G.
49th Infantry Brigade	California N.G. 4 November 1966.
49th Armored Brigade	Texas N.G.
53rd Infantry Brigade	Florida N.G. Formerly armoured 4 December 1964. An infantry unit since 25 July 1968.
67th Infantry Brigade	Nebraska N.G. 16 June 1964.
69th Infantry Brigade	Kansas N.G. 3 December 1964.
71st Airborne Brigade	Insignia of former 36th Inf. Div. Texas N.G. 10 March 1969.
72nd Infantry Brigade	Texas N.G. 18 September 1968.
81st Infantry Brigade	Washington N.G. Indian symbol of a raven. 27 May 1970.

86th Infantry Brigade	Vermont N.G. 1 July 1964.
92nd Infantry Brigade	Puerto Rico N.G. 16 June 1964.
157th Infantry Brigade	Pennsylvania A.R. 13 July 1964.
171st Infantry Brigade	Alaskan unit. 28 August 1963.
172nd Infantry Brigade	As above.
173rd Airborne Brigade	Also Plate 44. 29 July 1963.
187th Infantry Brigade	Massachusetts A.R. 3 October 1963.
191st Infantry Brigade	24 October 1963.
193rd Infantry Brigade	23 August 1962.
194th Armored Brigade	13 January 1966.
196th Infantry Brigade	Double-headed match for matchlock muskets. 29 October 1965.
197th Infantry Brigade	A cartridge. 14 December 1962.
198th Infantry Brigade	6 July 1967.
199th Infantry Brigade	10 June 1966.
205th Infantry Brigade	A unit of Minnesota. 1 November 1963.
256th Infantry Brigade	Louisiana A.R. 23 July 1968.
30th Artillery Brigade	Raised in the Ryukyus Islands. The three arrows (symbolising missiles) and the circle suggest the Brigade's number. 12 April 1966.
31st, 35th, 45th, 47th, 49th, 52nd	Army Air Defense Command (ARADCOM).
32nd Artillery Brigade	20 April 1966, became ARADCOM with its own patch on 16 July 1966.
38th Artillery Brigade	Insignia suggests the partition of Korea. 2 June 1961.
40th A.A. Artillery Brigade	10 June 1955. Later became part of ARADCOM and in 1971 was redesignated 13th Art. Group.
107th Artillery Brigade	Virginia N.G. 31 May 1967.

The Army Defense Command, divided into regions, secures the anti-aircraft defence of all the territory of the United States.

Plate 38. Shoulder Sleeve Insignia
Brigades

The patches of all the remaining brigades, of Engineers, Ordnance, etc., are illustrated in this plate.

7th Engineers Brigade	The saltire is the map symbol of a brigade. The seven stripes symbolise this Brigade number and red and white are the colours of the Engineers.
16th Engineers Brigade	The Roman number 'X' plus the six merlons on the towers form this Brigade's number. Ohio N.G. 9 July 1968.

18th Engineers Brigade	10 February 1966.
20th Engineers Brigade	Four Roman 'V's add up to the Brigade's number. 30 June 1967.
130th Engineers Brigade	23 September 1969.
411th Engineers Brigade	4 January 1967.
412th Engineers Brigade	Mississippi A.R. 8 November 1967. Later a Command.
416th Engineers Brigade	20 April 1967.
420th Engineers Brigade	18 December 1967.
57th Ordnance Brigade	Crimson-yellow patch with central grenade.
1st Signal Brigade	The electric spark combined with the army's sword.
7th Signal Brigade	16 March 1970.
1st Support Brigade	The millrind is a symbol of strength. 11 February 1966.
2nd Support Brigade	The chevrons simulate a belt supporting the sword and symbolise the unit's number. 15 February 1966.
3rd Support Brigade	Three lances supporting each other. 19 August 1966.
12th Support Brigade	2 February 1966.
13 Support Brigade	11 August 1966.
15th Support Brigade	A supporting arch. 19 December 1966.
35th Support Brigade	Insignia of former 35th Inf. Div. 23 July 1969.
103rd Support Brigade	Insignia of former 103rd Inf. Div. 4 January 1967.
167th Support Brigade	Symbolic support to the above combat section. 14 July 1969.
301st Support Brigade	The chain of supply, the chain symbolising strength. 19 January 1966. Formerly a Command since 21 March 1952.
311th Support Brigade	21 March 1968. Formerly a Command since 22 March 1955.
377th Support Brigade	21 September 1966.
15th M.P. Brigade	18 April 1966.
18th M.P. Brigade	The army's sword upon the magistrate's fasces. 1 June 1966.
43rd M.P. Brigade	Rhode Island N.G. Rhodes city walls. 18 May 1969.
220th M.P. Brigade	Located at Gaithersburg, Maryland, an A.R. unit.
221st M.P. Brigade	The griffin head above the Californian Sun. U.S.A.R.
258th M.P. Brigade	Insignia of the former 258th R.C.T. 24 September 1968.

290th M.P. Brigade	Nashville, Tennessee, U.S.A.R.
7th Medical Brigade	21 February 1966.
18th Medical Brigade	Entwined medical bandages. 25 October 1967.
44th Medical Brigade	5 October 1966.
1st Aviation Brigade	Formed in Vietnam. 2 August 1966.
107th Transportation Brigade	11 May 1966.
125th Transportation Brigade	The symbol of water and road transportation.
143rd Transportation Brigade	Roads and viaducts. 24 October 1969.

The 184th and 425th Transportation Commands (Plate 39) have recently been transformed into Brigades.

Plate 39. Shoulder Sleeve Insignia
Logistical Commands
The 1st Logistical Command was activated at Fort McPherson, Georgia, on 20 September 1950 and its patch was authorised on 12 May 1952. The Command was later transferred to Fort Bragg and subsequently to France. Back in the U.S.A., for a time it was part of 3rd Corps at Fort Hood, Texas, and in April 1965 it arrived in Vietnam. It was renamed 1st Field Army Support Command and replaced the 22nd FASCOM at Fort Lee, Virginia.

The 2nd Logistical Command was formed in Korea; thus the map of Korea is depicted in one of its shoulder patches, the Torii gate on the other.

A number of other commands have been formed since the 1950s in order to secure the supplies to the various U.S. Army units and all wear round-shaped shoulder sleeve insignia, 5 cm. in diameter.

A section of the Golden Gate bridge can be recognised on the patch of the 305th, and the silhouette of Morro Castle, in Puerto Rico, on that of the 324th Logistical Command.

Transportation Commands
The Transportation commands' patches show the colour of this branch of service, brick-red and yellow, and most depict wheels. However, a section of a railway track can be seen in the patch of the 3rd and the magnolia flower of Mississippi in that of 184th Transportation Command.

Plate 40. Shoulder Sleeve and Pocket Insignia
Commands
These last few patches illustrated were worn by personnel of commands whose badges could not be included in the previous plates. The 14th A.A. Command, for instance, is the only one of its kind and existed during and after World War 2.

The U.S. Army Investigation Command was organised on 15 September 1971 and is divided into six regions (1st U.S. Army, 3rd U.S. Army, 5th U.S. Army, 6th U.S. Army, U.S. Army Pacific and U.S. Army Europe and Africa), plus several field offices.

The abbreviation 'FASCOM' stands for Field Army Support Command.

Cavalry -- Armored and Airmobile

Only the 1st Cavalry Division saw active service during World War 2, although several cavalry units were deployed as independent armoured regiments or groups. In 1965 the 1st Cavalry Division became 'airmobile', thus adding another role to the cavalry. The great majority of the patches illustrated, mainly pocket patches, are those of armored cavalry regiments (A.C.R.) and some were also worn during World War 2. Some modified patches of the 1st Cavalry Division were used by the divisional artillery; the 'Medevac' patch was worn, numbered, by only twenty-six helicopter pilots, usually on the left pocket, on the right if the wearer had been previously shot down.

The patch of the 163rd A.C.R. is similar to that of the 163rd R.C.T. because they are technically one unit. It was raised in 1884–7 as the 1st Infantry Regiment of the Montana N.G.; redesignated 163rd Infantry Regiment in 1922, it was inducted into Federal service in 1940 as part of the 41st Infantry Division. After the War it became the infantry regiment of the 163rd R.C.T. and in 1953 an armoured cavalry regiment.

Plate 41. Shoulder Sleeve and Pocket Insignia
Armored Force

The tricoloured triangular insignia was adopted by the Armored Corps during World War 1; the colours, yellow, blue and red, are those of the cavalry, infantry and artillery, which are the basic components of the armoured formations.

The lightning, tank tracks and cannon, on round patches in branch-of-service colours, were the insignia of the 7th Mechanised Cavalry Brigade, formed in 1937 and composed of the 1st and 13th (Mech.) Cavalry Regiments, 68th F.A. Regiment, 47th Engineers Squadron and service units.

The Armored Force was formed on 10 July 1940 and its insignia, authorised on 7 May 1941, was the triangular patch of the former Armored Corps with the insignia of the 7th Mechanised Cavalry Brigade in its centre.

Roman numerals in the yellow apex of the shoulder patch distinguished the Armored Corps: these patches have been made with numbers from I to V and XVIII, although such corps never existed. The I Corps was disbanded in 1943, after the invasion of Sicily and the II, III and IV Corps became the 18th, 19th and 20th Army Corps respectively, with different patches altogether. The V Corps was never formed.

During World War 2, divisional patches were made numbered from 1 to 22, although only the divisions 1 to 14, 16 and 20 actually existed. The divisions numbered 27, 30, 40, 48, 49 and 50 belong to the National Guard. Many shoulder patches have straight tabs at the bottom, with black or dark blue lettering on yellow background. Also khaki tabs with yellow lettering have been used.

The following are the divisional titles embroidered on the tabs:

'OLD IRONSIDES'	1st Armored Division
'HELL ON WHEELS'	2nd Armored Division
'SPEARHEAD'	3rd Armored Division
'BREAKTHROUGH'	4th Armored Division
'VICTORY'	5th Armored Division
'SUPER SIXTH'	6th Armored Division
'LUCKY SEVENTH'	7th Armored Division
'IRON DUCE' 'IRON SNAKE' 'THUNDERING HERD' }	8th Armored Division
'PHANTOM' 'REMAGEN' }	9th Armoured Division
'TIGER'	10th Armored Division
'THUNDERBOLT'	11th Armored Division
'HELLCAT' 'SPEED IS THE PASSWORD' }	12th Armored Division
'BLACK CAT'	13th Armored Division
'LIBERATOR'	14th Armored Division
'EMPIRE'	27th Armored Division
'VOLUNTEERS' 'DIXIE' }	30th Armored Division
'GRIZZLY'	40th Armored Division
'HURRICANE'	48th Armored Division
'LONE STAR'	49th Armored Division
'JERSEY BLUES'	50th Armored Division

More than 200 shoulder patches of armoured battalions exist as well, with numbers running from 41 to well over 800. Some have additional tabs, for instance:

'BATTLEAXE'	526th Armored Battalion
'FLAME THROWER'	713th Armored Battalion
'DAREDEVILS'	740th Armored Battalion
'LITTLE DIVISION'	771st Armored Battalion

Shoulder patches with red numerals are worn by units of Armored engineers or artillery. A few regimental patches exist as well, as in the case of that of the 1st Bn/151st Armor, a unit of the Alabama N.G.

Personnel serving at the U.S. Army General Headquarters have 'GHQ' embroidered on the yellow apex of their insignia, while personnel of the Headquarters Armored Force have the letters 'HQ' only. The personnel of some other major organisations wear tabs below the patch, instead of letters on the patch, for instance, 'USATC ARMOR', 'USA ARMOR CENTER', 'THE ARMORED CENTER', 'THE ARMORED SCHOOL', 'THE ARMOR SCHOOL' and 'HONOR GUARD'.

The 112th Armored Cavalry Regiment wears the tank insignia with its regimental title on the tab, as a pocket patch, while the 5th and 7th Armored Cavalry Regiments have the regimental number and abbreviation 'CAV' embroidered on the patch, the latter in yellow.

The following letters can also be found embroidered on the shoulder patches: 'S' (School), 'DR' (Demonstration Regiment), 'RCN' (Reconnaissance). The latter title can also be shown by a 'RECON' tab. All personnel of the 7th Army Tank Training Center have the letters 'TTC' on the yellow apex of their patches and '17/GP' stands for 17th Armored Group.

The Airborne tab above the triangular patch was worn by a special unit just before the invasion of Japan.

A great number of pocket patches are worn by personnel of the various tank battalions and armoured cavalry regiments (Plate 40) of the armoured divisions. A yearly tank qualification course is held at Grafenwöhr, Germany, and a badge is issued afterwards with the year of the course at the bottom and often with 'DISTINGUISHED CREW' embroidered at the top. Illustrated below is the patch of the 14th Armored Cavalry Regiment which belongs to the same course.

Plate 42. Shoulder Sleeve and Pocket Insignia Para. Glider, Abn Infantry, Glider Infantry and Para. Infantry Regiments

The titles of the regiments of the Airborne divisions are related to their roles: thus they are known as Airborne Infantry (A.I.R.), Parachute Infantry (P.I.R.), Glider Infantry (G.I.R.) or Parachute Glider Infantry regiments (P.G.I.).

During World War 2, and since then, many regiments have changed their roles, some have been disbanded or absorbed by others, and most have worn more than one insignia. The 187th, 188th, 503rd and 511th were regiments of the 11th Airborne Division and battalions of the 187th, 188th and 511th were later part of 11th Air Assault Division (Test) which subsequently became the 1st Air Cavalry Division.

The 503rd P.I.R. was dropped in 1945 on the narrow highland on the western side of the fortress island of Corregidor. The dropping zone was very narrow and windswept and therefore the troop carriers flew in a single line and only six men could be dropped on each pass. After the war the 503rd adopted a new patch to commemorate the assault on the Rock of Corregidor.

The regiments of the 11th Airborne Division have also worn patches similar to the divisional one, but with the regimental number instead of the divisional number in the centre. The Division occupied Japan, so the 511th A.I.R. wore a patch with a Torii gate in its centre. The 187th Regiment also took part in the Korean War.

The 327th, 501st, 502nd and 506th were regiments of the 101st Airborne Division; the 325th, 504th and 505th belonged to the 82nd Airborne Division. During the North African/Mediterranean campaign part of the 509th P.I.R. was attached to the latter division and later, in North Western Europe, some other regiments (502nd, 506th, 507th, 508th and 517th) became provisionally part of the 82nd Airborne Division.

There are variations of the smaller patch of the 504th P.I.R. with company letters ('A', 'B', 'C', 'D', 'E', 'F', 'G', 'H', 'I', 'K', 'L', 'M', 'H and J HQ') on the shield and also a regimental patch of German manufacture. The third patch on the right was worn in the Lebanon in 1958.

The 509th was an Independent Parachute regiment. Some of its personnel wore the shoulder patch of the 5th Army below a scroll with the title 'PARACHUTE' during World War 2. A variation of the pocket patch of the reconnaissance platoon of the 509th has the figures '2/509' embroidered at the bottom.

Large cloth replicas of the distinctive insignia (D.I.) have been used as pocket patches by most regiments. I have illustrated only some examples of these as the D.I., and not the patch, is the original badge.

Plate 43. Shoulder Sleeve and Pocket Insignia
Airborne and Parachute Infantry Regts and Miscellaneous Para. Units

The 13th Airborne Division was formed by the 189th and 190th G.I.R. and by the 513th P.I.R. and, eventually, the two Glider Infantry regiments became the 326th G.I.R. The 513th P.I.R. was transferred to 17th Airborne Division, replaced in the 13th by the 515th P.I.R. The Division arrived in Europe in 1945 but only its 517th Combat Team saw combat action.

The 17th Airborne Division consisted of the 193rd and 194th G.I.R.; the 507th (Plate 42) and, since March 1944, the 513th P.I.R. also joined its numbers. The 550th Airborne Infantry Bn was attached to the Division during the Battle of the Ardennes and the Crossing of the Rhine.

Patches of the 542nd P.I.R. exist on blue or on grey background and there is a patch of the 550th P.I.R. with the motto 'A BOLT FROM THE BLUE' embroidered on a scroll below the shield.

The parachute field artillery battalions and the airborne engineers were part of the divisions: some other patches, mainly D.I. replicas, exist as well.

The green Aerial Supply badge was worn by the airborne detachment of U.S. TASCOM, Europe. A pocket patch of the Golden Knights, with the knight's helmet, has no 'AIRBORNE' designation above the parachute.

Plate 44. Shoulder Sleeve and Pocket Insignia
Airborne Divisions, Brigades and Other Units

In 1946 the former 80th, 84th and 100th Infantry Divisions were reactivated as airborne divisions of the Organised Reserve, as well as the 108th, a new division with a new shoulder patch. They became infantry divisions in 1952.

The 1st Battalion of the 225th Infantry Regiment wore the patch of the 46th N.G. Division (Plate 35) with an 'AIRBORNE' tab.

The 6th, 9th, 18th, 21st and 135th are known as 'ghost airborne divisions' because, although a great number of their patches have been made, the divisions have never existed (see also Plate 35).

A miscellany of patches has been illustrated under the heading of Airborne Brigades and Other Units, starting with the shoulder patch of the 2nd Airborne Brigade, worn during World War 2. The two pocket patches of the 173rd Airborne Brigade have been worn unofficially in Vietnam and the fourth is the pocket patch worn by personnel of an airborne unit of the 24th Infantry Division. The patch of the 24th, with an 'AIRBORNE' tab, has been used by the 187th (1st Brigade) and by the 503rd Airborne Infantry Regiment, in several variations, with attached and detached tabs. The 509th A.I.R. wore the patch of the 8th Infantry Division as well, with an 'AIRBORNE' tab attached.

The airborne patch of the 2nd Field Force was worn by personnel of 'D' Company, 75th Infantry Regiment.

A selection of shoulder sleeve and pocket insignia of units of the 82nd and 101st Airborne Divisions are illustrated in this plate. Both Divisions have coloured and subdued patches and the 101st has two versions of the latter, the first with 'AIRBORNE' and the eagle's head in black on an olive-green background and the other in reversed colours. Some coloured and subdued patches of the 101st have 'VIETNAM' on the tab and subdued patches exist with the eagle facing left or right and with the following abbreviations on the tab: '327th INF', '501st INF', '502nd INF', '506th INF', '787th INF', '320th ARTY', '326th ENGR', '101st AVN BN', '101st MP CO', '101st QM CO', '801st MAINT' and 'ABN SPT CMD'.

The patch of the 7th Ranger Bn was worn during the Korean War.

Italy

King Victor Emmanuel II was the creator of the Italian nation. When, in 1849, he succeeded to the throne as King of Sardinia (and Piedmont), the Italian peninsula was still divided into several independent states, which were slowly annexed to Piedmont until finally, in 1861, the Kingdom of Sardinia became the Kingdom of Italy.

After the Wars of Independence came the period of the Wars of Expansion, by which the Italians struggled to conquer an empire of their own. Italy was, however, a poor nation, dependent in many ways on the good will of the great powers, and the time came when the Italian leaders and the people did not know whether they were fighting for independence, expansion or survival. By 1943 Italy had collapsed, the country had become a battlefield, and Italian soldiers wore foreign uniforms. No national traditions seemed to be left.

The Italian soldiers who, in the van of the Allied armies, finally occupied Northern Italy wore British uniforms with Italian badges. The cap badges and collar patches remained those they wore before 1943 and, after the War, many officers were still wearing the old grey-green uniforms. The first Italian-made uniforms were very similar to the British battledress but without patch pockets on the trousers; the khaki blouse had two patch pockets with rectangular flaps. Summer uniforms were made of a greenish-yellow material and were composed of shirt and tie, and trousers. The forage cap was standard army head-dress but personnel of the armoured units wore a black beret.

Soon after the war a new khaki uniform was introduced for the officers, warrant officers and N.C.O.s and it is still issued today in winter and summer versions. It is composed of a peaked cap and a single-breasted jacket with open collar and four patch pockets with rectangular flaps; all buttons are gilded and bear the arm-of-service badge. This jacket is always worn with a belt of matching material and the trousers are also made of the same material.

The greatcoat is also made of khaki material; it is double-breasted, with side pockets and shoulder straps. The same pattern of greatcoat is worn by all ranks, although that of the soldiers is made of a coarser material and is fastened with plastic buttons, whilst the officers, warrant officers and N.C.O.s' greatcoat has gilded buttons.

Several other utility garments have been adopted since 1945, for instance the sleeveless leather jacket of the tank troops (used during the war by the British Army), camouflage overalls and olive-green jackets.

A new ceremonial uniform for officers was adopted in 1956. It is basically black, although a white jacket is prescribed for summer wear. A dark blue (infantry blue) greatcoat has to be worn with this uniform. The winter version consists of a black peaked cap and a black double-breasted jacket with open collar showing the white shirt and black tie. The trousers and shoes are also black. The lapels of the jacket are pointed and small rectangular ornamentations are worn in place of the shoulder straps on both the jacket and greatcoat.

All Bersaglieri still wear the wide-brimmed black hat with cockerel feathers when on parade or special duties; ordinarily they wear the red fez with blue tassel. Mountain troops usually wear their traditional feathered hat although several patterns of mountain field cap, with folding sides, have also been adopted in turn since the end of the War. In the 1950s the stiff kepi, now lined with khaki material, was reintroduced as parade head-dress of the horse artillery. The parachutists wore khaki berets until 1960; then they adopted grey-green berets and, finally, maroon berets in 1968. The British helmets worn during the latter stages of the war by the Royal Italian Army were soon replaced by Italian helmets whilst, by contrast, the webbing equipment of British pattern is still used nowadays.

Plate 45. Cap Insignia

In June 1946 Italy became a republic and therefore the Royal Crown and all the symbols of the House of Savoy were eliminated from all official Italian emblems. However, part of Italy had temporarily become a republic some years before and the same process had already taken place then. The crown was cut off the generals' cap badges in 1943 and the year after new badges were made without the Cross of Savoy. Thus, after 1946, entirely new cap badges were adopted for the generals. They represent the eagle superimposed on a wreath of laurel and oak leaves, with a shield charged with the letters 'R' and 'I' (Repubblica Italiana) interlaced on its breast. The generals' cap badges are usually embroidered in gold or silver wire on a red background but white and gilded metal cap badges can be found as well, without coloured backing. The Generals of Brigade and Division wear silver cap badges, the senior generals gold badges. All the officers, including generals, wear woven cap bands with oak leaf design on the peaked cap, while the other ranks wear a ribbon-type cap band. The chin strap has lost its original supporting role and it is now an ornament which shows the rank and class of rank of the wearer. The generals wear three silver twisted cords, the senior officers two gold twisted cords and the junior officers a stripe of gold lace. One, two or three narrow stripes of gold lace with black edges, all woven in one piece, show the rank. Two are worn, slipped one on each side of the chin strap. The warrant officers wear leather chin straps with one, two or three stripes of W.O.'s lace at the sides. All the other ranks wear plain leather chin straps. Illustrated in this plate are the chin straps of a General of Brigade, a Lieutenant-Colonel, a Captain and a Warrant Officer. The rank badges illustrated below the chin straps have been worn on a variety of head-dresses (khaki, black, grey-green and maroon berets, mountain field caps and forage caps) which I have loosely described as field caps, although they are not necessarily worn only with the field uniform. These badges used to be worn on the left side of the head-dress and were abolished in February 1971. The officers' rank was shown by gold-embroidered stars, the warrant officers' rank by stripes. The generals' stars were embroidered on silver lace, the senior officers wore stars surrounded by a rectangular gold frame (3 × 5–6 cm., depending on the number of stars) embroidered in gold on khaki, black, etc. material, matching the colour of the head-dress. The three stars of the Colonel Regimental Commander were edged in brick red. The stars of the junior officers were embroidered individually and then stitched on the cap. The Aiutante di Battaglia had three W.O.'s stripes on a red backing. The officers of the mountain troops wear gold lace stripes on the left side of the grey-green cap, behind the gilded feather holder. The centre of the officer's feather holder is usually blank but holders with the Cross of Savoy in its centre are still worn. The O.R.s' feather holder is an oval woollen pompom, of a different colour for each battalion. Enamel badges (Plate 50) are worn pinned on the left side of the cap.

Plate 46. Officers' and Warrant Officers' Rank Badges

In March 1945 the officers' rank badges were moved once again onto the shoulder straps, as they used to be worn before 1934. The generals wear from one to three gold stars on silver lace shoulder straps; Army Corps Generals with Special Appointments (i.e. Army Chief of Staff, Defence Chief of Staff) wear another gold star but with red edging. The same generals wear a fourth stripe with red edging also on the sides of the chin strap.

The senior officers wear gold stars with a stripe of gold lace around the loose ends of the shoulder straps and junior officers wear the stars only. The warrant officers already wore their own gold and black stripes on the shoulder straps, those of the Aiutante di Battaglia being on a red background.

Plate 47. Officers' Rank Badges (Black Uniform)

When the black uniform was first adopted the rank badges were worn on the shoulders of the jacket and greatcoat, and small gilded arm-of-service badges (miniature replicas of the cap badges) were worn on the lapels of the jacket, below the national stars. The rank badges were rectangular (about 3 × 6 cm.) and the stars and frames embroidered on black or white background, depending on whether they had to be worn on black or on white jackets. The generals' badges had a silver background.

In 1963 all the badges of the black uniform were modified. Sleeve rank badges, similar to those worn from 1934 to 1945, were readopted and the arm-of-service badges were moved onto the shoulder frames where the rank stars were previously. Thus the generals now wear small embroidered eagles in the frames and the traditional *greca* and stripes on the sleeves. The stripes are commonly called *lasagne* and the Army Corps General with Special Appointment wears four, the top horizontal stripe edged in red. The senior officers wear a large (1·5-cm.-wide) stripe and from one to three narrow (6-mm.-wide) ones, the regimental commanders on a brick red background. The junior officers wear from one to three narrow stripes.

Sergeants and Corporals

The sergeants of the Italian Army wear V-shaped gold chevrons formed by a large stripe and one or two smaller ones, which are woven in one piece and then stitched into shape on khaki cloth.

The corporals wear black chevrons, except for those of the Parachute Brigade who wear red chevrons on sky blue cloth.

The chevrons are usually worn on both upper sleeves, below the formation sign, if any is worn. On the camouflage overalls and olive-green field jackets only one chevron is worn, stitched above the left pocket. Only one chevron is worn with the summer uniform, stitched below the formation sign onto a 'tongue' hanging from the shirt's left shoulder strap.

Cadets

The three badges illustrated at the bottom of this plate are made of metal and are sewn on slip-ons worn on the shoulder straps of the summer shirts. The letters 'AUC' stand for Allievo Ufficiale di Complemento and are worn by conscripted officer cadets. The N.C.O. cadets wear the letters 'AS', standing for Allievo Sottufficiale, and the cadet squad leaders wear the letters 'ACS' – Allievo Comandante di Squadra.

Gold or silver stripes of lace on the collar of the jacket, blouse or great-coat replace the badges on the winter uniforms. The gold stripe of the A.U.C. and A.S. is stitched along the edges of the collar, all around, starting from below the collar patches if they are worn. The silver stripe of the A.C.S. is worn only at the front, from below the collar patches to the level of the shoulder straps.

Cap Badges

Until 1946 the army was officially known as the Regio Esercito, or Royal Army, and when Italy became a republic the title was changed to Esercito

Italiano, Italian Army. During 1945 and 1946 three types of cap badges were made on a khaki background: large badges, embroidered in gold wire, worn on the peaked cap by officers, warrant officers and sergeants; small gold-embroidered badges for field caps; and the black machine-embroidered badges for corporals and soldiers. Previously they had worn their old badges embroidered on grey-green on the khaki uniform. In 1946 all crowns and royal emblems were abolished; thus the Infantry and the Lancers had their crown replaced by flames; but most army services (Medical, Administrative, etc.) replaced the Royal Crown with the new Crown of the Republic. Cap badges which had no royal emblems (Bersaglieri, mountain troops, Grenadiers, Dragoons, Artillery, Engineers, etc.) remained the same. Since 1945 some of the badges illustrated in these plates have been abolished and others have been adopted in the meantime.

The officers, warrant officers and sergeants wear hand-embroidered badges; large ones embroidered on khaki, black and brick red are found on the peaked cap, and smaller ones on the field cap. Also plastic imitations of gold-embroidered cap badges are used at present and will eventually replace the hand-made ones.

In the last twenty-eight years corporals and soldiers have worn several different types of cap badge, ranging from small brass badges and machine-embroidered badges to plastic and white metal badges. On 15 February 1971 new regulations were published which prescribe the last type, still in use at present.

Plate 48. Cap Badges

A selection of different cap badges is illustrated here: the gold hand-embroidered badges of Infantry, Bersaglieri, Grenadiers, Lancers and some of the badges of the Artillery and Engineers.

The infantry, artillery and engineers of the Folgore Infantry Division wear special cap badges granted to commemorate the exploits of the old Folgore Division at the Battle of Alamein. The infantrymen wear the old divisional cap badge but without the Royal Crown. Artillery men wear Field Artillery cap badges superimposed on crossed swords. The divisional engineers wear the badge of the Pionieri d'Arresto (Plate 49). The khaki beret is the divisional head-dress.

The Lagunari are the amphibious troops of the army. They were formed in 1951 and are stationed and trained on the lagoons of the Northern Adriatic. All ranks wear black berets with gold or yellow thread embroidered cap badges.

The white metal parachutists' badge illustrated is currently worn on the maroon beret by all ranks of the Parachute Brigade. Previously a bi-metal badge was worn by the other ranks on the grey-green beret, whilst the officers, W.O.s and N.C.O.s had gold and silver hand-embroidered badges which, previously, were also embroidered on khaki, for wear on the khaki beret. A new badge for all the Armoured Cavalry was adopted in 1971 and another of these newly-adopted white metal badges is that of the A.A. Artillery. A roundel with the regimental number is fixed onto the centre of the badges. The Dragoons and Engineers' cap badges shown respectively in the 2nd and last row were used soon after the War. They were made of brass and had some small holes for stitching them on the head-dress. Later the O.R.s' cap badges were machine-embroidered in yellow thread on a black background for all armoured units (see Armoured Artillery) and in black thread on khaki for the rest of the army (Plate 49, Medical Service). Subsequently other badges were made in yellow or gold plastic (see Territorial Air Defence) and black plastic (Plate 49, Clerks and Supply Service).

The tank troops for a time wore a brass badge which in the 1930s used to be worn by officers on metal shoulder boards. The badge of the 1930s, however, used to be gilded.

The Heavy A.A. Artillery and the Light A.A. Artillery have been amalgamated and now wear the cap badge of the latter.

Plate 49. Cap Badges

The branch of the Engineers now known as Pionieri d'Arresto wear a special cap badge which is a combination of the Engineers' cap badge and the arm badge of the Guastatori (Plate 54).

Until 1946 a cog-wheel used to be in the centre of the Motor Transport's badge with the Savoy Knot just below. In 1946 the knot was abolished and the cog-wheel became a steering wheel.

The cap badge marked as N.B.C. is worn by personnel of the Nuclear, Biological and Chemical Defence units and, together with that of the Military Postal Service, was adopted in 1971.

The kepi badge worn by the cadets of the Modena Academy is illustrated in the bottom row. It is always superimposed on the national cockade.

Plate 50. Mountain Troops' Cap Badges

The mountain troops still wear their own traditional cap badges on all forms of head-dress. The Mountain Infantry (Alpini) cap badge shows an eagle clutching a bugle, superimposed on crossed rifles; the Mountain Artillery's badge has the eagle and bugle above crossed cannons, and the Engineers and Signals, the eagle and bugle above crossed axes. The latter has electric sparks added all around the axes. There are badges of the Motor Transport with and without the bugle and in all other cases the eagle is depicted just above the arm-of-service badges. The officers, warrant officers and N.C.O.s wear badges embroidered in gold on grey-green felt for the traditional grey-green hat, embroidered in gold on khaki for the khaki peaked cap and on black felt for the black peaked cap. There also exist some small gold-embroidered cap badges for the khaki mountain field cap. The Alpini wear machine-embroidered or black plastic cap badges with a green centre on the grey-green hat. The cadets at the Mountain School wear gold plastic badges. They wear smaller gold or black plastic badges and badges embroidered in black thread on khaki on the mountain field cap. The regimental commanders wear large gold eagles embroidered on brick red felt. The generals of the Mountain Medical Service have the gold eagle embroidered on amaranth felt.

Enamel Badges

All ranks of the mountain troops wear enamel badges on the grey-green hat, near the feather holder. Initially there was one badge for each alpine battalion and mountain artillery group, but a great number of badges have been made in recent years to commemorate the brigades, the regiments, the companies and various support services of each brigade. These badges are usually self-explanatory, depicting regimental and company numbers, feathers and coloured feather holders, local mountains, mottoes, etc. For instance, the badge of the Agordo Group shows its regimental number (it is the 6th Mountain Artillery Regiment) and demonstrates that the group is formed by the 41st, 42nd and 43rd Batteries. The coat of arms of Agordo is shown and the regimental motto, in the local dialect, reads 'Men, rocks and guns, all one piece.'

Some other army units have adopted enamel badges which are usually worn pinned on one of the breast pockets. Illustrated on the left is a badge of the Territorial Air Defence and one of a unit of self-propelled guns.

Collar Patches

These patches are worn on the collar of jackets, blouses and shirts and for a time some larger ones were also worn on the collar of the greatcoat. Smaller patches, usually made of plastic or metal and enamel are used for summer uniforms, on the shirt collar. The Infantry regimental patches are made of felt and Russia braid, or are woven or made of printed ribbon. After the war patches were made of metal, painted in regimental colours, and later, for almost two decades, they were made of plastic. A number of different types of plastic were used and the badges were also made in different sizes. Some recent regulations, however, have introduced a new standard type of collar patch made of metal and coloured enamels. Technically the collar patches are of rectangular shape and in Italy are known as *mostrine*. The collar patches of the Grenadiers, also rectangular, are, however, called *alamari*. The pointed patches are known as 'flames'.

Plate 51. Collar Patches

The Infantry collar patches were adopted in 1902 and at that time were much longer than the present patches; they used to have pointed ends and a small silver button on one side, and a star on the other side, at the front. Plain rectangular collar patches were adopted in 1934 and are still in use at present. After 1946 the Re (King) Brigade, with the black patch with two red stripes, was re-titled Piemonte, and the Regina (Queen) Brigade, with white collar patch, became the Bari Brigade. A great number of Infantry regiments have been formed and subsequently disbanded in the last twenty-eight years and due to the fact that a modern division is composed of three Infantry regiments, the brigade system has ceased to exist. The complete range of the Infantry collar patches can only be illustrated in a volume dealing with World War 1, as most regiments were disbanded in 1919 and never raised again.

All the Cavalry flames which have existed since 1945, have been illustrated. The first four regiments were Dragoons, the 5th, 6th, 7th and 8th regiment were Lancers, the 19th used to be a regiment of Guides and all the others Light Cavalry. The 3rd Savoia Cavalry Regiment was renamed Gorizia and later it became Savoia again, but the collar patch was slightly changed. The Cavalry flames and all the other two- or one-pointed flames are made of coloured felts, plastic or metal and enamel. The Signals, which used to be part of the Engineers, became an independent branch of the army in 1955. All ranks of the Armoured Infantry wear a small brass tank in the centre of their Infantry cap badge, in place of the regimental numbers.

Plate 52. Collar Patches

The Artillery, Engineers and all the services of the alpine brigades and armoured troops wear their original collar patches, superimposed on a rectangular green or blue background respectively. There is no Veterinaries patch with blue background for the armoured troops.

The parachutists of the Parachute Brigade wear special collar patches: the winged sword and parachute could be found embroidered in gold and silver on the patch or, made of metal, can be pinned onto the patch. Some years ago members of the Parachute platoon of the alpine brigades used to wear the green flames on the para. patches, but without parachute. They also used to wear a special enamel badge. Personnel of the Folgore Infantry Division wear similar collar patches, also without the parachute. All the personnel of both the Parachute Brigade and Folgore Infantry Division, except infantrymen, wear their special patches on the blue patch, below the star. Infantrymen of the 183rd Infantry Regiment of the Folgore Division wore plain collar patches whilst infantrymen of the 53rd and 82nd regiments of the same division now wear a small regimental patch below the winged sword; the first, green with a white stripe, and the second, blue with a yellow stripe.

There is only one cap badge for all the Technical Services (Plate 49), while the collar patches are black with piping in the colour of the arm of service, as follows:

yellow	Artillery Service
crimson	Engineers Service
red	Chemical Service
green	Geographical Service
light blue	Signals Service
blue	Motor Transport Service

Plate 53. Miscellaneous Insignia

Until 1964 all qualified parachutists wore an embroidered or brass parachute on the left upper sleeve; the background of this badge was usually sky blue, but the Alpini parachutists wore it with a green background. A new badge was adopted in 1964 to be worn above the right breast pocket and was in gilded metal for officers and silver or white for the other ranks. The badge with the star is worn by the parachutists of the Parachute Brigade and the other, without star, by qualified army parachutists not belonging to that brigade.

The Military Parachute Centre, formed on 18 January 1947, was the first military parachute establishment. All its members wore a special badge made of metal and enamel. The badges for Riggers and Parachute Saboteurs are made of brass and enamel, the breast wings of the 1st Tactical Group are made of bronze and all the other badges are embroidered on the uniform material except for the badge of the Parachute Artillery which is embroidered on sky blue cloth.

The officers, warrant officers and sergeants of the Lagunari wear patches on the collar of their winter jackets, whilst the other ranks wear smaller patches on the cuffs. When in summer uniform, all ranks wear a badge on the breast of the shirt. These latter badges are made in brass and enamel or in brass, with the background painted red. Patches and badges show the winged Lion of St Mark on crossed rifles and an anchor. The collar patches are embroidered in gold, whilst the cuff patches are embroidered in yellow thread or made of plastic.

Plate 54. Specialists' Badges

Only a small selection of specialists' badges have been illustrated in this plate as a great number of such badges have been adopted since 1945.

Most are unofficial, some have been abolished and others have been changed. There are three types of specialists' badges, made of metal or plastic or embroidered.

Amongst the tank badges illustrated the only official one is the brass breast badge surrounded by the wreath and motto, worn by officers in brass or gilded brass, and in silver or white metal by the other ranks. The tank and dragon badge is also made in two variations, of brass and of white metal, and it is often worn, although unofficially. The Anti-Tank badge is made of brass and coloured enamels. The plastic arm badges for tank and armoured car crews are also unofficial; like the others they are made of plastic stamped onto khaki material. There also exists another triangular badge with the title 'Istruttore Milit. di Sci. e Alpinismo', with two skis in the centre as well. Motor-car and motorcycle drivers wear gold-embroidered arm badges as well; the small brass motor-car illustrated was worn until the 1950s, and other badges, embroidered in red thread, used to be worn during the War. That car was older in style and another one, older still, was worn in the early 1930s, embroidered in yellow. A vintage car, embroidered in wool, was worn on the arm during World War 1.

Specialists' Arm Shields and Pocket Badges

A great number of different specialists' arm shields have been worn since the end of the War. The tank crews wear four similar shields on which only the appointment title of the wearer is different, i.e. Tank Chief, Driver, Signaller and Gunner. The size of these shields is 5 × 6 cm. Some smaller shields have been made in recent years in two versions: one made of brass and enamel and the other made of brass and coloured plastic.

Plate 55. Arm Shields.
Infantry and Armoured Divisions and Brigades,
Mountain Brigades and Miscellanea

The Italians call their formation signs *scudetti*, i.e. small shields, and they wear them stitched on the left upper sleeve or, with summer uniform, on a cloth tongue suspended from the shoulder strap.

After World War 2 Italy had five Combat Groups and three formations called Internal Security Divisions; the former eventually became infantry divisions and the latter infantry brigades.

Originally there were six Combat Groups: Folgore, Cremona, Legnano, Friuli, Mantova and Piceno, but the last became a training unit in January 1945.

Later another infantry division was formed, the Granatieri di Sardegna, stationed in Rome and composed of Grenadiers and the 17th Infantry

Regiment. The Aosta, Avellino, Pinerolo and Trieste are independent infantry brigades.

The Ariete and Centauro are armoured divisions, formed by tank and armoured cavalry regiments, while the Pozzuolo del Friuli Armoured Brigade is formed by regiments of armoured cavalry only. The Italian units stationed in Somaliland (Corpo di Sicurezza della Somalia), before this former colony became independent, wore a special blue and red shield with a leopard in its centre.

The five alpine brigades wear shields with the brigade emblem on a green background, which is the colour of the mountain troops.

The Folgore Parachute Brigade consists of the brigade headquarters, the 1st Parachute Regiment, units of airborne artillery and engineers, and support services. The 1st Parachute Regiment was formed in 1962 and the year after all parachute units were formed into a brigade. A yellow thunderbolt (*folgore*) was added some years later to the original arm shield. The 1st Tactical Group is the spearhead of the Brigade. The 3rd Missile Brigade also has an independent unit of parachutists, the Gruppo Acquisizione Obiettivi (Acquisition–Objective Group). These men are initially trained by the Italian Parachute School and subsequently they undertake further training with the U.S. forces of SETAF. Therefore they wear the U.S. Parachute badge as well.

All troops of the garrison in Trieste wear a special badge which depicts the white halberd, taken from the town's coat of arms, on a shield divided into the national colours.

In the late 1940s the officers, warrant officers and sergeants used to wear hand-embroidered shields and the corporals and soldiers used to wear woven ones. Later, woven badges were replaced by plastic badges. Some shields have also been made of metal, usually brass, with painted background.

Plate 56. Training Schools' Arm Shields

These come in three variations: hand-embroidered, woven and plastic, although some O.R.s' shields exist only in two variations, woven or made of plastic. For instance, the first O.R.s' pattern of the Armoured Troops School badge was woven whilst the second pattern was only made in plastic. There is also a similar badge for mechanised troops with 'SC. TR. MECCANIZZATE' written above the shield. These arm shields are mostly self-explanatory.

Germany

Before and during World War 2 Germany expanded territorially in Central Europe but by the spring of 1945 it was completely overrun by the Allied armies which, after the German surrender, assumed supreme authority. It was divided into zones of occupation administered by British, American, Russian and French Military Governors. The capital city of Berlin, in the heart of the Russian Zone, was similarly divided among the victors.

They also formed a Control Council for the administration of Germany as a whole, but the Russians withdrew from it in March 1948.

Since the Fusion Agreement signed in December 1946 the British and U.S. Zones, and later the French Zone, joined in an economic union and subsequently a Parliamentary Council elected by the Diets of the western zones drafted a provisional constitution. The first Federal Government came to office after the publication of the Basic Law, in 1949.

In the zone occupied by the Soviet Army, the People's Council, appointed in 1948, became the People's Chamber, which approved the first Constitution in 1949. The German Democratic Republic was founded on 7 October 1949.

Meanwhile, in Western Germany, when the Federal Government took office, the Allied Military Governors became High Commissioners and when, in 1955, the Federal Republic of Germany became a sovereign nation, they became Ambassadors.

German Federal Republic

The armed forces of the Federal Republic are known as the Bundeswehr and were raised in accordance with the 1955 treaties which provided for Germany's military contribution to NATO.

The first dress regulations are dated 23 July 1955 and the first uniforms were shown to the public on 12 November 1955. The new uniforms adopted in 1955 had no connection whatsoever with the traditional German military dress: all ranks wore grey service and walking-out uniforms, olive-green fatigue uniforms and a camouflage battledress. The grey jackets were double-breasted with two rows of buttons and an open collar, showing the shirt and tie underneath. Officers and sergeants wore longer walking-out jackets than the other ranks, who had only one jacket, considerably shorter, which technically was the service dress jacket worn by all ranks.

The walking-out uniform consisted of the peaked cap, jacket, trousers and shoes. Officers wore white shirt and grey tie and the other ranks grey shirt and tie.

The 'mountain cap', with soft peak and folding sides, was worn with service dress, together with a cloth belt and boots with leggings, the latter subsequently being replaced by jackboots. The new steel helmet, on the American pattern, replaced the mountain cap on armed duties.

An olive-green mountain cap was worn with fatigue uniform, and the helmet with battledress. A grey winter greatcoat and a raincoat were also adopted in 1955 for all ranks' use and both are worn currently.

In January 1957 variations of traditional German collar patches replaced the metal collar badges previously worn and in the summer of the same year a new jacket was adopted for all ranks and is still in use nowadays. It is single-breasted with open collar, four metal buttons at the front and four patch pockets with flap and button. The grey of this jacket is a shade lighter than that of the trousers and head-dress. At the same time a black leather belt, with rectangular voided buckle, replaced the cloth belt previously worn with service dress. The pointed shoulder straps were changed back to the rounded shape in 1962 and during subsequent years other details of the uniform have been changed and new badges adopted. The peaked cap, which originally was round, has now resumed its original German shape and, in the meantime, the side cap has been readopted as well.

New uniforms were introduced for wear on special occasions and others to fit the needs of specialised warfare. The camouflage battledress was replaced by olive-green battledress, issued in summer and winter variations and considerably different for different branches of the army (i.e. airborne and mountain troops, and tank crews).

Plate 57. Cap Badges

The standard cap badge, worn by all ranks of the Bundeswehr, is the yellow, red and black national cockade which usually is worn above the crossed swords, the emblem of the army. When worn on the peaked cap, the crossed swords are superimposed on a wreath of oak leaves and they are worn on their own − below the cockade on all the other types of head-dress except the side cap, on which generally only the cockade is worn at the front. In certain cases, however, the swords are also worn on the side cap, above the cockade. They have to be bent in order to fit the top of the narrow front of the cap.

The peaked cap was introduced in 1955, to complement the walking-out dress and, at the same time, the grey and olive-green mountain caps were introduced respectively for service and fatigue uniforms. The generals wear gold-embroidered cap badges and the officers silver-embroidered cap badges on the peaked cap, both with embroidered cockades. The other ranks wear metal badges. The swords and oak wreath were of a yellow-brownish colour, known as 'old gold', until 1962 when new 'bright old gold' cap badges were issued to the other ranks. The peaked cap piping shows the class of rank of the wearer, i.e. gold piping for the generals and silver for the other officers. In 1955 the generals were granted a double row of gold-embroidered oak leaves on the visor of the peaked cap while all the others wore plain black visors until 1962, when one row of silver-embroidered oak leaves was granted to the senior officers and a silver ornament to the junior officers. The same ornament has also been worn by senior cadets (Oberfähnrich) since 1966.

Gold or silver piping is also worn on the grey mountain and side caps. A metal cockade and crossed swords are worn on the former and all mountain troops wear their traditional edelweiss as well, pinned on the left side. Olive-green and field-grey mountain caps are worn with the fatigue uniform and battledress respectively; their badges are coloured cockade and grey swords, machine-embroidered on one piece of material, the colour of which matches the uniform. The same composite badge was also worn until recently on the beret by tank troops who, together with reconnaissance troops, now wear a black beret with metal cap badge. Since 1971 all rifle units (Jäger) have been issued with green berets and airborne troops with Bordeaux-red berets, both with metal cap badges.

The side cap was originally adopted by the air force and later by the army. There are two army types, one made of grey cloth and worn with grey uniform and another, olive-green, worn by some units with battle-dress. A machine-embroidered cockade is worn on the latter.

Plate 58. Officers' Rank Badges (1955–62)

The standard jacket, adopted in 1955 by the Army of the Bundeswehr, had pointed shoulder straps on which the officers' rank was shown by an arrangement of stars and oak wreaths. The square-shaped stars were similar to those used until 1945 whilst the wreaths were new badges, adopted in order to distinguish the senior ranks.

The generals wore a piping of twisted gold cords around the loose sides of the shoulder straps, gold buttons, gold oak wreaths and stars. Initially there were only three generals' ranks. The rank of full General was created in 1956 and, as the standard stars (21 mm. in diameter) were too large, some new smaller stars (19 mm.) were made for this new rank.

The officers wore a silver cord piping around the shoulder straps with old gold buttons and old gold wreaths and stars. It should be noted that the first senior officers' wreaths were straight. On 1 February 1956 the officers' rank badges were changed to silver and rounded oak wreaths were adopted for the senior officers. In 1959 the buttons of the shoulder straps were also changed to silver.

Plate 59. N.C.O.s' Rank Badges (1955–7)

Three different types of N.C.O.s' rank badges were introduced in 1955: the four senior N.C.O.s wore their rank badges on the shoulder straps in the form of small old gold metal chevrons, in singles and doubles one above the other. The Stabsunteroffizier and Unteroffizier wore chevrons on the upper sleeves and the others wore stripes (half chevrons) on the upper sleeves. These chevrons were made of old gold lace (10 mm. wide) and were woven in a single stripe or in two and three stripes with a dark grey line in between.

1957–9

On 26 July 1957 the new rank of Hauptfeldwebel was created and a new rank badge devised for senior N.C.O.s. It was a diamond-shaped loop made of metal with a brownish old gold finish. The small metal chevrons and the lace chevrons and stripes remained unchanged.

Plate 60. Officers' Rank Badges (1962)

In 1962, new shoulder straps with rounded ends were adopted by all ranks, with gold and silver piping for generals and officers respectively. Piping in arm-of-service colour was added in the form of a cloth underlay protruding all around the shoulder strap. However, many officers for a time wore the old pointed shoulder straps to which they had added the coloured underlay.

The standard old gold buttons were changed in 1959 to gold for generals, silver for officers and grey metal buttons for the other ranks. Later, in 1962, new wreaths and stars were adopted as well. They were both made of a lighter metal and the wreaths were narrower and the stars considerably smaller.

Plate 61. N.C.O.s' Rank Badges (1962–4 pattern)

Between 1957 and 1962 a new regulation, dated 8 June 1959, modified the N.C.O.s' rank badges. The N.C.O.s from Oberstabsfeldwebel to Unteroffizier, were now ordered to wear an old gold stripe around the loose sides of their shoulder straps. The individual rank badges, worn on the shoulder straps or on the sleeves, remained the same.

In 1962 the new rounded shoulder straps with coloured piping were adopted and the N.C.O.s' rank badges were also changed by the 12 November 1962 regulations. The Stabsunteroffizier and Unteroffizier's chevrons were abolished and all the N.C.O.s from Oberstabsfeldwebel to Stabsunteroffizier were entitled to the lace stripe all around the shoulder straps, while the Unteroffizier retained the stripe only around the loose ends of the straps. Thus the wearing of chevrons became unnecessary.

In practice the N.C.O.s, now entitled to the stripe all around the shoulder straps, added the short missing segment of lace on the old pointed shoulder straps, which were kept for a time until they wore out and new ones were made.

In 1964 the old gold badges and stripes were discarded. The new N.C.O.s' badges, still used nowadays, were similar in shape to the former types but made of oxidised white metal (technically called 'old silver') and in relief, whilst the former badges were flat. The stripes are narrower, only 8 mm. wide, made of greyish-yellow lace (bright old gold). The design of the lace has also changed. On 14 May 1973 the stripes on the sleeves were replaced by small old silver metal bars on the shoulder straps.

Plate 62. Officer Cadets' Rank Badges

The officer cadets wore a silver stripe slipped on the shoulder straps until 1962, when they adopted silver stars, worn on both forearms.

Since 1 February 1956 there have been two cadets' ranks: Fähnrich and Fahnenjunker, the former with a small metal chevron on the shoulder straps and the latter with one lace chevron on both upper sleeves.

The letters 'OA' stand for Offizieranwärter (officer candidate). They wore stripes on the upper sleeves.

The cadets' ranks went through stages of insignia changes just like those of other N.C.O.s. In 1959 both Fähnrich and Fahnenjunker adopted old gold stripes around the loose sides of their shoulder straps and, in 1962, the former started wearing the stripe all around the shoulder straps, whilst the Fahnenjunker lost the lace chevrons.

The rank of Oberfähnrich was instituted on 5 May 1966. Its insignia is the diamond-shaped loop, made of old silver, and worn on officers' shoulder straps.

Non-Commissioned Officer Cadets

Until 1 January 1973 the N.C.O. cadets wore a cuff title on both sleeves with the inscription 'Unteroffizierschule' followed by the Roman numerals I or II, embroidered in silver on a dark grey background. The cuff title is 30 mm. wide with silver edgings. Since 1958 the N.C.O. cadets have been appointed to corporal ranks after school training and their appointment is shown by a 6-cm. horizontal stripe above the usual corporal's stripes.

The letters 'UA' stand for Unteroffizieranwärter (N.C.O. candidate). On 14 May 1973 the stripes of the Gefreiter UA were replaced by small bars made of metal, worn on the shoulder straps.

Field Uniform Rank Badges

The generals, officers and sergeants wear different rank badges on field and fatigue uniforms whilst the corporals wear their usual stripes. The badges (wreaths, stars, etc.) are machine-embroidered on ready-made patches which are worn slipped on the shoulder straps or, in the case of uniforms without shoulder straps, stitched on the upper sleeves, below the national colours. The generals' rank badges are embroidered in yellow thread. As no arm-of-service badges are worn on field uniforms, since autumn 1962 a coloured band has often been worn slipped on at the end of the shoulder straps.

The national insignia is worn on both sleeves of the field uniform, at 6 cm. below the shoulder; it is a small machine-embroidered national flag, 5 × 2.5 cm. in size.

Plate 63. Collar Badges

In 1955 the new German Army was issued with metal collar badges, which were worn by all ranks on the collar of the grey jacket and of the fatigue uniform.

The generals wore their traditional gold-embroidered collar patches and officers of the General Staff Service also wore collar patches (Plate 64), whilst all the others wore metal badges. Personnel of the armoured units and of the Medical Service wore badges made in pairs, with the tanks and the snakes facing outward respectively; all the others were made in singles. Personnel of the Armoured Infantry should have worn a tank above crossed sabres and Reconnaissance Troops a shield superimposed on crossed lances, but due to the fact that metal badges were worn only for a short time the latter two badges were never used. The collar badges were made of solid metal with brownish old gold finish.

Miscellaneous Insignia

Before the adoption of divisional arm badges the mountain troops and the airborne troops wore distinguishing oval-shaped arm badges featuring an edelweiss and a parachute. The first one later became the divisional badge and the airborne troops adopted a parachute on a blue shield (Plate 66) as their divisional badge.

Qualified Mountain Guides wear their badge on the right breast pocket; it is very similar to that worn during the War but is now embroidered. The Hand-to-Hand Combat badge is also embroidered and worn on the right breast pocket.

The Marksman's lanyard was reintroduced in the early 1960s and it is worn attached to the right shoulder strap and to the first button of the jacket. The lanyard is made of twisted matt silver cords and is awarded in three classes, shown by a gold, silver or bronze badge pinned onto it at the shoulder.

The belt buckle is made of old silver metal and the same buckle is worn by all ranks, except generals who wear gold buckles.

Plate 64. Collar Patches

In 1955 only the generals and the officers of the General Staff Service wore collar patches. The first G.S. collar patches were embroidered on grey background cloth, later changed to the traditional crimson. On 1 January 1957 the traditional German double bars, embroidered on rectangular coloured patches, replaced the metal collar badges previously used. The arm-of-service colours adopted in 1957 were the following:

rifle-green	Infantry
grass-green	Armoured Infantry (Panzergrenadiere)
dark green	Anti-Tank Units
pink	Armoured Troops
golden-yellow	Armoured Reconnaissance
red	Artillery
coral-red	Army Anti-Aircraft
lemon-yellow	Signals
black	Engineers
Bordeaux-red	Atomic-Biological-Chemical Defence Troops

blue	Technical Troops
dark blue	Medical Troops
light blue	Quartermasters
orange	Military Police
light grey	Army Aviation
white	Military Bands

Subsequently, the collar patches of the Armoured Infantry, Anti-Tank units and Quartermasters were discarded and the first two became part of the Infantry, adopting its patches. The same green patches are also worn by rifle units, grenadiers, mountain and airborne troops. The remaining thirteen arm-of-service colours have also been shown on the shoulder straps since 1962, when piping was adopted.

The officers wear matt grey hand-embroidered collar patches, slightly longer than those of the other ranks, which are woven and measure 5.5 × 3 cm. in size.

Two O.R.s' collar patches have been illustrated in the bottom row of patches, at the left; the following three on the right are no longer in use, and like the others are now worn by officers.

Plate 65. Parachutists' Wings

The first type of parachute insignia (1) was adopted very early and vaguely resembles the wartime Close Combat clasp. It was worn above the right breast pocket of the jacket and it was made of old silver metal, although an embroidered type also existed for fatigue or field uniforms. Later, another breast badge was adopted (2), embroidered on grey felt in matt silver for officers and grey thread for other ranks. The third and final pattern (3) of parachutist's badge was adopted in 1965. It is a silver-embroidered badge and is issued in three classes, represented respectively by a gold, silver or bronze wreath. It is still worn above the right pocket.

Arm Badges

These arm badges are worn on the left forearm by specialised personnel and are usually hand-embroidered for officers and machine-embroidered for other ranks on a circular grey background. They were initially adopted by the Medical Service in four variations: for Doctors and medical personnel, Veterinaries, Pharmacists and Dentists. The generals of the Medical Service wore a badge embroidered in gold, officers wore silver-embroidered badges and the other ranks wore badges embroidered in grey thread. Veterinaries, Pharmacists and Dentists are always officers. By a new regulation of April 1972 Doctors, Veterinaries, Pharmacists and dental officers were granted new metal badges to be used on the shoulder straps instead of arm badges. The design of the badges remained unchanged, although the new badges are smaller and made of old silver for officers and gilded metal for generals. Some badges worn by the other ranks only show a letter of the alphabet, which stands for the wearer's qualifications, in the following order:

S	Schirrmeister	Storekeeper (vehicles, cars, etc.)
F	Feuerwerker	Artificer
I	Instandsetzungstruppführer	Repair Maintenance Fitter
W	Wallmeister	Fortification Maintenance
P	Prüfer	Equipment Inspector (Parachute units)
A	Absetzer	Rigger (Parachute units)

Cuff Titles

Another two cuff titles exist besides those of the N.C.O.s' schools. One is worn by the Guards Battalion stationed in Siegburg, near Bonn, and the other by all personnel of the Army Aviation. They are both 30 mm. wide, with silver edgings and lettering or wings hand- or machine-embroidered on a dark grey background.

Plate 66. Formation Badges

The formation badges were adopted in December 1962 and are still worn on the left upper sleeve by all ranks of the German Army.

The badges of the staff headquarters always have the German spread eagle in the centre; those of the training schools and depots have crossed swords in the centre while divisional badges show the emblem of the division.

The first badge illustrated is worn by personnel serving at the Ministry of Defence (*Bundesministerium der Verteidigung*) and it has a golden-yellow border with black lines. The same badge, but with a silver and black lined border, is worn by personnel of the Territorial Defence Command (*Kommando der Territorialen Verteidigung*); the personnel of the Bundeswehr's Central Military Stations (*Zentrale Militärische Bundeswehrdienststellen*) have a red border on the badge. The same badge, but with a dark blue border, is also worn at the Central Medical Stations (*Zentrale Sanitätsdienststellen*). Personnel of the six Military District Commands (*Wehrbereichskommandos* I–VI) wear the same badge with silver and black lined border and Roman numerals (from I to VI) below the eagle.

The third badge illustrated in this plate is that of the 1st Corps Headquarters. There are similar badges for the 2nd and 3rd Corps H.Q. The same badge with a pink border is worn by personnel of the 100th, 200th and 300th Tank Regiments, respectively part of the 1st, 2nd and 3rd Corps.

Personnel serving at depots wear crossed swords with a small flaming grenade beneath. The same badge, but with an 'L' or 'S' below the swords, are used by training and demonstration units. The badge with the 'L' is worn by soldiers serving in training brigades, or by demonstration units in training schools. The 'S' is worn by training staff, instructors and N.C.O. students. Identical badges, but with different borders, stand for different branches of training, as is explained below:

Border Colour	Branch of Training
silver/black stripes	Army Officers and N.C.O.s' Schools
	Heeresoffizierschulen
light grey	Army Aviation School
	Heeresfliegerwaffenschule
lemon-yellow	Signals School
	Fernmeldeschule
orange	Military Police School
	Feldjägerschule
rifle-green	Combat Schools I, III and IV (Infantry)
	Kampftruppenschulen I, III and IV
pink	Combat School II (Armour)
	Kampftruppenschule II
brick-red	Artillery School
	Artillerieschule
brick-red/blue stripes	Rocket School
	Raketenschule
green/white stripes	Airborne–Air Transportation School
	Luftlande–Lufttransportschule
coral-red	Anti-Aircraft School
	Flugabwehrschule
black	Engineers' School
	Pionierschule
Bordeaux-red	Atomic–Biological–Chemical Defence School
	A.B.C.–Abwehrschule
blue	School of Technical Troops
	Schule der Tech. Truppen I–III

The Army of the Bundeswehr has twelve divisions each with its divisional emblem on the badge. However, the personnel of the divisional headquarters of each division wear the badge with a silver border and black lines, those of the 1st brigade in each division, a plain white border, those of the 2nd brigade, a red border, and those of the 3rd, a yellow border. There are thus the following divisional-brigade badges:

Division	Brigade	Coloured Border
1st Armoured Division	H.Q.	silver/black lines
	1st Brigade	white
	2nd Brigade	red
	3rd Brigade	yellow
2nd Armoured Infantry Division (now Rifle Division)	H.Q.	silver/black lines
	4th Brigade	white
	5th Brigade	red
	6th Brigade	yellow
3rd Armoured Division	H.Q.	silver/black lines
	7th Brigade	white
	8th Brigade	red
	9th Brigade	yellow
4th Armoured Infantry Division (now Rifle Division)	H.Q.	silver/black stripes
	10th Brigade	white
	11th Brigade	red
	12th Brigade	yellow
5th Armoured Division	H.Q.	silver/black lines
	13th Brigade	white
	14th Brigade	red
	15th Brigade	yellow
6th Armoured Infantry Division	H.Q.	silver/black lines
	16th Brigade	white
	17th Brigade	red
	18th Brigade	yellow
7th Armoured Infantry Division	H.Q.	silver/black lines
	19th Brigade	white
	20th Brigade	red
	21st Brigade	yellow
1st Mountain Division	H.Q.	silver/black lines
	22nd Brigade	white
	23rd Brigade	red
	24th Brigade	yellow
1st Airborne Division	H.Q.	silver/black lines
	25th Brigade	white
	26th Brigade	red
	27th Brigade	yellow

10th Armoured Infantry Division (now Armoured Division)	H.Q.	silver/black lines
	28th Brigade	white
	29th Brigade	red
	30th Brigade	yellow
11th Armoured Infantry Division	H.Q.	silver/black lines
	31st Brigade	white
	32nd Brigade	red
	33rd Brigade	yellow
12th Armoured Division	H.Q.	silver/black lines
	34th Brigade	white
	35th Brigade	red
	36th Brigade	yellow

The average armoured division is formed by one armoured infantry (*Panzergrenadiere*) brigade and two armoured (*Panzer*) brigades, while the armoured infantry division is formed by two armoured infantry brigades and one armoured brigade. The rifle division has two rifle (*Jäger*) brigades and an armoured one, although the 2nd Rifle Division is still in the process of reorganisation.

The airborne division consists of three airborne (*Luftlande*) brigades and the mountain division is formed by two mountain (*Gebirgsjäger*) brigades and one armoured infantry brigade, which used to be an armoured mountain (*Geb. Pz.*) brigade.

All the formation badges, except that of the 1st Mountain Division, are shield-shaped and can be obtained in two versions: hand- and machine-embroidered.

German Democratic Republic

In January 1956, the People's Chamber of the G.D.R. sanctioned the establishment of the Ministry of National Defence and of the National People's Army (*Nationale Volksarmee* — N.V.A.) and in January 1962 legislation was passed which introduced general conscription. The Border Police came under the control of the Defence Ministry in September 1961.

The G.D.R. has been a member of the Warsaw Treaty since its establishment in May 1955; thus the N.V.A. automatically became associated with the armed forces of the U.S.S.R. and of the other Eastern European countries, under the united command of the member states of the Treaty.

The uniforms adopted by the N.V.A. are very similar in style to the traditional German uniforms which were in use until 1945, although the colour of the material is now different — stone-grey, the uniform collar being made of a darker material.

All ranks are entitled to wear service, walking-out, parade and field uniforms. They also have a double-breasted greatcoat with two rows of five buttons and a darker collar, buttoned up to the neck.

The ordinary tunic is single-breasted with five buttons and four patch pockets. The tunics of the walking-out and parade uniform have cuff patches and coloured piping on the cuffs. The officers have piping around the collar also. The tunic of the service uniform has no cuff patches and has piping only around the shoulder straps, which are the same for all uniforms.

All ranks can also wear an off-duty double-breasted jacket with open collar and two side pockets. Cuff patches are worn on this jacket, together with coloured piping around the cuffs and the top of the collar. This jacket is optional and must be bought privately if wanted.

The colour of the piping was the arm-of-service colour until 1962 but since then the uniform piping has been light green for the Border Troops and white for the rest of the army. The arm-of-service colours have been retained around the shoulder straps and on the collar and cuff patches only.

The peaked cap is worn with the service and walking-out uniforms: the side cap is usually worn by soldiers with service uniform and by all ranks with the field uniform. The helmet is worn by all ranks with the parade and field uniforms. The parachutists initially wore stone-grey berets; the beret worn with the parade and walking-out uniforms had white piping all around the sides. In 1968 they were issued with red berets. During the winter months all ranks wear a fur cap with folding sides together with the greatcoat.

The traditional mountain cap, with folding sides, was reintroduced in 1956 but a different mountain cap was adopted later. It is round, with folding sides joined at the top, and it also has a narrow cloth chin strap.

The standard Eastern European field uniform, made of striped cloth, is currently worn together with special camouflage overalls or utility garments.

In 1966 the sports overalls were adopted: the N.C.O.s wear a small silver-grey stripe on the left upper sleeve and the officers, two stripes.

Plate 67. Cap Badges

The national cockade surrounded by a wreath of oak leaves is worn on the peaked cap by all ranks; it is embroidered in gold wire for the generals and silver for officers, and made of white metal for the other ranks.

Initially the cockade consisted of the black, red and yellow national colours, later changed to the coat of arms of the G.D.R.

The generals wear gold twisted cords above the visor while the officers wear silver cords and the O.R.s wear a plain leather chin strap. The cap band is made of dark grey material with the exception of that of the Border Troops who wear light green cap bands, generals included. All other army generals wear red cap bands, and thus their cap badges are embroidered on red felt. A narrow coloured piping is worn around the crown of the peaked cap and on the upper side of the cap band.

The same type of cap badge is also used by all ranks on the mountain cap and by officers on the fur cap, while the O.R.s wear only the cockade on the latter. The cockade on its own is also worn on the side cap.

Breast Badges

A number of breast badges are worn by army personnel, usually above the right breast pocket of the tunic as the ribbons are worn on the other side.

All officers who have attended courses at the General Staff Academy and the Military Academy of the Soviet Army are entitled to wear special diamond-shaped badges made of metal and red and white enamel. They are both worn above any other badges already worn above the right breast pocket. The triangular badges of the Military Academy are also made of metal and enamel. As it is customary in the G.D.R. to name military institutions and units after socialist heroes, the Military Academy is named after Frederick Engels and his portrait is present in the centre of the badge. Similarly the portrait of Ernst-Moritz Arndt is on the badge of the Military Medical Section of the E.-M. Arndt University in Greifswald. The third badge is worn by officers who have graduated at a civilian university or high school.

Other badges are granted to individuals in order to stimulate their enthusiasm and keenness. The parachutist's badge is worn on the left breast.

Plate 68. Officers' Rank Badges

The N.V.A. officers display their rank on the shoulder straps, which in appearance conform with German military tradition.

The general's shoulder strap is made up of three interlaced cords, two gold and one silver, on which the individual rank is shown by five-pointed stars, or pips, made of silvered metal. Initially, in 1956, the stars were worn pointing outwards, whilst now they point inwards towards the collar. The backing material is red for army generals and light green for the generals of the Border Troops.

The senior officers' shoulder straps have two interlaced silver double cords while the junior officers wear the same silver cords straight, on a cloth underlay of arm-of-service colour. Both senior and junior officers' rank is shown by gold four-pointed stars.

The N.V.A. has three lieutenants' ranks in order to comply with Eastern European custom.

Medical officers now wear the Staff of Aesculapius on the shoulder straps, above the stars.

The officers and sergeants used to wear different rank insignia on the field uniform: these were stripes worn on the upper sleeves. At that time there were only three sergeants' ranks and, therefore, the Unteroffizier had one stripe, the Feldwebel two stripes and the Oberfeldwebel three stripes. The junior officers wore a thicker stripe with from one to four stripes above it, and the senior officers wore two thicker stripes with from one to three normal stripes above it. At present the usual rank badges are worn on the shoulder straps, but are embroidered in grey thread.

Plate 69. N.C.O.s' Rank Badges

In 1956 only three sergeants' ranks were adopted and only later, in 1962, were the ranks of Stabsfeldwebel and Unterfeldwebel added. From July 1960 until 1 January 1971 the Artillery sergeants had the title of Wachtmeister instead of Feldwebel: thus their rank titles were Stabswachtmeister, Oberwachtmeister, Wachtmeister and Unterwachtmeister. The infantry private was known as Schütze and the artillery private as Kanonier but, since 1971, all privates have been called Soldat.

An Oberfeldwebel can be appointed to the rank of Hauptfeldwebel (or Hauptwachtmeister) and consequently he can wear a stripe of lace above the cuffs. Corporals show their rank on the shoulder straps in the form of one or two silver stripes. The shoulder straps are typically Germanic, with rounded ends and piping in arm-of-service colours. Bandsmen wear the lyre on both straps, together with the usual rank badges.

Cadets' Rank Badges

The officer cadets have a silver stripe all around the loose sides of their shoulder straps on which they also wear a gothic 'S' made of white metal. The stripes at the outer ends of the shoulder straps represent the years of training and N.C.O. rank to which they are appointed (i.e. one stripe Unteroffizier, two stripes Feldwebel, etc.). The training to become an officer usually takes four years, the exception being medical officer training, which takes six years.

The N.C.O. cadet can be recognised by the coloured stripes he wears at the outer ends of the shoulder straps. The colour of the stripes matches the piping and shows the rank to which the cadet is appointed.

On 1 September 1956 a cadet school was opened for the training of young people and it existed until June 1960, when it was finally abolished. The boys wore army uniforms without collar patches and with a white metal 'K' on both shoulder straps. The junior cadets could reach the rank of Gefreiter and then wear a stripe of silver lace on the shoulder straps. The senior cadets wore a silver stripe at the front of the collar and around the shoulder straps, the Unteroffizier cadet wore the stripe around the loose sides of the straps, the Feldwebel cadet all around the shoulder straps with one silver star.

Service Stripes

The first pattern of service stripe was adopted in 1956: V-shaped chevrons worn on the left forearm. The one-stripe chevron was worn by personnel with more than three years' service; after five years' service the two-stripe chevron was worn.

On 1 January 1965 two different chevrons were introduced and are now worn on the right forearm. The one-stripe chevron is worn by soldiers who volunteer for three years service and the two-stripes chevron is worn by professional N.C.O.s, usually sergeants, who serve for a twelve-year period.

Plate 70. Patches/Arm-of-Service Colours

The generals of the N.V.A. wear the traditional German general's collar and cuff patches embroidered in gold. The collar patches of the generals of the Border Troops are embroidered on light green material while those of generals of the rest of the army are embroidered on red.

The officers and other ranks wear the traditional double bars on the collar and also on the cuffs of the 'dress' uniforms. The double bars are embroidered, woven or stitched on a background material the colour of which matches the material of the collar or cuffs.

The officers' collar and cuff patches are embroidered in silver while the other ranks wear grey woven patches or silver lace bars stitched on dark stone-grey patches. Some examples of each type have been illustrated. Initially the parachutists wore the same collar patches as the rest of the army, with white arm-of-service colour, from 1962 until autumn 1964 when the colour was changed to orange. On 1 November 1969 the patches were changed to the pattern illustrated. The officers wear the same patch with silver twisted cord piping all around.

The following are the arm-of-service colours:

white	Infantry (now Motorised Rifles)
red	Artillery and Rocket Troops
pink	Armoured Troops
black	Engineers, Chemical Service and all Technical Services
yellow	Signals
dark green	Medical, Legal and all other Non-Combatant Services
orange	Parachutists
light grey	Air Defence (and Missiles)
light green	Border Troops
olive-green	Pioneers

Plate 71. Miscellaneous Insignia

Both the proficiency and qualification badges are worn above the right breast pocket of the tunic and are awarded in three classes.

The Marksman lanyard is made of twisted matt silver cords and it is worn from the right shoulder to the second button of the tunic. Infantry, artillery and armour marksmanship are represented by different badges which are applied on the knot at the top of the lanyard. It is awarded in three classes which are distinguished by one (2nd class) and two (1st class) acorns.

There are three types of belt buckles: a gilded metal one for generals, and a silver for other officers, worn on the lace belt of the parade uniform, and the rectangular white metal buckle for other ranks. Officers wear a leather belt with plain Sam Browne type belt buckle with the service uniform.

Plate 72. Arm Badges

The badges illustrated are those worn at present on the left forearm of the tunic. The badges adopted initially were embroidered in yellow and were those of the medical and radio-location services now still in existence. There was also an oval badge for Helmsman, a round badge with a gothic

'F' for Artificier and another round badge with crossed guns for the Ordnance personnel. The first two were similar to those previously in use until 1945. Subsequently, the Helmsman badge was abolished and the other two were modified.

From 17 December 1957 to the beginning of 1966 the badges (Signals, Motor-Driver Technician, Radio Technician, Radio-Location, Medical, Armour and Reconnaissance) were embroidered in arm-of-service colours. Since 1966 all these badges have been machine-embroidered in silver thread, although there are also in existence hand-embroidered badges with silver piping all around the edges, for officers of the medical and legal services. The badge is now worn on the shoulder straps instead of on the arm.

Before November 1969 the parachutists wore an oval arm badge, depicting the parachute above the wings, which was later transferred onto the collar patches.

All ranks of the Guards Regiment stationed in Berlin wear white piping and officers' belt buckles, and on special occasions they wear white belts with cross strap. They also have a distinctive cuff title, with the inscription 'NVA-WACHREGIMENT', which they wear on the left sleeve.

U.S.S.R.

The Red Army of Workers and Peasants was renamed the Soviet Army in 1946. The Red Army traced its origins to the Red Guards, which were revolutionary formations active in Russia long before the 1917 Revolution. The Red Army was born officially in February 1918 and, although Russia had disentangled herself from World War 1, conscription was reintroduced in April 1918 in order to quell the anti-bolshevik movements and internal disorder.

Initially, the new army was mainly formed by infantry and, in order to create a separate striking force, all the cavalry units were gathered to form a Cavalry Corps which later, during the war against Poland, expanded into two Cavalry Armies.

The Red Army went through a period of redevelopment and mechanisation during the 1930s but it was during the Finnish War and subsequent World War 2 that Russian industrial resources, combined with battle experience, built the great military power which we know now. In 1945 the Red Army consisted of more than 500 infantry divisions, plus cavalry and artillery divisions, tank and mechanised corps (equivalent to divisions), anti-aircraft divisions and a great number of tank brigades and independent tank regiments.

In 1946 the STAVKA (Headquarters of the Supreme Commander of the Armed Forces) was replaced by the Military Council, and many other administrative changes and reorganisations have taken place since. In 1952 the airborne forces, previously under the Air Force, became a separate arm.

At the end of World War 2 officers of the Red Army were provided with a parade/walking-out uniform, an ordinary uniform and the field uniform. A white peaked cap and jacket were worn during summer in hot climates and a fur hat and greatcoat in winter.

The other ranks were issued with ordinary and field uniforms. The former were also used for parades and ceremonial occasions.

In April 1955 a new parade uniform was adopted by the marshals and generals: it was similar to the 1943 pattern but made of dark bluish-green material and now was double-breasted with two rows of six buttons. The gold ornamentation on the peaked cap, the shoulder boards and all the other details relating to the rank of the wearer remained the same.

In the following years an entirely new style of khaki uniform came into use. It was very similar to a civilian double-breasted suit; the jacket had an open collar with pointed lapels and two rows of three buttons. It was adopted in 1949 initially by the generals and officers of the Air Force and Armoured Corps, and it later became standard issue.

In April 1954 this new jacket, made of dark bluish-green material, was adopted by all the marshals and generals as a parade/walking-out uniform and with a khaki version for ordinary wear. During the following months summer uniforms in the same style were adopted as well; made of light grey material for the Marshal of the Soviet Union and white for the other marshals and generals. Later, in 1955, grey or khaki uniforms were adopted for all officers of the ground forces, including the generals whose dark bluish-green dress was replaced by a grey one.

The parade and the walking-out uniforms are very similar. For example the parade uniform of the marshals and generals consisted of the peaked cap with gold ornamentation, jacket, breeches and cavalry boots and was worn with decorations, medals and gold waist belt. The same dress, but with trousers instead of breeches, with medal ribbons only and without the waist belt, was the walking-out uniform.

The ordinary uniform consisted of the khaki peaked cap, khaki double-breasted jacket and dark blue trousers or breeches.

Three years later the officers' jacket was modified to the pattern which is in use currently: it is single-breasted with four buttons and without pointed lapels. The cuff patches have been abolished and the badges considerably simplified.

By a decree of 26 July 1969 of the Ministry of Defence, the uniforms of the officers and long-serving N.C.O.s were divided into service/parade and parade/walking-out uniforms, plus the ordinary and field uniforms.

The other ranks (conscripted N.C.O.s and soldiers) have a parade/walking-out uniform, the ordinary uniform and the field uniform.

Although the shirt-tunic is still worn, it has been widely replaced by some more comfortable jackets and tunics. The O.R.s' khaki jacket is similar to that of the officers, with an open collar showing shirt and tie and without breast pockets. It is worn together with the helmet, breeches and high boots, with the personal weapons for parade duties and with the peaked cap and trousers as a walking-out uniform.

A tunic with buttoned-up folded collar, and without breast pockets, is worn together with forage cap as the other ranks' ordinary uniforms, which is the only uniform usually possessed by the conscripted other ranks.

The airborne troops wear light blue berets, light blue collar patches and shoulder straps.

New field uniforms have also been adopted for winter and summer and special overalls are worn by airborne and armoured troops. The fur hat and greatcoat are still worn during winter.

Plate 73. Service Chevrons (26 November 1945)

The first decree on dress regulations to be published after World War 2 appropriately granted service chevrons to be worn on the left upper sleeve, just above the elbow, by the war veterans. The chevrons consisted of silver or gold stripes of lace, 15 or 25 mm. in width, V-shaped at an angle of 95–105 degrees. One narrow silver chevron was worn after one year's service, one wide silver chevron was added after the second year, one narrow gold one after the third and a wide gold one after the fifth year of service.

Shoulder Boards

On 31 January 1947, due to the post-war reorganisation of the Soviet Army, the generals and officers of the Reserve and Retired Lists were distinguished from those in active service by the adoption of 28-mm. lace stripes worn across the shoulder boards. The reservists wore plain stripes while the others had a zigzag motif woven on the same stripe as the former: silver stripes were worn on gold shoulder boards and vice-versa.

Arm Badges

Two new arm badges were authorised, for parachutists and personnel of the Railway Military Transport, on 18 August 1947 and 13 February 1951 respectively.

The badge of the parachutists measures 5.5 × 11 cm. and the winged parachutist in its centre 3.7 × 8 cm., and the surrounding edging is 2.5 mm. wide. The badge is worn on the left upper sleeve.

The badge of the Railway Military Transport was 4.5 × 10.5 cm. in size, surrounded by a 2-mm. edging all around.

Plate 74. Railway Military Transport

The railway system has always been the most important, vital service of Russia due to the vastness of its territory. As early as 1919 the personnel of the railways wore their own special badge on a red armband which, together with the red star, is one of the first badges to have been officially adopted by the Red Army. The badge is the winged wheel, then made in white metal and affixed on a diamond-shaped patch with yellow or green edging. Later, during World War 2, the same badge, always on the diamond-shaped patch, was worn on the left upper sleeve of the uniform and the winged wheel, on its own, on the red crown of the peaked cap. Small metal winged wheels were also worn as collar badges before 1936.

A new badge, for wearing on the sleeve and on the collar, was adopted in 1936 by the combined Railway–Road–Waterways Communications Service. It depicted a star superimposed on an anchor and crossed hammer and spanner, with side wings.

On 13 February 1951 new regulations prescribed the wearing of the composite badge described above on the arm and shoulder straps and of the winged wheel on the crown of the peaked cap, above the red star. New collar patches and cap bands were adopted as well, in the colours previously used by the engineers in the 1920s: black with blue piping. The new arm badge therefore is mounted on a diamond-shaped backing (4.5 × 10.5 mm.) which is black with blue edging, and blue piping surrounds the shoulder boards.

Service Chevrons

New service chevrons were authorised on 31 March 1952 for personnel serving longer than their period of conscription. One narrow gold chevron was awarded for the first two years of re-enlistment, and two narrow chevrons for the next two years. One wide gold chevron was worn by personnel re-enlisting for a further period of from four to ten years' service and, finally, two wide chevrons were awarded to personnel who served for over ten years. The narrow lace stripe was 10 mm. in width, the wide one 25 mm., and the finished chevron was 10 cm. in length.

Parade and Ordinary Uniforms (9 April 1954)

The jackets of the pattern already introduced in 1949 were adopted by the marshals and generals in 1954 as part of the dark bluish-green parade/walking-out uniforms and khaki ordinary uniforms (as described in the introduction to this section). The Marshal of the Soviet Union had an oak leaf motif embroidered in gold on the collar and cuffs of the dark bluish-green jacket, while the other marshals and generals had a laurel leaf motif, combined in both cases with double gold piping and red piping.

The khaki ordinary uniform did not have gold-embroidered trimmings. Instead it was worn with collar patches and a red piping on the peaked cap, collar and cuffs of the jacket. The Marshal of the Soviet Union wore red patches with gilded buttons surrounded on three sides by gold piping, and the other marshals and generals patches in arm-of-service colour with gilded buttons and gold piping.

Plate 75. Lapels and Cuffs

On 10 June 1954 new regulations were issued and during that summer new ordinary uniforms were introduced for the top ranking officers. Those of the Marshal of the Soviet Union were made of light grey material and the others of khaki. Gold oak and laurel motifs replaced the patches on the collar and the small left breast pocket of the previous jacket was ultimately abolished.

The same style of uniform, similar to a civilian double-breasted suit, was officially adopted by all officers on 25 February 1955. It came in two versions: grey for parade/walking-out uniforms and khaki for ordinary wear.

A leaf ornamentation was present on the collar and on the cuffs of the former, with gilded collar badges, while collar patches with the arm-of-service badge at the apex were worn on the khaki uniform. The officers of the armoured troops had black facing around the collar of the grey uniform.

Visors, Chin Straps and Belts

The regulations of 10 June 1954, previously mentioned, also prescribed gold ornamentation on the visor of the peaked caps.

Gold and silver cords were authorised in 1940 for the Marshal of the Soviet Union and generals, together with new round cap badges. Three years later the oak and laurel motifs were adopted, embroidered on cap bands, collars and cuffs. On 20 February 1949 the officers of the armoured troops were granted one row of gold oak leaves on the visor of the parade peaked cap, the marshals and generals of the same service with the addition of a double gold piping around the rim.

Thus in the summer of 1954, the same ornamentation was granted to the marshals and generals of the rest of the army.

Gold waist belts with gilded belt buckles were adopted on 25 February 1955 as part of the marshals' and officers' parade uniform.

Plate 76. Parade Peaked Caps (1955)

The ornamentation of the peaked cap was modified further by some new regulations during 1955.

The new oval cap badge (see also Plate 83) was adopted on 25 February 1955 to be worn on its own on the cap band of the officers' khaki ordinary peaked cap. This peaked cap has a black leather visor and chin strap. A gold twin-cord chin strap was added to the officers' grey peaked cap of the parade/walking-out uniform and the cap badge was now applied onto an ornament of gold leaves. The gold ornamentation was adopted on the visor the previous year.

On 3 March 1955 a new gold chin strap was introduced for the grey peaked cap of the parade/walking-out uniform of marshals and generals. The new oval cap badge was applied on the gold oak or laurel leaves ornamentation already adopted in 1943. The same regulations also prescribed an ornamentation of gold oak leaves on the visor of the grey peaked cap of the Marshal of the Soviet Union and an ornamentation of laurel leaves on that of the other marshals and generals.

All marshals and generals have the new cap badge on a plain red cap band, together with gold cords and black leather visor, on the ordinary khaki peaked cap.

Plate 77. Arm-of-Service Badges (1955)

These small badges are worn on the shoulder straps or on the collar patches and show the branch of service of the wearer. They are considerably different from those used during the War, even for the branches of service which still exist today. A tank, for instance, is still the badge of the armoured troops, but it is an entirely different tank from that previously used.

Often one badge is worn by personnel of several different services, as in the case of the crossed hammer and spanner of the technical troops, worn by chemical and smoke units (toxic, smoke producing and incendiary warfare), electric line-of-communications layers and technical engineers. The badge of the Engineers–Technical Troops is worn by fitters, builders and maintenance units. All these badges were authorised on 23 June 1955.

Collar Patches for Overcoat (23 June 1955)

A new overcoat was introduced for summer wear in June 1955 and some special collar patches (7.5 cm. in length) were authorised at the same time. The marshals and generals were granted gold or silver piping on three sides of the patch. That of the Marshal of the Soviet Union had a golf leaf motif; the others had a laurel leaf motif. The marshals and generals of the non-combatant services (Medical, Veterinary and Legal) had a silver motif and silver piping.

On 1 August 1955 similar collar patches were adopted for the officers' overcoat, worn with arm-of-service badges at their apex. Such patches were made only in three colours, raspberry-red, black and dark green, which do not necessarily match the colours of the marshals' and generals' services. The branch of service of the wearer was further distinguished by its badge.

Plate 78. Orchestra of the Regimental Garrison at Moscow (11 March 1955)

The musicians of this orchestra had a special parade uniform with red cap bands, shoulder boards and cuffs, and blue piping. Their tunics were double-breasted with six buttons on two rows, and white waist belts.

They also wore the Bandsman badge, the lyre, on the peaked cap and on the collar.

The Honorary Guards (1 August 1955)

All ranks of this unit were issued with new parade uniforms in August 1955. These uniforms were grey, with red cap bands on the peaked cap and with red collar, shoulder boards and cuffs and red plastron edged by a stripe of gold lace, on the double-breasted tunic. Similar trimmings used to be part of the Russian Guards' uniforms before World War 1.

Later, the Soviet Guards adopted khaki uniforms slightly modified. The other ranks had only the red star on the cap band and the tunic lost the red cuffs and collar. The latter is now khaki with red patches. The plastron remained the same, but the gold piping and the regimental number is no longer worn on the red shoulder boards.

Plates 79 and 80. Officers' Rank Badges
Parade and Walking-Out Uniforms

Since the introduction of the jacket with open collar, the inner ends of the shoulder boards were covered by the collar. Thus the shape of the inner part of them became irrelevant and the button was discarded.

New regulations issued on 22 September 1956 prescribed a new shape of shoulder boards for the marshals and on 29 March 1958 the same were extended to the generals and officers as well.

In 1958 new khaki parade/walking-out and ordinary uniforms were adopted for the officers and sergeants. The new jackets were single-breasted with four buttons and an open collar showing the shirt and tie, and without breast pockets. Coloured piping was abolished and all the badges considerably simplified.

The shoulder boards illustrated in this plate and the first four in the following plate all belong to the parade and walking-out uniforms and are woven in gold or silver.

The coat of arms on the shoulder boards of the Marshal of the Soviet Union are 47 mm. in width and the star, embroidered in gold on red background, is 50 mm. in diameter.

The rank badge of the Supreme Marshals is a gold star 40 mm. in diameter surrounded by a wreath, while the marshals wear only the star. Both wear the arm-of-service badge also, on the shoulder boards, and piping and edging around the star in the colour of their branch of service.

The marshals' and generals' shoulder boards are 65 mm. in width, the officers', only 60 mm. The generals and officers of non-combatant services have silver boards with rank stars and badges made of gold, the others have gold shoulder boards and silver stars and badges.

Plate 80. Officers' Rank Badges
Ordinary Uniforms

On 29 March 1958 new shoulder boards were also introduced for all ranks' ordinary uniforms: plain officers' shoulder boards had already been introduced in December 1956 for use on the ordinary, sports and field uniforms. The background of the new shoulder straps matches the colour of the ordinary uniform; the stars and other badges are gold.

Also conventional shoulder boards with buttons have been made for wearing on tunics and shirt-tunics.

The arm-of-service badges are worn on the shoulder boards or on the collar patches, depending on the type of uniform or by the rank of the wearer. They are never worn on both the shoulder boards and collar of the same uniform.

Plate 81. Officers' Rank Badges
Field Uniform
The shoulder boards for field uniforms were also adopted on 29 March 1958 and are always worn on tunics. They are very similar to those of the ordinary uniform but with the rank stars and badges made of tarnished metal. The coat of arms of the Marshal of the Soviet Union is the only fully coloured badge worn on the shoulder boards of this uniform.

N.C.O.s' Rank Badges
Parade/Walking-Out and Ordinary/Field Uniforms
The coloured shoulder boards for the parade/walking-out uniforms were adopted on 30 December 1955 and were similar to those previously worn except for the piping, which was abolished. The arm-of-service badges used to be worn pinned below the rank stripes, whilst after the new regulations they had to be worn above the stripes, below the button.

Coloured boards with gold stripes and badges were worn on parade/ walking-out uniforms, khaki boards with red stripes and tarnished badges on the others.

The 29 March 1958 regulations granted the use of an officers' jacket to the regular sergeants (serving longer than the period of conscription) also, and new shoulder boards were adopted as well. The gold rank stripes were replaced by khaki stripes and the arm-of-service badges were transferred onto the collar, pinned on collar patches. The tarnished metal badges were still worn on the shoulder boards of the field uniform.

The rank insignia of the Sergeant-Major was modified in 1963 (Plate 82).

Plate 82. Cap Badges and Lapels
On 29 March 1958 new khaki uniforms were adopted for officers and sergeants as parade/walking-out and ordinary uniforms. The jackets were single-breasted with four buttons, with an open collar showing the shirt and tie, and without breast pockets. Coloured piping was abolished and all the badges were considerably simplified.

The officers retained their oval cap badges, with the red star in its centre: it is worn on the peaked cap of the parade/walking-out uniform together with a metal wreath which replaces all the gold ornamentation adopted in 1955, with the exception of the gold cord chin strap. The oval badge, which is made of red and white enamel and anodised gold, is worn on its own on the coloured cap band of the ordinary peaked cap, with a black leather chin strap. The same cap badge but in a colour matching the peaked cap was adopted for the field uniform peaked cap, which has a khaki visor and chin strap.

The cap badge of the other ranks is the red star which is worn together with a gold anodised metal wreath, as is that of the officers, on the peaked cap of the parade/walking-out uniforms.

New oak and laurel motifs of the marshals' and generals' ordinary uniforms were adopted, made of tarnished metal instead of the gold ones adopted in 1954. The officers and sergeants (later all ranks) adopted raspberry-red or black patches, with arm-of-service badges, on the collar of the khaki jackets. A narrow gold piping was added on three sides of the patch worn on parade/walking-out uniform, plain patches on the ordinary uniform.

Shoulder Boards and Service Chevrons

Until 1963 the Sergeant-Major wore a large and a thinner stripe arranged in a T shape but since that year his rank has been identified by only a large stripe, worn all along the centre of his shoulder boards.

The Russian soldier now wears the brass letters 'C A', which stand for the initials of the Soviet Army, at the outer ends of the shoulder boards of his greatcoat and of all uniforms except field.

A Warrant Officer rank was created on 1 January 1972 with two stars on the shoulder boards, and provision is made for the future establishment of a Junior W.O. rank with only one star. The Warrant Officer wears also service chevrons on the left lower sleeve, above the cuff. They are made of gold lace stripes on red background. One narrow chevron is added for each year of service until three are reached. The fourth year is represented by a large chevron and a gold star is added for service between five and nine years. On the tenth year and over a large chevron below two stars is worn. These chevrons are not worn on the field uniform.

Breast Badges

The Extended Service badge was adopted on 1 August 1957. It is made of metal and enamel, 26 × 60 mm. in size, and a small triangular plaque attached below the badge shows the number of years of service it is awarded for.

Later, another wing-shaped badge was introduced for the tank crews, divided into four classes, the top class with an 'M' in the centre of the shield.

The badge of Infantry Specialist, the Proficiency badge and all other badges of this type are usually worn on the right breast of the jacket or tunic.

Plate 83. Arm Badges (1972)

The shield-shaped arm badges were introduced in 1972 and are worn on the left upper sleeve of the jacket and greatcoat. They are all similar in design, with the branch-of-service badge in the centre, all on a background of arm-of-service colour. The branch-of-service badges in most cases are similar to those previously used on the collar and shoulder boards, although new badges were introduced in order to distinguish the various specialities of the technical troops.

The Traffic Controller wears a round badge with a yellow 'P' enclosed in a shield-shaped border.

Belgium

The present Belgian Army is descended from the army of 1940, whose traditions were loyally maintained through the war years by the Belgian forces raised in the United Kingdom. They were considerably reinforced during the closing months of the War after the liberation of Belgium. At the same time, between January and June 1945, another five infantry brigades, each comprising 4,300 men, were raised and sent to Northern Ireland for training.

An agreement was signed on 1 December 1944 between SHAEF and the Belgian Government, by which Belgium provided the Liberated Manpower Units (L.M.U.) that, equipped by Britain, were used to maintain the Allied line of communications. However, several of these units also fought bravely beside British, American and Canadian troops.

When peace came at last, the Belgian troops were wearing British uniforms with the traditional Belgian badges.

The khaki battledress was the field uniform of all ranks. The officers, warrant officers and sergeants also had another uniform which consisted of a jacket with four patch pockets, shoulder straps and open collar showing the shirt and tie, peaked cap and trousers. This uniform, with slight variations, was worn for various duties and special occasions. It was worn as full dress uniform, together with white shirt and black tie, decorations and medals, shoulder cords instead of shoulder straps and, in the case of officers, with lace waist belt also. For ceremonial duties it was worn with white shirt and black tie and lace waist belt and ribbons instead of metal decorations. A khaki shirt and tie and the Sam Browne belt, or a plain khaki cloth belt, were worn with the walking-out uniform.

Officers and warrant officers wore battledress with peaked caps as their service dress; with the beret or steel helmet as field uniform. They both had the battledress blouse with open collar, while the O.R.s' blouse was buttoned up to the neck.

The webbing equipment was khaki, the exception being the webbing of military policemen, regimental policemen and bandsmen who had white webbing. The Chasseurs of the Ardennes wore their traditional green berets, tankmen wore black berets, parachutists maroon berets and the rest of the army, khaki berets.

Plate 84. Generals' and Senior Officers' Rank Badges

Belgian rank badges did not change a great deal after World War 2 and are still worn on the collar patches, with the exception of the generals who also wear stars on the shoulder straps. Different chin-strap cords, bars and bands on the peaked cap distinguish the classes of rank.

All ranks wear the Belgian national cockade on the peaked cap. There are now three ranks of generals, all wearing amaranth red cap bands with two gold double bars and gold piping around their base, and gold chin strap on the peaked cap. They also have the 'thunderbolt' badge, unique to their rank, on the cap and on the collar patches; on the latter it is worn together with gold-embroidered double bars and stars. Their collar patches are black with a 2-mm. amaranth piping at the top.

All the senior officers, including the Colonel-Brigadier, wear two single vertical bars, gold or silver chin-strap cords and piping on the peaked cap and, in the case of the Colonel-Brigadier, an additional coloured cap band. At the front, between the bars, the arm-of-service badge is worn pinned or embroidered above the chin strap.

As the different corps have different patches and different badges, the collar patches illustrated only depict the rank of a particular corps. The rank of Colonel is represented by a patch of a Colonel of Infantry who has qualified at the Staff College: thus he wears the infantry patch with the G.S. badge, known as *demi-foudre*. Next are the collar patches of a Lieutenant-Colonel of the Engineers and of a Major of the Grenadiers. The Grenadiers wear a gold flaming grenade on the scarlet blue-piped collar patches of the infantry.

All ranks of the Infantry and Artillery respectively wear scarlet patches with royal blue piping and royal blue patches with scarlet piping, without the arm-of-service badges, which however are worn on the peaked cap and on the shoulder straps. Thus I have illustrated the crown of the Infantry and the crossed cannons of the Artillery as worn on the peaked cap by a Colonel-Brigadier and by a senior officer of these corps.

Plate 85. Junior Officers' and Warrant Officers' Rank Badges

All ranks of the Cavalry and the warrant officers and sergeants of all corps wear silver or white metal insignia (badges, chin-strap cords, stars, etc.) while the rest of the army wears gilded or brass insignia.

Both junior officers and warrant officers wear gold or silver chin-strap cords on the peaked cap. Officers wear six-pointed stars on the collar patches and the 1st Captain, in some corps known as Captain Commandant, has the three stars of the captains surrounded by a thin (2 × 30 mm.) horizontal bar. Warrant officers wear silver badges: the W.O. one silver star and the W.O. 1st Class, the star below a small bar (2 × 16 mm.).

Other Collar Patches

The personnel of the Legal Service wear royal blue patches with ultra-marine blue piping on which they wear the appointment badge above a gold bar 30 mm. in length. The Judge Advocate General and the Judge Advocate wear the *faisceau de licteur* surrounded by wreaths of oak and laurel respectively, above a thick bar, whilst the Clerks of the Legal Service wear only the *faisceau de licteur* without wreath, above a thin bar.

The Ingenieurs des Fabrications Militaire are officers specialised in mechanics, electronics, etc., who study and control the production of equipment supplied to the army. They have royal blue collar patches with scarlet piping, the usual stars and bars and the cogwheel on crossed hammers badge.

Finally, a collar patch for other ranks of the Medical Service, in the shape as worn by the other ranks of all corps on the collar of the battle-dress blouse, is illustrated.

The colours of the remaining patches are as follows:

	Patch	*Piping*
Infantry of the Line } Grenadiers	scarlet red	royal blue
Carabiniers } Chasseurs-on-Foot	dark green	yellow
Chasseurs of the Ardennes	dark green	scarlet
Security Sections	dark green	black
Commandos	black	white
Parachutists	maroon	sky-blue
Guides	amaranth-red	green
Lancers	white	royal blue
Chasseurs-on-Horse	yellow	royal blue
Artillery Royal Military School } Cadets School	royal blue	scarlet
Engineers	black	scarlet
Signals	black	green
R.A.S.C.	ultramarine	orange
R.E.M.E.	black	orange
Military Police	scarlet	white
Doctors	amaranth	amaranth
Pharmacists	emerald-green	green
Stomatologists	dark violet	amaranth
Veterinaries	ultramarine	royal blue
Medical Service (O.R.s)	amaranth	royal blue
R.A.O.C.	grey	amaranth
Commissariat	royal blue	sky-blue
Administrative Service	royal blue	grey-blue

The officers and warrant officers of the Engineers and Signals, and the Doctors, Pharmacists, Stomatologists and Veterinaries (all officers) have velvet collar patches, while the patches of all the others, including generals, are made of felt.

Badges are worn on the collar patches in order to specify a particular appointment, rank or service (G.S. Officers, Advocates and Clerks of the Legal Services, Commissaries, etc.) or in order to distinguish one corps from another in the case when both wear the same patch. The Grenadiers, for instance, wear an infantry patch with the grenade, and the Carabiniers wear the same patch as the Chasseurs-on-Foot, but with an additional bugle.

The Engineers wear the traditional helmet as their badge.

Most of the arm-of-service badges illustrated in the following plates are worn on the shoulder straps and on the collar of the greatcoat.

Plate 86. Sergeants' and Corporals' Rank Badges

The sergeants and corporals of the Belgian Army wear rank stripes on both forearms, above the cuffs, pointing inwards at a 30-degree angle. Khaki stripes are worn on the field uniform and silver ones, considerably smaller, are worn on the other uniforms. Regular sergeants and bandsmen, and all ranks of the Military Police, wear the peaked cap with a brown leather chin strap, while corporals and privates are entitled to wear the peaked cap, with khaki cloth chin strap, only after ten and fifteen years of active service respectively. No rank badges are worn on the beret.

Front Line Wound Stripes and Service Chevrons

The stripes are worn in the same manner as the rank stripes but on the left upper sleeve: they are made of gold or silver lace and each measures 4 × 40 mm. The chevron is also 4 mm. in width and each arm is 32 mm. in length, with a 120-degree angle between the arms, and it is worn on the left sleeve.

Armlets

There are two police organisations in the Belgian Army: the Military Police, which is an independent organisation, and the Regimental Police, whose personnel is part of the various regiments and units.

The military policemen have their own badges, white webbing equipment, armlets and peaked caps with a red cover, when on duty. The regimental policemen wear only white webbing equipment and the armlet when on duty, together with the badges of the corps and regiment they belong to.

The armlets of both organisations are black with red letters 'PM' and

'PR', standing for Police Militaire and Police Régimentaire respectively. Both measure 6 × 39 cm.

Plate 87. Miscellaneous Badges
Royal Military School's Shoulder Cords and Badges

The cadets of the Royal Military School wear plaited cord colours at the shoulder indicating the year of the course. All cadets wear a sprig of laurel in white metal (2.8 × 1 cm.) and the qualified N.C.O. instructors wear two sprigs of laurel instead. The Polytechnic Branch of the same school wear a diamond-shaped badge, 3 × 3 cm. in size.

The students of other training schools wear coloured bands, slipped on the outer ends of the shoulder straps. The Physical Training Instructors have two badges: the N.C.O. instructors wear a sword (5 × 1.6 cm.), while the officers wear two crossed swords and the crown.

Three types of Belgian wings, the badge of the Commandos Training Centre, and the wing worn by parachute instructors, have also been illustrated.

Plate 88. Formation Signs

Most formation signs depict the Belgian Lion, or just his face, the exception being those of the parachutists and commandos which were adopted in Britain during the War. Formation signs are worn on the left upper sleeve of the battledress.

The badge of the Ground Forces Base was adopted in February 1959 and depicts the Lion's head on a shield divided into the colours of the five components of that organisation: Engineers, Signals, Quartermasters, Ordnance and Security Section. In 1969 it was replaced by another sign showing a hand supporting a sword which suggests the role of this logistical organisation.

The round formation sign is no longer worn as the Home Defence Forces now wear the sign of the former 2nd Corps.

The Lion's head appears on all the divisional signs, on a different coloured background for each division. The amaranth and white of the 16th Armoured Division's badge are the colours of the Guides and Lancers whose regiments originally composed the division.

Arm-of-Service Badges

The badges illustrated in this and the two following plates could be divided into corps and service badges, and appointment badges, known in Belgium as *Attributs des Fonctions*. They are worn at the front of the peaked cap, some on the shoulder straps, some on the collar patches and also on the collar of the greatcoat.

The badges illustrated in this plate are worn by officers only. That of the generals is known as *foudre* (thunderbolt), and that of the General Staff as *demi-foudre*. The latter is worn on the collar patches of the corps of service of the wearer.

The Commissaries and the Doctors, Veterinaries and Pharmacists wear their gold badges on the cap and collar and their unit's badge on the shoulder straps. The cadets of the three latter services wear a silver badge and the 2nd Lieutenant cadet wears the officer's gold badge but with a silver mirror.

The badge of the Substitute Judge Advocates has a silver axe.

Plate 89. Arm-of-Service Badges

Silver and white metal badges are worn by the cavalry and by the warrant officers and sergeants of all corps, gilded and brass badges by personnel of the rest of the army.

Many new badges have been introduced since the War and the structure of the army has also been modified and modernised. However, most of the old badges are still used nowadays, such as the crown of the Infantry of the Line, the bugle of the Carabiniers and Chasseurs-on-Foot, and the beautiful badge, the boar's head, of the Chasseurs of the Ardennes. Among the cavalry badges only that of the Chasseurs-on-Horse has been modified, as previously it depicted a sword across a bugle. The badges of the Artillery and Engineers remain those in use before World War 2.

Some badges were introduced during or soon after the War when the Belgian Army was connected with the British Army and new corps were formed as a result.

The Pioneers badge is now a skill-at-arms badge and is worn on the sleeve.

Plate 90. Arm-of-Service Badges

There are three types of badges worn by different categories of Clerks of the Legal Service. One is made of gold, one is gold with a silver axe, and a third is all made of silver. The warrant officers and sergeants of the Medical, Veterinary and Pharmacist Service wear silver badges, the lower ranks brass badges.

The Logistical Corps (CORLOG) has been formed recently by the amalgamation of the Quartermasters and Ordnance Corps. The helmet on crossed cannons badge was worn in the early 1950s by personnel of the Tank battalions attached to the infantry divisions; the badge is now obsolete.

Shoulder-Strap Numerals

Some examples of units using Arabic and Roman numerals have been illustrated. They are all 19 mm. in height and are made of brass or white metal; divisional numerals are on a rectangular background (26 × 22 mm.) and brigade numerals are on a disc (27 mm. in diameter).

Beret Badges

The beret is worn as a complement to the battledress and in general it is the head-dress usually worn by the soldiers. The Chausseurs of the Ardennes wear dark green berets, parachutists, maroon berets, personnel of the armoured units, black, and personnel of the Army Aviation, light blue. Khaki berets are worn by the personnel of the rest of the army.

The badges are made of different metals depending on the rank or corps of the wearer and most are worn on a shield-shaped coloured backing, with the exception of those worn on coloured berets.

The badges of the Infantry of the Line, Grenadiers, Artillery and Military Police, for instance, are worn on a red backing, the badges of the Royal Military School, Cadets School, R.A.S.C., Signals and Administrative Service on a blue backing, dark blue for the badge of the latter. The beret badges of the Engineers and R.E.M.E. have a black backing and that of the R.A.O.C. a grey backing; the Medical badge is worn on an amaranth backing and the Carabiniers wear a green backing. The Chasseurs-on-Horse have yellow, the Lancers white and the Guides amaranth backings.

Beret Badges

The beret badges of the R.A.S.C., of the R.E.M.E. and of the R.A.O.C. are not in use anymore. The former, with the motto 'VICTORIAM ALO', was worn for a time by the Quartermasters which later joined the personnel of the R.A.O.C. to form the new Logistical Corps. The Engineers and signallers used to wear similar badges but now a new badge has been adopted by the Signals.

Plate 91. Beret Badges
Chasseurs-on-Horse

Five regiments of Chasseurs-on-Horse have existed since the War; the badge of the 5th Regiment is that of the 2nd with the figure '5' below the scroll. The 1st and 2nd Chasseurs-on-Horse were formed in 1830 from former hussars regiments. The 2nd Regiment, for instance, was raised by Prince Victor Philip de Croy on 1 March 1814 and after the disbandment of the Belgian Legion of Napoleon's army, it became the 8th Hussars Regiment of the Army of the Netherlands, and subsequently the 2nd Chasseurs on Horse of the new Belgian Army.

The 3rd Regiment originates from the 3rd Lancers and existed briefly in the 1920s: it was re-raised in 1952 together with the 4th which, formed in 1913, was in existence during World War 1. The 5th was formed in 1957.

Guides
The 1st and 2nd Regiments of Guides were raised in 1830 and 1874 respectively. The former was originally known as the Cossacks of the Meuse, and became a regiment of guides on 24 January 1833. The 1st Regiment was reformed on 8 March 1946 from the Armoured Car Regiment and retains the traditions of the former Armoured Squadron of the Belgian Forces in the U.K.

The 2nd Regiment was re-formed in 1952, the 3rd was raised in 1957 and the 4th in 1961.

Lancers
The 1st and 2nd Lancers were formed in 1830 by the Provisional Belgian Government, although the former traces its origins to the Van Der Burch Light Cavalry, raised in 1814. The 3rd was raised in 1830 as a regiment of cuirassiers, converted to lancers on 1 January 1863. The 2nd Lancers was reformed in 1949 and the 3rd the year after.

The 4th Lancers was, until 1863, the 2nd Regiment of Cuirassiers which was raised in 1836.

The modern 4th, 5th, 6th, 7th and 8th Lancers were all formed in 1952; the 9th and 10th in 1961, but the former wore the beret badge of the 4th Heavy Tanks Battalion.

The 5th Lancers was raised in 1913, disbanded in 1923 and reformed in 1939. The 6th Lancers descended from the 2nd Lancers, became a regiment on 1 January 1920 and disbanded three years later.

Plate 92. Beret Badges
Infantry
Thirteen infantry regiments have been raised since the end of the War. However a beret badge for the 10th Infantry Regiment does not exist, as before the war this unit became the Regiment of Chasseurs of the Ardennes and adopted the boar's head as its insignia. The 13th existed for only a few months after the War. The 6th Infantry Regiment has worn in turn two badges, both of which are illustrated.

The grenades of the Grenadiers and the Mortar Company are worn on a red backing as these units are part of the infantry.

Three regiments of Chasseurs-on-Foot, each wearing different badges, have existed since the War and each of the three para-commando battalions wears a different badge. The 3rd Parachute Battalion is famous for its participation in the Korean War. The Chasseurs of the Ardennes exist at present as battalions, not as a regiment. The 'B' in the centre of the Carabiniers badge stands for the King's name, Baudouin.

Plate 93. Beret Badges
Schools and Training/Armoured Units

These badges are worn on patches of their own arm-of-service colour, blue in the case of the Royal Military School and Cadets School. The badge of the Armoured Troops Training Centre can be worn on yellow, white or crimson backing by chasseurs, lancers and guides respectively.

The Armoured School traces its origins to a cavalry school created in 1842 at Brussels and, after many changes and conversions, it became the School for Armoured Troops in 1945.

The Armoured Troops Training Centre and the Armoured Troops Demonstration Detachment were formed in 1951 and amalgamated in 1961. The latter was an international establishment, thus the letters 'JTTC' in the scroll stand for Joint Tank Training Center, which was a Belgian–American establishment. A similar badge, but without the scroll, was worn by the personnel of the Armoured Centre (1954–8).

The 1st Heavy Tanks Battalion was created in 1951 as the armoured support of the 1st Infantry Division. The first badge illustrated on the left was never worn and the second was later replaced by a third pattern.

The personnel of this battalion wore the knight's helmet on crossed cannons on the peaked cap and on the shoulder straps. The 4th Heavy Tanks Battalion was created on 1 April 1952 as part of the 4th Infantry Division and was subsequently disbanded in 1956.

The 1st and 4th Reconnaissance Squadrons of the 1st and 4th Infantry Divisions were also formed in the early 1950s, each with its own beret badge, with squadron number, on white backing. In 1953 both adopted a badge without a squadron number.

Bibliographical Note

Among the many publications which could further enlarge one's knowledge of the subject I have dealt with, I would like to mention the following:

Regimental Badges, by Major T. Edwards, several volumes (later revised and edited by A. L. Kipling), dealing with British cap badges.
Heraldry in War and *Badges on Battledress*, both by Lt-Col. H. N. Cole, in several revised editions, dealing with British formation signs.
Military Badge Collecting by J. Gaylor, dealing with British cap badges.
German Army Uniforms and Insignia, by B. L. Davis.
Orders, Decorations, Medals and Badges of the 3rd Reich, by Littlejohn and Dodkins.
Uniforms of the SS, a series by A. Mollo and other authors, illustrating in great detail the uniforms, badges and equipment of the German SS.
American Badges and Insignia, by E. E. Kerrigan.
Emblemes de Cavalerie, by J. P. Champagne, a very good publication on Belgian cavalry badges (Editions G. Everling, Arlon).
Żołnierz Polski, by K. Linder, H. Wiewióra and T. Woźnicki, an illustrated book, showing Polish uniforms and badges used in the period 1939–65 (Wydawnictwo Ministerstwa Obrony Narodowej, Warsaw).
Uniformi Militari Italiane, by E. and V. Giudice, Volumes I and II, dealing with all the Italian uniforms worn from 1861 to 1968 (Bramante Editrice, Milan).

Other good publications on military subjects might be available and I do not list them solely because I do not know them, or because they do not concern the armies I have dealt with in my own books.

As a member of the American Society of Military Insignia Collectors I have gained much useful information from their remarkable periodical, *Trading Post*. I would also like to mention the marvellous pamphlets of the Military Heraldry Society.

Index

This is not a complete index but is intended only as a
cross reference between illustrations and description